D0952967

the LEADERSHIP GAP

the LEADERSHIP GAP

*Building Leadership Capacity
for Competitive Advantage*

Dr. David S. Weiss
Dr. Vince Molinaro

John Wiley & Sons Canada, Ltd.

Copyright © 2005 by Dr. David S. Weiss and Dr. Vince Molinaro

All rights reserved. No part of this work covered by the copyright herein may be reproduced or used in any form or by any means—graphic, electronic or mechanical—without the prior written permission of the publisher. Any request for photocopying, recording, taping or information storage and retrieval systems of any part of this book shall be directed in writing to The Canadian Copyright Licensing Agency (Access Copyright). For an Access Copyright license, visit www.access-copyright.ca or call toll free, 1-800-893-5777.

Care has been taken to trace ownership of copyright material contained in this book. The publishers will gladly receive any information that will enable them to rectify any reference or credit line in subsequent editions.

National Library of Canada Cataloguing in Publication

Weiss, David S. (David Solomon), 1953-
        The leadership gap : building leadership capacity for competitive advantage / David Weiss, Vince Molinaro.

Includes index.
ISBN-13 978-0-470-83568-0
ISBN-10 0-470-83568-0

    1. Leadership. I. Molinaro, Vince, 1962- II. Title.

HD57.7.W525 2005   658.4'092   C2005-900326-X

Production Credits
Cover design: Mike Chan (with a contribution from Joseph Weissgold)
Interior design: Interrobang Graphic Design Inc.
Printer: Friesens Printers Ltd.

John Wiley & Sons Canada Ltd.
6045 Freemont Blvd.,
Mississauga, ON
L5R 4J3

Printed in Canada
10 9 8 7 6 5 4 3 2 1

Contents

Preface

The Leadership Gap addresses one of the most mission critical business issues facing organizations today—building leadership capacity. Organizations are experiencing significant leadership gaps, which is undermining their ability to succeed. However, many executives either are not focusing on this issue or are not satisfied with current approaches to building leadership capacity. What is especially alarming about the leadership gap is that despite widespread investments in management and leadership education, companies still are not able to deal with this gap.

Executives and HR professionals need to rally around the leadership gap issue and not allow it to jeopardize their business success. Some executives may believe that this is a soft business issue. We suggest that, quite to the contrary, the leadership gap should be one of the top priorities for executives now and into the future.

The Leadership Gap challenges the traditional views and approaches of building leadership capacity with a new integrated perspective that recognizes leadership as a source of competitive advantage.

To this end, *The Leadership Gap* presents the case for a new framework for responding to this gap. Based on our extensive work and research in this field, we provide the practical strategies necessary for business executives and HR leaders to bridge the gap.

THE PURPOSE OF THE BOOK

The Leadership Gap helps leaders and their organizations respond to the leadership crisis in an effective and sustainable manner. The unique contribution of this book is that it recommends a dual response to bridging the leadership gap in organizations: a response on the part of individual leaders for self-development and a response on the part of organizations to establish the infrastructure that enables the leaders to learn. One of the unique contributions of this book is that it champions this balance. Many leadership books present what leaders need to do to develop their capacity as individual leaders. Other books focus on the organizational responsibility to provide leadership development and manage key leadership talent. They do not create a complete picture of what is needed to build leadership capacity. This book integrates the two areas and gives each equal prominence as part of the leader-organization partnership to build leadership capacity.

It provides a comprehensive approach—a much-needed road map—to enable organizations to build strong leadership capacity. For this approach to be successful, both individual leaders and their organizations must commit to it. Individual leaders must become *holistic* leaders, and the book explains how this is possible through using our Holistic Leadership Framework. Organizations must also respond, and we show the most effective way to develop a more complete and integrated approach to building leadership capacity.

A DESCRIPTION OF THE BOOK

This section presents a brief overview of the four parts of the book and a description of each chapter. We believe it is best to read the book in its entirety for a full understanding of our integrated solution. However, we also are aware that some readers may want to dip into the book and explore

specific topics of particular need. The following descriptions should guide
the reader to determine what will address their needs most effectively.

Part One—The Business Imperative highlights the mission critical
business imperative of building leadership capacity and provides an
overview of our approach to bridging the leadership gap.

Chapter 1: Mission Critical

This chapter explores the dynamic nature of business environmental
changes and the significant implications of these changes that all leaders
should know about. It shows why "leadership capacity" is such a crucial
strategy for an organization's success.

Chapter 2: Bridging The Leadership Gap

We spotlight four aspects of the leadership gap that organizations must
address in order to bridge the gap successfully: (1) The *Talent* aspect,
(2) The *Capability* aspect, (3) The *Development* aspect and (4) The
Values aspect.

Part Two—The Leader's Response presents what individual leaders
must do to become holistic leaders. The seven chapters in this section
provide insight into our Holistic Leadership Framework, consisting of
six integrated elements: (1) customer leadership, (2) business strategy,
(3) culture & values, (4) organizational leadership, (5) team leadership
and (6) personal leadership. The six elements focus individual leaders on
driving business results and creating the conditions for an organization
to achieve sustainable business success.

Chapter 3: Holistic Leadership: An Overview

This chapter gives you a look into the future role of leadership. It
introduces the need for leaders to focus on driving business results by

delivering customer value. We introduce our *Holistic Leadership Framework* and bring its various components to life with real-life stories and anecdotes.

Chapter 4: Customer Leadership

Customer leadership requires a relentless focus on directing all work to deliver external customer value. This chapter provides the concepts and ideas that can help leaders position their organization as a leader in the eyes of the customer. It also helps leaders understand what they need to do to distinguish their organizations by delivering a higher level of value to achieve customer loyalty.

Chapter 5: Business Strategy

This chapter explains that holistic leaders need to know how to partici-pate in all phases of business strategy. This chapter shows the importance of thinking strategically and gives an action plan for execut-ing the five-phase business strategy process.

Chapter 6: Culture and Values

Culture and values represent a living, vibrant force that distinguishes one organization from another. This chapter explains how leaders can build dynamic and enduring organizational cultures by effectively lead-ing culture change, integrating values into the organization, and driving employee engagement.

Chapter 7: Organizational Leadership

Organizational leadership means being able to lead an organization as an entire enterprise. This chapter explores how leaders can effectively create high-performance organizations characterized by high alignment and engagement to a common business strategy. It shows leaders how to operate with an enterprise-wide perspective and work in the interest of the whole organization.

Chapter 8: Team Leadership

This chapter shows how leaders can leverage the potential of four different types of teams. The chapter also presents the eight tactics that leaders can use to build strong team leadership throughout their organizations.

Chapter 9: Personal Leadership

This chapter shows how leaders can be more capable personal leaders by learning to lead in a more reflective and conscious manner so that they can effectively manage the pressures they face on a day-to-day basis.

Part Three—The Organization's Response consists of five chapters that explore what organizations must do to successfully implement strong leadership capacity.

Chapter 10: Leadership Capacity Implementation: An Overview

This chapter presents a leadership capacity framework that will shape the overall approach business leaders and senior HR executives need to implement to achieve strong leadership capacity.

Chapter 11: Embedding Leadership in the Organization

Embedding leadership is a process by which leadership capacity is recognized as critical and is made an integral part of the very fabric of an organization. In this chapter we explain how to embed leadership so that organizations can support the development of holistic leaders. More specifically, the chapter shows how organizations can secure a supply of leadership talent, develop a compelling leadership story, and how to embed leadership capacity into well-established processes.

Chapter 12: Focus on Critical Positions and Key Talent

In this chapter we provide steps to help organizations engage in succession management for critical positions and examine strategies for retaining key talent. This chapter provides the templates and processes to help organizations identify critical positions, succession candidates and development strategies. It also explores how to engage and retain key talent.

Chapter 13: Integrated Leadership Development

This chapter discusses the limitations of traditional approaches to leadership development. It then explains the eight steps necessary to effectively implement an integrated approach to leadership development.

Chapter 14: Accountability For Leadership Capacity

One of the key reasons the leadership gap continues to exist is the confusion over who should own leadership capacity. This chapter explores who is accountable. It also provides a comprehensive set of questions that can be used to conduct a leadership capacity audit and assess its effectiveness.

Part Four—The Epilogue consists of one chapter that reflects on the societal implications of the leadership gap.

Chapter 15: The Leadership Economy

In this chapter we consider the societal implications of the leadership gap and explore the emerging "leadership economy." We also discuss the critical need for business, government and academia to work together to address the leadership capacity gap and build a vibrant society.

WHO WILL BENEFIT FROM THIS BOOK

Readers hungry for information, ideas and techniques to advance the leadership role in organizations will find *The Leadership Gap* very helpful both conceptually and practically. It can be valuable to people in many different roles:

- *Executives and managers* seeking to understand the changing leadership role and the new value that leadership must provide.

- *Boards of Directors* who have responsibility for the recruitment and ongoing review of leadership performance of its senior executive officers.

- *Human Resources, talent management, and leadership development professionals—internal and external to an organization*—interested in understanding a new role for leaders to attract, develop and retain them.

- *Associations* that are concerned with leadership, strategy and organizational issues related to leadership capacity.

- *Members of the academic community* interested in a well-researched and practical text to teach their students about the changing role of leadership.

- *Students in MBA, Organizational Psychology and Human Resources Development programs* interested in books to support their understanding of the challenge to build leadership capacity.

- *Management consultants* seeking ideas and guidelines to provide advice to organizations about how to transform leadership to drive results.

HOW TO READ THIS BOOK

Most readers will benefit from reading the book cover to cover. However, others will find they can dip into the book for specific ideas and information, and it will add value. Here are some alternative ways this book can be read:

- Some readers—those responsible for the development of leaders—may want to use the book as a study guide. A suggested approach would be to ask leaders to read Part One for the first discussion. Part Two and Part Three can be read and discussed one chapter at a time. The audit questions presented in Chapter 14 can be explored after the completion of each chapter.

- If the readers are primarily interested in leading-edge elements for holistic leadership, they may want to focus on reading Part Two (Chapters Three to Nine), which describes the Holistic Leadership Framework.

- Other readers may want to understand how the organization can create a leadership culture and what it needs to do to build leadership capacity (Chapters Ten to Fourteen).

- Still other readers may want to explore the topic of integrated leadership development and how it is done, which can be found in Chapter Thirteen.

- Some readers may want to focus on the many leadership stories (*in italics*). These stories may be helpful for readers to help them develop their own leadership stories to embed leadership in their organization.

- Finally, readers may want to study a topic of their own interest. A detailed index has been prepared for referencing specific topics.

This book is a road map for executives and HR leaders who are considering how to build leadership capacity for competitive advantage. It will help leaders create an understandable leadership story of how leadership contributes value to the organization and the customer. And most important, it will provide leaders with a solid, effective approach for "bridging" *The Leadership Gap*.

Acknowledgements

This book is a product of a combined forty years of consulting and managerial experience within organizations and over three years of writing. We have had numerous opportunities to work with other individuals and leaders to whom we want to express our appreciation and acknowledgement.

A great deal of the development and refinement of our ideas for the book came from our association with the clients with whom we have worked. One of the joys of executive and human resource consulting is the privilege that comes from working with ambitious, dedicated and intelligent leaders with the genuine desire to continually take their organizations to higher levels of performance. In particular, we thank our clients who had the confidence in us and the courage to champion leadership capacity innovations within their organizations. It was through their experiences that we gained insights that helped us validate the concepts appearing throughout this book. We are grateful for your ongoing support and friendship.

Our appreciation also goes to the entire team of dedicated professionals at Knightsbridge Human Capital Management. In particular, we want to thank our president, David Shaw, and the Operating Council for their support of this book. Special thanks also are extended to our colleagues who directly contributed to the development of this book—Monika Berger, Malcolm Bernstein, Joanne Berry, Brad Beveridge, Janet Burt, Cathy Gareau, Judy Hemmingsen, Mary Kelly, Janine Lang, Janice McNabb,and Ralph Shedletsky. We would also like to acknowledge our colleagues from across our entire firm—we are proud to work with such fine professionals.

We also thank our publisher, editors and internal support staff, who contributed greatly to this project. A special thank you is extended to Karen Milner and the John Wiley & Sons team for their confidence and support of this project. We thank Mary Jo Beebe for challenging our ideas, her attention to editorial detail and guidance in refining the thoughts throughout the book. Also, a very heartfelt thanks to Michele Allan for continually going above and beyond the call of duty in the creation of graphics, editing and layout of the final manuscript and to Susan Beckley for her continual support throughout this project.

We also thank the many graduate students who have taken graduate courses with Vince at Brock University and the many professionals who have participated with David in executive development sessions at Queen's University and in programs at the Technion Institute of Management. Their ideas and questions have been a source of learning and refinement of thought.

We also would like to thank the people who have been a constant support and inspiration for our individual professional and personal learning.

From David, deep appreciation is extended to Dr. David Bakan for his words of wisdom as my study partner and friend over the past twenty-five years; to Dr. Carol Beatty, Brenda Barker Scott, and Yoram Yahav for their support professionally; to my brother Avi Weiss, who gives me ongoing encouragement; and to Dr. Vince Molinaro for his insights and drive to make this project a reality and for his wonderful approach to collaborative writing.

From Vince, a special thank you to Dr. Susan Drake for her constant guidance and inspiration over the years; to Dr. Jack Miller for his contribution to my understanding of the holistic aspects of leadership; and to Dr. David Weiss for his tremendous energy, passion and insight. I especially valued David's collaborative spirit throughout the writing process.

The writing of this book has been an invigorating and gratifying experience. We extend our deep appreciation to all those who contributed to this work. We wish to dedicate the book, with deepest gratitude, to our families.

From David: to my wife Dr. Nora Gold— my true friend, partner, and love, whose creativity is a constant source of inspiration. And to my son Joseph Weissgold—my source of pride and joy, who also contributed artistically to the cover of this book. I am deeply grateful to you both.

From Vince: to my parents, for their continual support in everything I've done. My final heartfelt thank you is to my wife and children. To Elizabeth—this work was only possible because of your unending encouragement, direction and guidance. Thank you, Liz. To my children, Mateo, Tomas and Alessia—you always help me keep things in perspective and remind me of what is truly important. I am blessed to have you in my life.

To all of you, our thanks and love.

David Weiss and Vince Molinaro
Toronto, Ontario, Canada

part one

THE BUSINESS IMPERATIVE

CHAPTER ONE

Mission Critical

During a recent international conference on talent management and leadership development, a panel session was taking place that consisted of several CEOs and VPs of Human Resources. Each of these panelists discussed the challenges that their companies were currently facing in building leadership capacity. A CEO from a global retail organization commented:

I've come to learn that our success as a company is a function of one fundamental variable—the quality of our leadership. When you think about it, differentiating ourselves from our major competitors is a big challenge! We sell the same products, we pretty much have the same technology as they do and we generally have the same number of retail outlets. In the end, it's the leaders in our organization who make the difference. When you put things in context, we have over 200,000 employees. Who guides their performance and direction? It's about 300 leaders. These leaders are the ones who shape our organization and who inspire our employees to deliver value to our customers. So our success as a company is based on our ability to continually build our leadership capacity. We work hard to bring our leaders new skills, ideas and competencies that, in the end, will help them collectively drive higher levels of performance. Leadership has become our competitive advantage.[1]

The insight expressed by this CEO is starting to be shared among business leaders in organizations around the world: leadership has become the primary source of competitive advantage in today's economy. However, the track record of many organizations is not good in terms of their ability to build the leadership capacity they need to succeed.

In another situation, the executive leaders of a financial company thought they had an approach that would solve their problem—but they were wrong. Here is their story:

The executives were encountering fierce competition, and they needed to cut costs. Their solution was to downsize most of their middle management. As a result, the gap between the leaders and the next level was huge. Many of the leaders possessed highly specialized talents that would be hard to replace. Some had very little confidence in the ability of the managers who were left to lead the organization into the future. The leaders suddenly realized that this "leadership gap" could threaten the viability of the company after their tenure. The executive team at this financial company rarely paid attention to their leadership capacity; but now they were worried, and some began to panic. They tried several approaches to either acquire or develop leaders, but none were very effective. They sent some of their more talented people to a two-week executive development course at a university. However, the instruction was generic and without specific application to the company environment. It was of little value in developing executive skills for the company's specific challenges. The executives felt the pressure. They also realized that leadership capacity was a critical business issue. Only time would tell how this company would fare in the future.

1. This case example is based on the experience of an actual client. Throughout this book we describe other case examples and anecdotes based on direct client experiences. In all cases we have changed some of the details to maintain client confidentiality. We also present composite examples based on the common experiences of several client organizations.

LEADERSHIP CAPACITY AND THE LEADERSHIP GAP

This second story is not unique. Many companies and public sector organizations throughout the world are struggling with similar leadership challenges. Building leadership capacity has become one of the most challenging business issues today—one that can threaten long-term organizational survival.

We use the term "leadership capacity" to mean the extent to which organizations can optimize their current and future leadership to drive business results and successfully meet the challenges and opportunities of an ever-changing business environment. The "leadership gap" refers to the "shortfall" between the required leadership capacity and the current and forecasted leadership capacity. As reflected in Figure 1.1 below, the leadership gap is preventing organizations from effectively building the leadership capacity they need to succeed in changing business environments.

Figure 1.1 *Bridging the Leadership Gap*

This book will explore how organizations can successfully "bridge their leadership gap" and ensure they have the current and future leadership capacity they need to succeed in changing business environments.

Many senior Human Resource professionals link the effectiveness of responding to business challenges to the strength of the leadership capacity that exists in their organizations. They also recognize that traditional strategies to build leadership capacity are inadequate to address the leadership gap that exists in most organizations. However, there are still many business executives who do not recognize the potential of leadership as a business driver and the strategic imperative of bridging the leadership gap. Our research suggests that this perspective is short-sighted. Leadership capacity and bridging the leadership gap will be critical in a new and fast-changing business environment.

THE CHANGING BUSINESS ENVIRONMENT NECESSITATES NEW WAYS OF THINKING

Change in the business environment is not new, but the speed and complexity of change is escalating dramatically. What worked in a previous business environment is outdated today and will be an antique collector's item tomorrow. The challenge is to stay ahead of the change sufficiently so that the business does not become irrelevant.

One buy-and-sell company of electronic video accessories quickly went out of business because they lost a key leader who kept them abreast of the latest consumer trends in digital technology. The company's existing accessory products were of an excellent quality but useless for the new technologies. Sales people noticed the trend as buyer interest waned, but the organization's leaders did not foster the open dialogue that would allow people to speak about the impending business crisis.

Another company had a highly respected CEO who retired due to ill health after many years of leadership. His approach had been to centralize all decisions around himself and to take a personal interest in all matters of the company. The model worked well as long as he was the leader. Once he retired, the new leaders were at a loss to know what they needed to do, where they could find information and how to rebuild the company's leadership. Although the former CEO tracked the environmental changes and responded to them, most of the other leaders were in the dark. The company's value dropped rapidly, and eventually, the company was acquired by a competitor.

The challenges and risks in the new business environment are vast. Companies' short-term and long-term viability will depend on the senior leaders' skill in recognizing and responding to the challenges. The new business environment necessitates key changes that include:

- A different kind of organizational response

- A different kind of leadership

Figure 1.2 shows a visual of the factors to consider in organizational and leadership change.

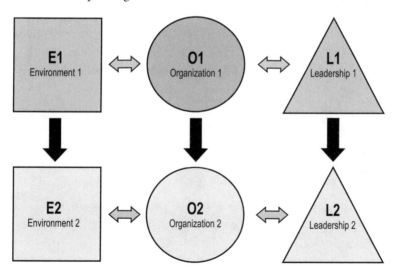

Figure 1.2 *Changes in the environment and its relationship to the organization and to leadership*

The first line shows the current environment, organization and leadership (E1, O1, and L1). The second line shows the new environment and required organization and leadership (E2, O2, and L2). The downward arrows indicate the transition from the current to the future state as follows:

- **From E1 to E2:** The transition from the current business environment to the new reality business environment

- **From O1 to O2:** The transition from the current organizational design, systems and processes to the new organizational design, systems and processes

- **From L1 to L2:** The transition from the current leadership capacity to the required level of leadership capacity

From E1 to E2
(Current business environment to the new environment)

One aspiring global company realized that their business environment (E1) was changing rapidly. They needed to respond quickly and with focused determination to this new environment (E2). Two sectors for their business were emerging:

1. A small number of dominant companies in the industry that would grow by volume and market share, and

2. A large cluster of "niche" players that would grow by specialization and margins.

The company leadership needed to choose a sector and then focus their strategy and organization on that sector. They chose to strive to be a dominant global player.

They realized that implicit in this decision was a competitive dynamic that would result in one global leader that would outdistance its rivals. The other global leaders would be fighting daily with each other and with niche players for survival. The company's desire to achieve global leadership in terms of customer satisfaction, growth and profitability necessitated leadership commitment to accomplishing that goal.

They recognized that the quality they achieved in leadership had to be similar in excellence to the quality of their products and processes. Their approach to the new environment (E2) focused on both appreciating the E1 achievements of the past and, at the same time, helping people let go and embrace the new challenges of E2.

The company set a new standard for all leaders— to continually develop their range of skills and expertise to respond to the rapidly changing environment. They emphasized that human quality and technology productivity were synergistic and must be achieved simultaneously to succeed in a global marketplace.

In contrast, another company was growing rapidly in E1. However, as they reduced investment in modernization, competitors entered their market with substitute product lines that replaced several of the company's major long, cycle-time products. They were becoming stagnant. The new environment reality caught the company by surprise and, in this case, too late. They needed to galvanize their leaders to transform their business model to stop the decline. They implemented changes that attempted to refocus the organization on what the customer valued. However, the technology-based leadership was slow to respond, and the changes did not yield the benefits anticipated. Eventually, the company went into receivership.

Another organization focused their leadership on the anticipation of future environmental changes. Often, this company had responded too late and had missed major opportunities. Over time, however, they succeeded in building an expectation that their leaders would be strategic thinkers for the company. The leaders became the source of early warnings about the continual evolution of their business environment. In essence, their leaders were not only expected to forecast and be ready for E2, they also were expected to be ready for the next evolution, the E3, and create their E2 response in such a way that it would be useful in E3 as well.

From O1 to O2
(Current Organization to the New Organization)

Being comfortable and successful in the past can block a company's acceptance of a new environmental reality. Many leaders are reluctant to change organizations that worked effectively in the previous environment. However, if done properly, the changes should result in a better organizational fit (O2) that will optimize the performance of the company in the new business environment.

Perhaps the most common obstacle to organizational change (from O1 to O2) is the belief that organizational structure is enduring and has permanence. Organizational structure is a mechanism to divide an organization into discrete parts in order to manage the whole enterprise and deliver customer value. The structure that is chosen is the best approximation of what will work. In an ideal world, there would be no departments, just one organization delivering value to the customer.

However, many leaders become so enamored with their own part of the organizational structure that they believe their portion is meaningful and needs to be preserved. They come to believe they have responsibility over an area that has value and importance unto itself. As a result, business units and areas of focus take on personalized importance, and silos are created. Some leaders forget they need to be thinking about the total organization, and the integration of work. The fact that the organization is divided in a certain way is merely an approximation of the best fit to respond to environmental needs and to deliver the best service at that time.

There are other reasons why leaders resist changes from O1 to O2:

- *It may be difficult for them to deal with the complexity of the new organization:* Leaders often are able to get work done in a less complex and more predictable manner in O1. They may resist O2 because of the need for much more fluidity, resulting in greater complexity and less definition.

- *It may take a huge effort on their part to develop teams:* Individual performance is highly valued in O1. Some leaders may resist the need required in O2 to focus on building strong intact teams, project teams, cross-functional teams and virtual teams throughout the organization.

- *It may require them to develop a new sensitivity to diverse values:* Employee values often are set through long-standing relationships in O1. In O2, the diversity of the workforce often changes, both to secure new talent from a wider pool of individuals and, in many cases, to reflect the diversity of the customers that the organization serves. New workers join the organization with diverse ideas and different interpersonal styles, which can destabilize the organization. Also, many leaders are not used to working in a diverse environment and may resist being sensitive to differing values and leveraging the strengths of people who may do things in a different way.

From L1 to L2
(Current leadership capacity to the required leadership capacity)

Modifying the organizational response to fit the changing environment is not sufficient. Leadership change is equally important. In fact, the success of the organizational changes is dependent on leadership. As difficult as organizational change can be, leadership change (from L1 to L2) is exponentially more challenging. Leadership often is the slowest to change in response to environmental and organizational demands.

In one company, a well-intentioned Human Resources Vice President attempted to lead an organizational change without engaging the leaders to actively participate and take ownership of the changes. His attempts to change the culture, build alignment and implement change failed. He lost his job because he was leading the significant change but without the leaders working with him to implement those changes. He demonstrated leadership in a vacuum without any "followership."

Executive leaders are beginning to recognize the leadership gap problem and as a result are worried about motivating leaders and engaging them to participate actively in making changes. The E2-O2-L2 model helps leaders understand that the past organization and leadership methods (O1 and L1) are valued but that the new environment necessitates organizational and leadership changes to achieve continued success in the future. Executive leaders need to understand that a critical success factor in the transformation of the business strategy is their leadership capacity.

One executive team helped their leaders move toward a new way of operating by educating them about the changes in their environment from E1 to E2 and the need for new methods in their operations. The company's competitive environment was shifting radically. New legislation was introduced that moved this company from its comfortable position as a monopoly service provider in a regulated environment. The new regulations allowed competition to exist, which could seriously threaten the shareholder value of the company.

The leaders needed to reflect on the current environment (E1) and how it generated a certain kind of organization (O1), which shaped how the leadership operated (L1) in the company. They needed to acknowledge the past, appreciate that the previous solution was the right one for that environment and recognize that their leadership approach maximized the company position prior to deregulation. They then needed to explore the new environment (E2). Through this process they became aware that the new environment necessitated a more competitive and nimble organization (O2). It also required its leaders to focus on innovation, empowerment and change (L2) rather than the traditional approach of quality at any cost, control and status quo management (L1). It was a dramatic request, and a number of the leaders could not make the switch. But those who did adjust were able to leverage their historical knowledge with the new way of leading, which represented the best combination for this company as it transitioned to a new way of operating.

Another company needed to change their leadership approach without a clear understanding of the new environment. They needed to convince the middle manager leadership that a problem was looming, even though it was ill defined to them. They challenged the middle manager leaders to explore the extent to which the differences between E1 and E2 were meaningful enough to take action. They used extensive educational processes, customer feedback and competitive intelligence to orient the leaders to the new challenges that were expected. Experts presented their assessment of the new technologies that could replace the technologies offered by this company. Groups of leaders made on-site visits to see what was done in other jurisdictions. These leaders then became the internal influencers to help other leaders understand that the environmental threats were likely to materialize.

THE LEADERSHIP GAP IS MISSION CRITICAL

The consensus among leading business thinkers is that the leadership capacity gap (between L1 and L2) has become mission critical. However, many executives either are not focusing on this issue or are not satisfied with current leadership development approaches. Our research suggests that many organizations are struggling to bridge the leadership gap. What also is clear is that if this gap is not addressed, organizations may jeopardize their ability to remain competitive in the future.

Other research has resulted in similar findings. For example, the Conference Board in the United States found that senior leaders believe their organizations have a serious leadership capacity gap.[2] In 1997 only about half of the respondents to the Conference Board survey rated their companies' leadership strength as either excellent or good. In 2001 the results declined sharply. Just four years after the 1997 study, only about one-third of respondents rated their companies' leadership capacity as excellent or good. The trend line is negative, which should be alarming to executive leadership.

The findings from this research are consistent with similar studies conducted with business leaders in other countries. For example, research conducted by the Conference Board of Canada reports that 70 percent of Canadian CEOs have identified leadership as their top

---

2. Ann Barrett & John Beeson, *Developing Business Leaders for 2010* (The Conference Board: New York, New York, 2001).

business concern.[3] Many of these business leaders believe that their organizations do not have the leadership capacity to succeed in a highly unpredictable business environment. The Conference Board suggests that the problem represents a severe leadership gap. Furthermore, if this gap is not addressed, it will seriously affect the overall competitiveness of Canadian companies in the future.

In the UK, the Council for Excellence in Management and Leadership found a significant leadership capacity gap that is holding back economic performance of organizations. In addition, in 2003, the UK Secretary of State, Patricia Hewitt, launched the "Accounting for People Task Force," chaired by Denise Kingsmill CBE. This task force explored methods of requiring publicly traded organizations to report on their investments in people.

At the outset, the Accounting for People Task Force intended to develop a list of employee-friendly companies. Investors then could use the list as a guide to their investment decisions, the same way an "environmentally friendly" list of companies guides some investor decisions. The hope was that companies would invest in people and leadership because doing so could have explicit economic and investment implications.

Weiss and Finn, 2004 conducted research exploring the readiness of companies in the UK and Canada to meet the potential reporting requirements of the task force.[4] Overall, most companies do not want to report this kind of information to any governing body. However, if they are required to do so, they are able to report transactional metrics, such as head count, total compensation, etc. However, they are not capable of reporting on more strategic issues such as leadership capacity and effectiveness of change initiatives. Of particular note, the line executives in 69 percent of the companies indicated that the number one desired metric they want in the future is "leadership team capability." The HR professionals in the survey expressed even stronger interest (82 percent

---

3. Prem Benimadhu & Judith Gibson, *Leadership for Tomorrow* (Conference Board of Canada: Ottawa, Ontario, 2001).

4. David Weiss & Richard Finn, "HR Metrics that Count" *Human Resource Planning*, February/March 2005.

of companies). The implications of this research are that line executives and HR professionals need to identify rigorous methods to develop and assess their organizations' leadership capacity and to determine and measure the leadership capacity gap on an ongoing basis.

The results of this study are consistent with the research conducted by Molinaro and Weiss that found executives foresee a significant leadership capacity gap in the future.[5] Still other surveys indicate that senior leaders are not satisfied with current approaches to leadership development.[6] In addition, many executives believe that their leadership development practices have a low probability of delivering success for their organizations.[7]

CURRENT SOLUTIONS ARE NOT BRIDGING THE GAP

What is especially alarming about the leadership capacity gap is that despite widespread investments in management and leadership education, companies still are not able to deal with the "leadership crisis" in their organizations.

Executives need to rally around the leadership gap issue and not allow it to jeopardize their business success. Some executives may believe that this is the soft side of management. We suggest that, quite to the contrary, the leadership challenge is mission critical and should be one of the top priorities of executives now and into the future.

Executives need to study and discuss the E1-E2 transformations and involve all employees in the process of reflecting on their business, organizational and leadership implications. They also need to assess regularly the extent to which the leadership gap is evident in their

5. Vince Molinaro & David Weiss, "The Leadership Capacity Gap," *Leadership Compass, The Banff Centre.* Vol. 10., 2004.

6. Barrett & Beeson, *Developing Business Leaders*; Benimadhu & Gibson, *Leadership for Tomorrow*; Hewitt, *Leadership Development Ineffective*, (source:http://was.hewitt.com/hewitt/resource/newsroom/pressrel/2002/06-05-02.htm).

7. Douglas A. Ready & Jay A. Conger, "Why Leadership Development Efforts Fail," MIT *Sloan Management Review* 44, 3., 2003, p. 83-89.

organization and develop comprehensive and thoughtful strategies to respond to the gaps that are evident.

Bridging the Leadership Gap

In one company, the executives realized that their overall corporate performance was reaching a plateau and that if they did not change, their results would begin to decline. They developed strategies to help transform the company. Their focus was to implement innovation (new product introduction, process change, etc.), anticipate significant changes in the market early enough and be ahead of the curve by transferring knowledge and best practices internally. However, they had concerns that many of their current leaders had been hired to run a certain kind of organization that did not operate at all like the company they needed to become. They were worried that the leadership gap would be a major risk factor in the corporate transformation.

Many corporations have a similar story to tell. In this chapter we describe four aspects of the leadership gap and our approach to bridging it.

THE FOUR ASPECTS OF THE LEADERSHIP GAP

The leadership gap that currently exists in organizations can be better understood by actually thinking about it as a series of four interrelated aspects which is depicted in the figure below:

Figure 2.1   *The Four Aspects of the Leadership Gap*

The Talent Aspect of the Leadership Gap

Because of demographic changes, the pool of younger leaders with the talent to assume senior roles in organizations has been shrinking—creating a talent gap for organizations. The book *Boom, Bust and Echo* predicted this phenomenon, and it has come to fruition.[1] Essentially, the reduced birthrate (the "bust") after the post-World War II "baby boom" has many societal implications. The implication for companies is that there are not as many future leaders available to lead companies as there were in the "baby boomer" generation.

---

1. David K. Foote, *Boom, Bust & Echo: How to Profit from the Coming Demographic Shift* (Macfarlane Walter & Ross, 1996).

Furthermore, the exodus of leadership talent coupled with organizational restructuring has resulted in lean hierarchies and organizational structures. This development has left many organizations without the pool of leaders they once had who would be ready to move into senior leadership roles. In addition, without the hierarchical layers, leaders do not have the career opportunities to develop their skills, capabilities and maturity as they may have had in the past.

Byham correctly predicted that the business world would experience a critical shortage of middle and upper leadership.[2] The report also projected that many large companies might experience a departure of up to 40-50 percent of its senior executives due to retirement. The book *The War for Talent* predicted that a battle for executive talent would be a defining characteristic of the business world in the future.[3]

The talent aspect of the leadership gap is putting pressure on organizations to be vigilant in their efforts to attract, retain and develop a strong group of potential leaders both from within and outside their organizations.

The Capability Aspect of the Leadership Gap

Research studies have found that up to 70 percent of CEOs surveyed see their own organization's leaders as being fair or weak in their ability to build teams, gain employee commitment, and make employees feel valued.[4] These have been identified as the capabilities that will be especially important in years to come. Other research indicates a strong link between leadership, employee engagement and corporate performance.[5] In addition, we found that many leaders also need to develop the

2. W.C. Byham, "Grooming Next-Millenium Leaders," *HR Magazine*, February 1999.

3. Ed Michaels, Helen Handfield-Jones, & Beth Axlerod, *The War For Talent* (Boston, MA: Harvard Business School Press, 2001).

4. Benimadhu & Gibson, *Leadership for Tomorrow*; Barrett & Beeson, *Developing Business Leaders for 2010*.

5. Marcus Buckingham & Curt Coffman, *First Break All the Rules*, (The Gallup Organization, 1999).

capability to think strategically and to understand the business from a holistic perspective. All these are critical capability areas where a significant gap exists among many leaders.

Clearly, a priority for organizations will be to ensure that leadership development programs help leaders develop the capability to inspire, align and engage employees. This will be especially important in coming years, as organizations continue to contend with the talent aspect of the leadership gap as well (i.e., the shifting demographics and shrinking pools of leaders). Employee retention will be vital, and the organizations with leaders who can align and engage employees effectively will have a distinct competitive advantage.

The Development Aspect of the Leadership Gap

Leadership development practices are often fragmented and lacking an overall strategy that is embedded successfully within the organization. Also, HR leaders often do not know how to influence CEOs and Boards of Directors to assume responsibility and accountability for bridging the leadership gap.

Senior leaders have begun to recognize that current approaches to leadership development are not effective in developing the leaders they need. Existing strategies for building leadership capability are falling seriously short of the mark in many organizations.[6] A survey of CEOs and HR executives of 240 major U.S.-based, multinational companies found that just over two-thirds of respondents believed their leadership development programs were ineffective.[7] Common ineffective solutions for developing leaders include:

- *A focus on leadership at the top*

   In the current business environment, the focus is often on how to emulate charismatic CEOs and other top leaders who have achieved extraordinary results with their organizations. Nothing is inherently

---

6. David Ulrich, Norm Smallwood, Jack Zenger, *Results-Based Leadership*, (Boston, MA: Harvard Business School Press, 1999).

7. Hewitt, *Leadership Development Ineffective*.

wrong with this approach, but it has led to an overemphasis on solely understanding leadership as it exists at the top of organizations at the expense of building leadership capacity at all levels.[8]

How leadership permeates all levels of an organization is not as well understood.[9] As a result, there is less attention placed on developing the leadership capabilities of middle- and first-level managers and employees as a whole. Kotter suggests that leaders will be the key to creating successful organizations in the future.[10] However, it is not solely leadership at the top of the hierarchy (which he refers to as leadership with a capital "L") that will be important. Rather, leadership in a more modest sense (or small "l" leadership) will be required throughout an enterprise.

- *Adopting generic leadership models*

Organizations have a tendency to adopt leadership models and development strategies that are generic, outdated and overemphasize personal attributes. Many of the leadership models provide valuable insights; however, they tend to be too theoretical and often seem disconnected from day-to-day realities of the jobs and the problems that leaders face.[11] They often focus too much on generic leadership attributes at the expense of tangible business results.[12] Bennis[13] further adds that this focus has been slanted too much to the individual leader (the "overpeoplefication" of leadership). Ready and Conger suggest that this focus on generic models has led many organizations to think of leadership development as a product.[14] This has resulted in the tendency to view leadership development as "one-day, paint by numbers,

8. Ulrich, et al., *Results Based Leadership*.

9. Horst Bergmann, Kathleen Hurson, Darlene Russ-Eft, *Everyone A Leader*, (New York, NY: John Wiley & Sons Inc., 1999); Noel Tichy, *The Leadership Engine, How Winning Companies Build Leaders at Every Level*, (New York: Collins Harper Publishers, 1997).

10. John Kotter, *Leading Change*. (Boston, Mass: Harvard Business School Press, 1996).

11. Jay A. Conger & Beth Benjamin, *Building Leaders*, (San Francisco, CA: Jossey-Bass, 1999).

12. Ulrich, et al., *Results Based Leadership*.

13. Warren Bennis, "Leading in Unnerving Times," *MIT Sloan Management Review*, Cambridge: Winter 2001, Vol. 42, Iss. 2; pp. 97-102.

14. Ready & Conger, "Why Leadership Development Efforts Fail."

'edutainment' sessions" or merely as a hodgepodge of courses and seminars that often appear separate and fragmented to the participants taking the programs.

Shope Griffin adds that a focus on generic models of leadership has created a "one-size-fits-all" approach to leadership training programs. These programs are ineffective because they fail to address the environmental changes, organizational directions, ideologies and behaviors that affect an individual's ability to lead within a company.[15]

• *An over-reliance on classroom training*

When senior leaders are asked to describe the learning events that most contributed to their development as leaders, classroom training rarely appears on the list. Rather, experience is regarded as the best teacher.[16]

However, current practices focus primarily on classroom-based leadership development. For example, 70 percent of respondents in a Hewitt study said that internal classroom-based training was the primary strategy used to develop leaders, even though this approach to leadership development has questionable utility.[17]

Despite this pattern, companies still spend a substantial amount of money building their leadership development solely on classroom training. In addition, although the leaders who receive the training programs often find them entertaining, they tend to report that it was "useless or irrelevant" to their actual roles as leaders. In years to come, organizations will need to completely reinvent the classroom component of leadership development. It will need to be more relevant for time-strapped and pressured business leaders and be delivered in a way that grabs the attention of participants and motivates them to learn. In addition, it must be closely connected to issues and challenges that leaders deal with in their daily work lives.[18]

15. Natalie Shope Griffin, "Personalize Your Management Development," *Harvard Business Review*, March 2003.

16. Research conducted by McCall, M, W., 1997, *High Flyers: Developing the Next Generation of Leaders* (Harvard Business School Press: Boston, Mass), and McCall, M, W., Lombardo, M., & Morrison, A., 1998. *The Lessons of Experience: How Successful Executives Develop on the Job* (Lexington Books: Lexington, Mass).

17. Hewitt, *Leadership Development Ineffective*.

18. Mercer Delta Consulting LLC, "Principles of Leadership Training: Building High Impact Programs," White Paper, 2001.

The Values Aspect of the Leadership Gap

The values aspect of the leadership gap refers to the differing work-related values between the current executive leadership and younger middle managers.

For example, one major utility company decided to develop core values for their organization. They anticipated that the values for the executives would typify the values for the entire organization. As a result, they engaged in a detailed exploration of the executives' values. Through an interviewing process, they discovered that the executives' core values were very traditional, such as individualistic leadership, being competitive, driving for the top, and believing in every person for themselves. Essentially, these were the values that made them successful.

The company decided to investigate further and determine if the assumption was true that the executive values were representative of the company. They explored the values for middle managers and found distinct differences. The middle managers valued collaboration, stakeholder management, use of influence, and building leadership throughout the ranks. Perhaps they espoused these values because they did not have autonomy in their roles, and they needed to operate that way to be successful. The company decided to conduct the research further and found that front-line supervisors had values more similar to the executive values. The supervisors were oriented toward their own career development, training, and individualistic goals.

In another situation, we were presenting the leadership gap concept and research to a group of middle managers to solicit their ideas about the talent, capability, development and values aspects of the leadership gap. They agreed that they definitely had development and values challenges. The company's methods of education and support were not meeting their developmental need. They also believed there was a difference in values between levels and among different parts of their company. However, they questioned the talent and capability aspects of the leadership gap. One person said he believed the executives at the top had a distorted view. Others chimed in that the talent and capability deficiencies were not at their level but, rather, at the executive level.

They also expressed concern that the executives did not realize their own inadequacies and were therefore not making room for the middle managers to demonstrate their talents and capabilities to lead.

The work-related values difference between executives and middle managers is even more evident with younger middle managers. Many executives do not understand the motivations of younger managers. For example, many younger middle managers live in "two-adult working families" and being relocated is an unacceptable request. In all likelihood, the executives would not accept total mobility for themselves either, but they are often frustrated when direct reports do not accept mobility as a condition of employment.

The difference in work-related values is also affecting the ability of organizations to build future leadership capacity. At the heart of the issue is the value of work/life balance shared by younger leaders. In our experience, we are finding that many young leaders are consciously choosing not to pursue more senior leadership roles in their organizations. They see the extra demands and pressures that come with these senior leadership positions as being in direct conflict with their desire to live balanced lives. The work/life balance issue is a fundamental part of the values aspect of the leadership gap.

It is intriguing that the baby boomer executives, who lived through a generation gap when they were teenagers, now find themselves in a generation gap of their own. The challenge is to surmount the values aspect of the leadership gap and provide opportunities for middle managers so they can develop their leadership capacity in the organization.

BRIDGING THE LEADERSHIP GAP

The distinguishing feature of best-practice executives is their fundamental belief that strong leadership is an important source of sustainable competitive advantage. A focus on leadership capacity has to become part of the business culture and needs to be reinforced strongly by executives. Organizations that have well-developed leadership capacity have a distinct advantage over their competition. In contrast, organizations with poor leadership capacity are vulnerable and at risk. The challenge then is how to bridge the four aspects of the leadership gap. This book explores our approach based upon our research at our firm, Knightsbridge, and our experience as practitioners. It also is based on our own direct experience as business leaders working to build a world-class human capital management firm.

The foundation of our approach to bridging the leadership gap is a partnership between the leaders themselves and the organization. Both need to reinforce and balance efforts to respond to the challenge of the leadership capacity gap and to optimize performance of the organization.

Balance the Contribution Leaders and the Organization Make to Bridge the Leadership Gap

Some executives have made the error of assuming all leadership development is the responsibility of the individual. They believe that learning is primarily the leader's responsibility. In their view, if a shortfall in leadership capacity exists, then the challenge is to find another person who has developed him or herself already. These executives see the need to develop leadership capacity as a cost of doing business, but if there is a need to find extra capital, they will cut those costs. Their preference is to avoid the cost altogether. In these organizations, HR leaders fight for budget to develop the leaders, and the executives often do not understand what they are buying and how it benefits the organization.

Only in rare cases can an organization succeed with this approach. These organizations are characterized by leaders who have limited commitment to the organization and the organization has minimal commitment to the leaders. The leaders are committed to self-development because that is the only way they can stay marketable within their company and externally, in the event that they choose to leave. In other words, this reliance on self-development works when the leaders are highly motivated (for personal gain) to invest in their self-development. The development is not targeted to deliver organizational benefit, although it's possible the development may benefit the organization.

On the opposite side of the spectrum, some organizations view development as an entitlement of employment. The development is not focused on building specific leadership capacity to respond to the new business environment. In one situation, a company spent a great deal of money building their own leadership "school" with courses that anyone could take at a local community college. The company's thick catalogue offered over 400 courses. Managers enjoyed the courses as part of the perquisite of being part of the company. A day in the "school" was a free day away from work. It was a bonus if the manager learned anything. The leaders in an organization like this one view the money spent as a necessary part of doing business and part of their organizational culture. Overall, HR professionals and the executives have a general belief that what they are doing is delivering value (although they can not articulate how the value is demonstrated).

In another organization, the organizational expectation was much more controlling. The executives expected the leaders to take certain courses, acquire certain formal degrees and pass specific prerequisites. Individual choice was not an option and was taken away from the employees. The participants were not learning for their own development. They were forced to learn because they were required to do so as a condition of employment. Participants attended courses reluctantly, and the return on investment from the courses was minimal.

All of these methods of leadership capacity development were unsuccessful. A balanced approach is needed.

Balancing the Responsibility of Leaders and the Organization to Bridge the Leadership Gap

The recommended approach is to balance the responsibility of the leader for self-development and the organizational commitment to establish the infrastructure that enables the leaders to learn. In some respects, one of the unique contributions of this book is that it champions this balance. Many leadership books present what leaders need to do to develop their capacity as individual leaders. Other books focus on the organizational responsibility to provide leadership development and manage key leadership talent. They do not create a complete picture of what is needed to build leadership capacity.

This book integrates the two areas and gives each equal prominence as part of the leader-organization partnership to build leadership capacity. Part Two of the book focuses on what leaders need to learn to build their leadership capacity and Part Three focuses on the organizational expectation to bridge the leadership gaps and ensure that the required leadership capacity is available to the organization.

So read on—and let the journey over the bridge to build leadership capacity begin!

part two

THE LEADER'S RESPONSE

Holistic Leadership:
An Overview

Think about people in a forest and what they see there. Most see the trees around them. Perhaps they identify the specific kinds of trees and notice details about the trees—their growth patterns, how they battle for sunlight, what the bark looks like, the condition of the soil, where flowers are able to grow. All these perspectives are useful and natural.

However, if the trees begin to decay, will a focus on specific details about the trees be enough to determine how to save the trees? It may not be enough. The entire forest and the environment that surrounds it may have an impact as well. By examining this environment, scientists and researchers can determine causes of environmental changes that create stress for the forest and its trees. This is a more holistic perspective to the health of the forest.

Many organizations are in a "forest" like this. They have had great success studying trees, assigning some people to watch over the soil, some to study the flowers and some to monitor the growth patterns. However, the entire forest is decaying. Very few of the senior leaders are able to oversee the entire forest, and these leaders are aging. The future is at risk if something is not done. The younger leaders need to learn how to see the environment and the forest so that they can understand how to continue to make the flowers grow and the trees flourish. They need to understand the interactions of the various parts of the forest that create a chain reaction of potential growth or decay.

One of the fundamental premises of this book is that the decay in organizations can, in part, be explained by the inability of leaders to see both the environment and the "forest." They only see the trees and bark. They do not understand the interdependencies of what they do with the work of others. They may operate effectively as functional leaders, who see the trees and bark, but they do not function as holistic leaders who also see the entire forest and environment.

UNDERSTANDING HOLISTIC LEADERSHIP

Holistic leadership refers to a whole and complete way of thinking about organization and leadership. In our analogy, it is the leadership capability to see both the forest and the trees.

Organizations, people, and teams have two tendencies:[1]

- *Integrative:* The tendency to be part of a larger organization. Each functional department has the tendency to be part of the larger organization. Similarly, each employee needs to be part of a social network—to belong to a team, department, organization and community.

- *Self-assertive:* The tendency to exert their own ideas and expertise. Each functional department has the tendency to exert its own expertise on the organization. Similarly, individual employees want to exert their own ideas and expertise, to fulfill their self-assertive needs.

Holistic leaders are able to balance the dynamic interplay between the integrative and self-assertive tendencies that exist within themselves, within a team, within an organization and within an entire business. "Functional leadership" can be useful in solving technical challenges that leaders face. However, when functional leadership becomes an entrenched mindset, the leadership can become a source of organizational dysfunction.

---

1. Koestler, A., *The Ghost in the Machine* (Arkana Books, 1989) Koestler proposed the word "holon" to describe a basic unit of organization in biological and social systems. Koestler observed that individual units of organizations comprise more basis units. Each holon is characterized by an integrative and self-assertive tendency. We apply these concepts to organizations and holistic leadership.

FUNCTIONAL LEADERSHIP

For a great many years, the focus has been on functional leadership and the functional/technical expertise of leaders. Organizations have been traditionally structured around core disciplines of business such as sales, marketing, research and development, production, information technology, human resources, finance, etc. Functional leaders view these disciplines as separate from one another.

The emphasis on discrete and separate disciplines is fairly ingrained in most leaders. It often begins when they are fairly young and at an early stage of their leadership development. Our formal educational system and informal continuing education create a "mindset" that emphasizes functional leadership—often at the expense of a holistic perspective.[2] Many of the current leaders in organizations have been educated in a particular mindset, and it continues to be reinforced daily in their work world. This mindset, which made them successful in the past, is now a contributor to the leadership capacity problem.

Consider the experience of a student who wants to build a career in business. The student attends school and learns about the world through a set of distinct subjects. The student attends classes in math, history, science, English, and so on. Rarely are connections made among these distinct subjects. This pattern continues in university and graduate school. It is the way many business schools still structure their MBA curriculum. As a result, every year, new MBA graduates enter the workforce with highly specialized business degrees in separate core disciplines.

Let's take the analogy to the next stage of a graduate MBA student who is applying for work in the new environment that needs holistic leadership. This graduate has a specialization in Marketing Management and applies for a leadership role in a financial services company. During the interview, he is asked to provide a metaphor for the ideal financial services company. The candidate responds by saying, "I see the ideal financial services company like a wheel of a bicycle. At the hub of the wheel is marketing, and all the spokes represent the

---

2. "Mindset" is defined as the habits of mind formed by previous events or by an earlier environment (from the *New Shorter Oxford Dictionary*).

other departments that support marketing." The interviewer replies, "That is interesting; however, in our organization, we put the customer in the center." The candidate is surprised and even confused by the response. He continues to make the case that marketing is the intelligence of the organization and references several well-known marketing models to validate his argument. The interviewer listens patiently. When the candidate finishes discussing his points, the interview concludes and the candidate is not recommended for the next round of interviews.

The graduate student's training has ingrained a marketing perspective in his mind, and he has developed what we refer to as a "functional leadership mindset." He has been taught to see the world through a marketing lens. As a business leader, he will see business problems as marketing problems. He also will develop marketing solutions. However, as we discussed in Chapter One, a new business environment necessitates new ways of thinking. The entrenched functional leadership mindset blocks the ability of leaders to think in holistic leadership ways.

This gives rise to the entrenched "silo" mentality that lives in many organizations today. Functional leadership becomes "dysfunctional" leadership. A process that is useful to segment and micro-manage parts of an organization begins to impede the leadership capacity to rise above the situation and see the entire organization.

The problem does not seem to be abating. Even the executive development courses are broken into segments and are not providing a holistic perspective of the organization and of leadership. Here is another example of a Vice President in a company who invested considerable time and money to attend a week-long residential executive program on Strategic Leadership.

The executive program was held at a prestigious business school. The VP decided to attend in order to expand his mindset so that he could see "the forest from the trees"—the holistic leadership perspective.

The program was an intensive five-day seminar. Each of the five days began at 8:00 a.m., included a working lunch and dinner

*and ended at 8:00 p.m. The days were filled with back-to-back pre-
sentations by distinguished professors who provided many
stimulating ideas. Some seasoned executives representing some
very respected companies were in attendance. He hoped that this
week would finally pull together a holistic understanding of strategy so that he could apply it back in his own company.*

*The week unfolded in an organized and predictable manner.
By the end of the second day, the pattern became obvious, and it
began to worry the VP. The concern was that the week was too
focused on lectures, case studies and analytical debriefings of the
cases. The faculty members from the school of business delivered
the presentations, and their presentations were not connected in
any way. Furthermore, there was no time built into the agenda for
the participants to talk to one another, to share experiences and to
apply what they learned to their own work environment. The only
time they had to apply and link ideas was during breaks or while
waiting in line at the buffet table during lunch and dinner.*

*When the VP returned to his job, he had all the best inten-
tions to reflect further on some of the ideas, concepts and
models he had learned. However, he struggled to make it fit
together and to apply it to his work. He did not see how he could
apply what he learned to become a more effective strategic
leader. He placed the attractive thick binder from the program on
his desk, and it stayed there. The demands of his job prevented
him from getting back to it for several weeks. By that time, his
energy had waned. He decided to move the binder from his desk
to the shelf behind his desk so at least others could see that he
attended the course, even though it had minimal usefulness.*

This leader was not able to take the many intriguing ideas presented at the weeklong program and integrate them into his own role as a
strategic leader. The learning experience did not help him develop a
holistic understanding of leadership. This company also did not leverage the substantial investment in this program to strengthen the
leadership capacity of this leader.

The fragmented and micro way of thinking about leadership is at the heart of the leadership capacity gap facing organizations. Here are some common problems that result from a functional leadership mindset:

- **It can create both an intellectual and structural rigidity:** The intellectual rigidity refers to the inability of leaders to think outside of their own areas of expertise to tackle complex business problems. The functional leadership mindset has led to structural rigidity as organizations have been built along departmental lines that often do not intersect. This also creates an "inward looking" approach to leadership, often preoccupied with the inner workings of a department and an inability or unwillingness to work outside departmental boundaries. As a result, leaders and their organizations become less responsive to changing environmental events or evolving customer needs.

- **It has over-emphasized rigorous analysis in solving problems:** This process tends to break problems into smaller parts and attempts to resolve the parts of problems. There is tremendous utility in this approach to thinking about problems, and it works well when problems have manageable variables to consider. However, it is less effective for more holistic challenges.

- **It has emphasized the vertical view of organizations where top-down authority and decision-making rule the day:** In the past, leaders were largely promoted for their technical expertise, and so those with the most expertise rose to the highest levels in the organizational structure. Top-down decision-making became prevalent because the leaders with the most expertise occupied the top positions of the organization. This pattern, albeit successful in the past, has become a problem in the current business environment that is more ambiguous and complex.

In the book *Leadership Without Easy Answers*, Ronald Heifetz suggests that the over-reliance on the specialized technical expertise of leaders is becoming increasingly limiting in a more complex world and asserts that this specialization has created some leaders who can handle only technical challenges and problems.[3] (These technical problems are defined as those that typically have clear answers and solutions because there are generally few competing variables and therefore a few "correct" technical solutions.) Leaders are able to generate answers and solutions based largely on their past expertise and experience. Finally, leaders implement their solutions by exercising their formal power and authority within the organization.

However, as the world continues to become more complex and uncertain, specialized technical expertise (in our terms, the "functional leadership") has its limitations. Leaders today are confronted with an onslaught of what Heifetz refers to as "adaptive challenges." These challenges do not have clear answers. Furthermore, a leader's prior experience or expertise may be of little guidance in responding to adaptive challenges. In addition, exercising one's power and authority also is limited because leaders need to rely more on their ability to ask the right questions, create deeper conversations and influence key stakeholders to reach consensus on the best possible choices and decisions.

The fundamental challenge now is that the functional leadership mindset is deeply ingrained; most leaders are unaware of how this mindset influences their day-to-day business decisions. A new kind of dysfunction blocks holistic thinking and creates a leadership capacity void for many organizations.

AN EXAMPLE OF DYSFUNCTIONAL EXECUTIVE LEADERSHIP AND ITS IMPLICATIONS

Here is an example of a group of executives who were struggling because their entrenched functional leadership mindset led them to dysfunctional performance. The story revolves around the team's strategic planning process to shape the future direction for the company:

---

3. Ronald A. Heifetz, *Leadership Without Easy Answers*, (Cambridge, Mass: The Belknap Press of Harvard Press and personal conversations. 1994).

The members of the executive team in this telecommunications company were busy preparing their departmental business plans to present at their upcoming three-day strategic operations meeting, which was going to take place in a beautiful world-class golf resort in Florida. The agenda for the first two days consisted of back-to-back presentations of each departmental plan. The CEO expected all of his executives to present their departmental plans with some stringent conditions. Each had a maximum of two hours, which included thirty minutes of questions and answers. They also would have to be able to address the CEO's questions, and at times, harsh feedback. On the final day, the team was expected to identify five corporate strategies from the departmental plans. The meeting would then end with a "team building" event, which featured a round of golf.

It was not uncommon to see the executives locked away in their offices the week before the meeting, trying to get their presentations completed. They also held meetings with their staffs. They referred to these meetings as "pre-ops." Essentially, the purpose of these meetings was to develop a presentation and then cleanse it so that it would avoid any mention of either problems or limitations. The watercooler conversations among employees at the corporate office compared the executives' behavior to worried university students cramming for their final exams. Others compared it to an annual job interview. In some respect, both these analogies were correct.

The new VP Marketing was particularly nervous about the closing golf game. The CEO and VP Sales were excellent golfers and did a great deal of business on the golf course (the CEO had been the VP Sales before he was promoted to the top job). The VP Marketing rarely played golf and felt that he would be embarrassed on the course. He started taking golf lessons, but he was progressing slowly. Other members of the executive team had their own anxieties about the planning process—their only salvation was that they had to endure this process for just three days a year.

When the meeting actually took place, events unfolded as they always did. Each of the executives went through his or her slide presentation. The questions were kept to a minimum, and the CEO provided his cutting remarks. The first day was long and exhausting. By the end of the second day, the frustration and tension began to mount. The primary reason was that the VP Sales proposed that the call center be reorganized and moved from Operations into Sales. He presented the case that the call center had not been adding value to the company for some time because it had merely functioned as a vehicle for fielding customer complaints. He asserted that under his leadership, he could revitalize the call center and ensure that it would become more customer-focused and sales-oriented.

The call center idea was a shocking concept. No one had ever brought up an idea that could be controversial at the strategic operations meeting. The idea also did not sit well with the VP Operations. She was upset for two reasons. It was the first time she had heard of the idea, and she believed the idea was faulty. She also believed that the VP Sales was primarily motivated by self-interest and his desire to build his own empire, rather than having the best interest of the entire organization. During the breaks she discovered that her colleagues on the executive team also saw this as another power play on the part of the VP Sales. They speculated that the VP Sales had pre-sold the idea to the president on one of their golf outings and that it would be very difficult to stop this change from occurring.

Against the advice of her colleagues, the VP Operations decided to push back and challenge the VP Sales' idea and did so quite forcefully. She knew that she had to take a strong stand to communicate her disagreement with the strategy. The VP Sales responded with equal aggression. The argument went back and forth like a tape-loop, and finally they reached an impasse. The other members on the team rarely added to the conversation, except on one occasion the VP Marketing asked how the idea would affect his department. Strong unexpressed _territorial divisions surfaced within the team. A series of side conversations took place. Notes were passed between executive members, and the meeting lost its focus._

The CEO grew impatient and had enough of the discussion. He decided to intervene and exercise his "leadership." He sided with the VP Sales and declared that the reorganization of the call center would become one of the five organizational priorities in the strategic operations plan. The VP Operations became quite angry and expressed how the CEO once again sided with the position of Sales. The CEO disagreed with the VP Operations. He pointed out the merits of the reorganization of the call center and said his decision was final.

By this point, the VP Operations slunk down in her chair in complete silence. The VP Sales notched another victory, and the CEO continued to push forward the meeting's agenda. The team was deflated, but they managed to identify another four corporate priorities, closely watching for cues from the CEO for his approval. They also managed to participate in the "team building" activity that involved a round of golf. Fortunately, the VP Marketing did not have to play in the CEO's foursome.

By the time the executive team returned to the office, word spread quickly about what had transpired at the off-site meeting. The sales team congratulated the VP of Sales for winning the call center and for his victory over the VP Operations. The VP Operations vented to her management team, bad-mouthing the VP Sales and the CEO. The other VPs did not speak about the off-site in any detail and told their managers to focus their attention and energy on delivering their departmental business plans.

What Went Wrong?

The work of an executive team in developing an organization's strategy is probably the most important collective leadership task. Yet, in this case, significant leadership gaps within the team, and potentially within the organization, are evident. Here is an analysis of what went wrong.

- ***The executive team does not work well together:*** Actually, the executive team is dysfunctional. This team needs to address the core issue of how to leverage the talent on the team.

- ***The strategic operations planning process is flawed:*** Executive team members create the company's strategy in a fragmented manner. The executives work in isolation from one another. They also modify their reports before they present them to avoid controversy, which means that the planning session is not really truthful. The basic underlying assumption is that the company's overall strategy is a sum of distinct parts represented by the cleansed departmental reports.

- ***The CEO does not manage the team's dynamics:*** The CEO only manages the executives through tight controls. He seems incapable of managing this team of executives when conflicts arise. Instead of learning to manage the conflict, and even encourage healthy conflict (without contempt), he exerts his power and shuts down the conversation.

- ***The behavior of the executives back in the office is unprofessional:*** The personal leadership displayed by some of the members of the executive team when they are back in the office is problematic. They feel that bad-mouthing their colleagues and putting down the strategic operations planning process is legitimate behavior. However, it only serves to undermine their personal credibility and the credibility of the entire executive team.

- ***The executives are motivated solely by their own interests and the interests of their departments:*** Many of the executives direct their managers to focus on their own priorities and on making their department look good. The departmental focus will continue to foster deep divisions within the company. Furthermore, the executives fail on their primary responsibility, which is their obligation to lead the entire company to deliver customer value and ensure a return for shareholders. No one department will be able to achieve that outcome alone.

How Bad Could It Get?

What then are the implications to this company if this leadership capacity gap remains unresolved? Could it get worse than the case example description? In most cases, it does. The ripple effect of the dysfunctional performance of the executives often has a direct impact on all employees. Here are some examples of what could occur:

- *The employees start to lose confidence in the company's future:* The executive team begins to lack credibility. Some employees question the future viability and success of the company because their confidence in the senior leaders is eroded.

- *Other teams model after the dysfunctional behavior of the executive team:* The poor dynamics on the executive team become a frequent topic of conversation in the company's rumor mill. The conflicts that exist at the executive team level are legitimized within the organization. The executive rivalry between departments is played out throughout the lower levels of the organization. In some cases, middle- and lower-level teams engage in interdepartmental battles without fully understanding why they are fighting.

- *The flawed strategic planning process can generate wrong solutions and put the company at risk:* The way the executive team develops the company's business strategy is from a "silo" mentality, and it's also not truthful. Since the executives do not deal with the real issues in the company, they are at risk of not having all the information needed to make effective strategic choices.

- *The company fosters deep divisions among the departments:* From a leadership capacity standpoint, the company will be weak in its ability to work holistically across the organization. Employees will spend more time fighting internally, rather than focusing on what it will take for the company to succeed with customers.

- *Organizational change will be vigorously resisted:* The deep departmental divisions will make the company more inflexible and less responsive. Most organizational change efforts will be resisted.

For example, if the company continues to implement the reorganization of the call center, there will probably be a high degree of resistance and push back among employees in Operations.

What Would Be The Wrong Thing To Do To Fix The Problem?

The leadership capacity issues in this case example are very interdependent and interconnected. Most of the executives are only thinking about their part of the problem and not the entire problem; the deeper and subtler issues may go unresolved.

Consider how the executive team could respond if they decided to fix a symptom rather than address the problem holistically:

- The team could take part in an outdoor adventure-training, team-building intervention to learn to like each other and get along better.

- The team could take an external leadership course that would focus on how to enhance their emotional intelligence.

- The CEO could retain an executive coach to work with the VP of Operations and the VP of Sales to help them work together.

Would any of these strategies be able to strengthen the leadership capacity in this organization and on this executive team? It is doubtful. These ideas are too piecemeal and isolated. They don't address the holistic leadership issues within this organization. Nonetheless, this is how organizations have typically gone about strengthening their leadership capacity. They identify one leadership issue and respond by implementing a solution that often does not lead to sustained change.

How Could They Have Done It Differently?

Many issues explored in this case example would benefit from a holistic way of thinking. The strategic operations planning process, the ability of the CEO to build a strong executive team, the ability of the team to lead the entire company, the personal behaviors of each leader—all need to be integrated and be part of the holistic leadership of this organization. However, this organization does not think of leadership in this way. Instead, their leadership approach is fragmented.

Let's consider how holistic leadership could be applied to this case. First, the organization needs to see the strategic operations planning process as a process of developing strategies that benefit the company as a whole, and not a specific department. The executive team should be meeting regularly to track and discuss strategic operational issues and not just engage in strategy discussions once a year. They also should meet together before the annual strategic operations meeting to discuss the data in a candid manner at a high level and gain consensus on the priority business and organizational challenges. It is here that the team should discuss the perceived problem of the call center that was identified by the VP Sales. In many situations, the VP Sales and the VP Operations would hold joint meetings to do the analysis, understand the root causes of the problem and create the business case to rectify the issue.

Each VP on the executive team also should meet with his or her own departmental management team, and together, they should explore the priority challenges and create a high-level departmental plan demonstrating how the department could contribute to the overall strategy. As part of the plan, they should identify priorities they could deliver on their own, those that would involve the resources and support from other functions, and those priorities considered enterprise-wide which would require a cross-functional team to lead. The VPs should then meet with each other to share their plans and to discuss the feasibility of the priorities and what they would need from each other to be successful.

Let's assume that based on their analysis of the call center proposal, the recommended strategy was to keep the call center within Operations but to improve the linkages with the Sales Department. The executive team would meet to review the recommendation. This time they would integrate the work that was done and develop a true "corporate" strategic plan around which the entire executive team could align.

The approach described above is more effective for several reasons:

- It balances functional and holistic leadership, yielding a more thoughtful strategy and business plan.

- Since the departmental managers are involved in the process in a truthful way, the plan is a more effective response to the business and organizational challenges.

- The directors have greater buy-in to the process since they had a say in the priorities for the organization. The strategies will unfold more efficiently.

- Through the process the organization has been able to strengthen its leadership capacity by giving directors an opportunity to develop their strategic thinking and capacity as holistic leaders.

- The executive team has done a more effective job of modeling positive cross-functional team behaviors to the rest of the organization, which will have a ripple effect for how other cross-functional teams operate in the company.

THE NEED FOR HOLISTIC LEADERSHIP

Holistic leadership is not an *either/or* approach of holistic versus functional leadership. It emphasizes an *and/also* approach that validates functional leadership in the context of an understanding of holistic leadership. The new requirement for leadership capacity emphasizes the need to understand the big picture and/also to understand its component parts. One needs to see the environment and the forest and at the same time, fully appreciate the trees and its bark.

Many ideas have emerged in leadership and business over the past couple of decades. Some of the new innovations are the balanced scorecard, learning organizations, knowledge management, customer relationship management and so on. Each in their own way attempt to bring a more holistic way of thinking about organizations.

In contrast, the functional leadership mindset views problems as an either/or problem. Functional leadership struggles with "and/also" scenarios, choosing to create unnecessary dichotomies between issues. For example, for many years, organizations fundamentally believed that environmental responsibility was an either/or issue. Companies could not be seen as being profitable and/also environmentally conscious. As a result, many companies merely chose to focus on financial profitability and largely ignore their environmental responsibility. Today, the issue has evolved considerably, mostly because of government legislation that required these organizations to adjust. Most organizations now accept that they cannot treat this issue as an either/or problem. It is a holistic leadership challenge in which executives must resolve how to be financially viable, and/also be environmentally responsible.

Here are some characteristics of holistic leadership:[4]

- *Holistic leadership thinking strives for balance:* Often, when organizations are in trouble, it is because they do not balance the multiple business ideas. They latch on to a new idea or fad and abandon everything else. Sometimes the new approaches are too extreme and result in failure. It is not uncommon that these organizations end up reverting back to their old ways. Through the process they create unnecessary disruption that harms their organizations. A holistic leadership approach stresses balance. Instead of jumping from one fad to another, it is important to keep the organization steady during change.

- *Holistic leadership recognizes that the world is in constant flux:* To be effective, holistic leaders must have a flexible attitude towards their business environment. Leaders must be externally focused on their environments and their customers. This also means that they design

---

4. Vince Molinaro, "Holism at Work," University of Toronto: Unpublished Doctoral Thesis, 1997.

organizations to be flexible and responsive to change. They also must be personally open to change and willing to shift gears quickly, both in their thinking and their actions.

- *Holistic leadership balances the vertical view with the horizontal view:* At the heart of the horizontal view is the ability to see an organization as an interconnected system; decision-making and information must flow up and down and across organizational boundaries. The ability to influence stakeholders across the enterprise is critical to success.

- *Holistic leadership brings things together by examining how problems and their variables are interdependent and interconnected:* Functional leadership excels at analysis and breaking things apart. In contrast, holistic leadership recognizes that variables are interrelated, and changing one will change all other variables. Holistic leadership strives for synthesis, the essence of which is the ability to identify patterns and themes taking place in the business environment and in organizations and see the big picture.[5] Synthesis relies on intuition and creativity leading to a more integrated perspective of organizations.[6]

The Six Elements of the Holistic Leadership Framework

Through our own research and work with hundreds of clients over the past two decades, we have developed a holistic leadership framework that brings a more balanced and integrated perspective to an understanding of leadership capacity.

This framework can help organizations develop the holistic leadership capacity that is required to bridge the talent, capability, development and values aspects of the leadership gap.

---

5. Jagdish Sheth & Andrew Sobel, *Clients for Life*, (New York: Fireside Books Inc. 2000).

6. Henry Mintzberg, "The Rise and Fall of Strategic Planning," *Harvard Business Review*, November-December 1995.

Figure 3.1   *The Holistic Leadership Framework*

The *holistic leadership framework* consists of six integrated elements, symbolized in Figure 3.1 that are in constant movement and change. It will continue to change. The source of success today may become the source of resistance tomorrow. The holistic leader is very aware of the changing dynamics and the evolutions of the environment.

The six elements define the kind of leadership capacity needed by organizations in the new business environment:

1. *Customer leadership*—is at the center of holistic leadership. Creating a customer-focused organization is crucial to its success. (See Chapter 4 on Customer Leadership.) All the other elements of the framework contribute collectively to successful customer outcomes.

2. *Business strategy*—when effective, business strategy permeates everything in the environment and the organization (see Chapter 5 on Business Strategy). All business activities must be aligned with the overall business strategy.

3. ***Culture and values***—are meaningful when all leadership and employee behaviors are guided by the organizational culture and individual values (see Chapter 6 on Culture and Values).

4. ***Organizational leadership***—aligns and engages the entire organization to focus on delivering customer value and to achieving the business strategy. (See Chapter 7 on Organizational Leadership.)

5. ***Team leadership***—focuses on building motivated and productive work units and providing effective coaching and mentoring for its members. (See Chapter 8 on Team Leadership.)

6. ***Personal leadership***—focuses on who the leader is and wants to be. It challenges leaders to be self-reflective and more deliberate about how they practice leadership at a personal level (see Chapter 9 on Personal Leadership).

To be effective in building leadership capacity, a dual response is required. Individual leaders must commit to becoming holistic leaders and integrating the six elements of the Holistic Leadership Framework. Organizations must focus on helping their leaders develop each of these six elements because they are inextricably linked together and represent the leadership capacity required in the future. Collectively, the six elements of the holistic leadership framework will:

- Focus leaders on driving business results;

- Create the conditions for the organization to achieve sustainable business alignment, employee engagement and customer loyalty;

- Bridge the leadership gap.

> **The outcome of the successful implementation of holistic leadership is an organization in which leadership becomes a business driver of customer loyalty and of sustainable competitive advantage.**

The six elements of the holistic leadership framework are discussed in detail in the next six chapters.

Customer Leadership

In Chapter 3 we presented our model of the Holistic Leadership Framework, consisting of six elements essential to building leadership capacity in an organization. Customer Leadership is the centerpiece of that framework.

Figure 4.1 *The Holistic Leadership Framework*

Customer leadership means that all leaders align around the common understanding of how to deliver value to the external customer. If this alignment is lacking, even if leaders perform their role exceptionally well, ultimately, they will be a detriment to the overall success of the organization.

Executives must "model the way" to build a customer leadership culture and to create a customer-focused organization.[1] One president of a company models customer leadership consistently, and it has a major influence on the entire organization. She positions the customer at the center of the company's business model. She holds consultative meetings regularly with the top fifteen customer presidents (which represent about 80 percent of their revenue) to learn about their needs and to share with them the latest trends that relate to their businesses. She also creates a work environment in which all employees focus on how to deliver greater value to customers. She models customer leadership and in so doing influences the behavior of all employees to be customer leaders as well.

THE CHANGING CUSTOMER DYNAMICS

Organizations should take into account a number of customer dynamics that affect how organizations meet customers' needs. Many customers are very pressured, extremely time sensitive and intolerant of poor service. Customers demand that service providers deliver to their expectations of quality, speed, customization and intimacy. The pressure is increasing dramatically for every leader to focus on customer leadership.

Here are some of the changing customer dynamics:

- *The availability of information:* Customers are more knowledgeable today through Web-based information sources. This places great pressure on leaders to ensure they know their products and services better than their customers. For example, customers used to buy

---

1. James Kouzes and Barry Posner include "modeling the way" as one of the five fundamental practices of exemplary leadership in their book *The Leadership Challenge*, (Jossey-Bass Publishers, 1985) pp. 209–268.

product on the advice of a sales person. Today, many customers arrive at a store (if they go to a store at all) with Web pictures of their product choices and explicit expectations of and questions for sales people. Sometimes the sales people are just one step ahead of their customers; sometimes they are even behind. The same pattern occurs in industries such as health care. Patients arrive to see doctors with self-diagnoses, recommended treatment and preferred medications. Leaders within a variety of organizations are finding themselves in the same situation with their customers.

- *Expectation that a new service introduced by one business should be offered by another business:* The standard is not necessarily set by the competition (as it used to be); it can be set by any similar service or product. For example, if I can pump my own gas and pay by flashing a rubber key on the gas pump, why do I still need to wait in line to pay for groceries? Not only do supermarkets have to be competitive with other supermarkets, but they also have to be competitive with all service innovations.

- *Balancing customers' time spent as consumers with their need for "down time" from consumerism:* Ironically, many organizations do spend time considering the work/life balance issues of their employees, but they rarely consider their customers' "work/life balance" issues. For example, telemarketers call people at their homes during the dinner hour. They do this because this is when they have the greatest chance of getting potential customers at home. Yet, almost all potential customers are frustrated by this practice and are searching for the way to eliminate this sales intrusion. One person who received frequent calls was delighted to find that the response, "We do not take unsolicited phone calls," caused the telemarketer to immediately say "thank you" and hang up. The customers' need for "downtime" has generated new industries based upon call screening, Internet security and other protective measures to preserve the personal space of customers and to fend off offensive business behaviors.

IMPLICATIONS OF CUSTOMER DYNAMICS

These customer dynamics have direct implications for the behavior of leaders within organizations. In the past, the term "customer" was used to refer to anyone who received your work. The concept of "internal customer" was developed and was useful in that business environment. In the current business environment, the new external customer dynamics and demands create the need for all leaders and employees to have a common focus on the external customer. For this reason, we prefer to use the term "customer" to mean the external customer—those outside the organization that receive the value from your work. It is not the adjacent internal departments with whom one works. Those groups are the partners with whom you co-create value to deliver external customer value.

Leaders who excel at customer leadership have a clear line of sight to the external customer, regardless of where those leaders work in the organization—manufacturing, R&D, HR, finance. Here is an example of an internal department within an organization that was struggling with the need to change to an external customer leadership perspective.

> *The legal department within a global technology business boasted privately that they had one of the largest corporate law firms of any company in the world. Eventually, the executives heard the message and asked: "Why do we have so many lawyers in our company?" They commissioned a study to determine the value of an internal law firm versus using an external law firm.*
>
> *Part of the study included detailed interviews with the company's most senior lawyers globally, the country presidents and the functional vice presidents. Two of the questions asked were "Who are the customers for the legal department?" and "Who is the competition for the legal department?"*
>
> *The lawyers identified many customers for their services—all internal. Their perception of their customers included the company presidents, the various functional vice presidents and the employees within the company. They believed that their competition was*

the external law firms who could replace them and take away their work, the paralegal professionals who worked in each geographical area, and, in some cases, the line managers who subcontracted legal services work without making it known to the legal department.

The presidents and functional vice presidents had quite a different perspective. They believed that the legal department had the same customers they had—their external customers. Both their customers and the legal department were working to sell product to various telephone companies globally. The legal department worked with their business partners to deliver value to the external customers. The competition for the legal department was the competitors' legal departments, not the various groups from within their own company or external law firms.

A number of the executives also complained about the perfectionism of the legal department. One example cited was that the legal department was an important factor in several lost opportunities to acquire intellectual property. Apparently, the legal department negotiated aggressively and then required an intellectual property (IP) owner to sign a detailed 80-page contract, which could take a week to prepare. On several occasions, the competition's legal department succeeded in acquiring the IP because they were friendlier negotiators and offered the IP owner a four-page IP contract that was easy to understand and was prepared within a day. The competitor's legal department became a source of competitive advantage in the acquisition of intellectual property. The legal department was informed that they either needed to learn how to be flexible with IP owners or some significant changes would need to be made.

The legal department leaders were perplexed by the feedback from the presidents and functional vice presidents. They saw their role as the protectors of the company from any risk or liability, and they believed they performed that role exceptionally well. They were unclear about their role as part of the growth engine of the business.

This case example illustrates a common "customer leadership" problem. The legal department succeeded as an internal control and as a service organization, which had met the needs of the organization for a long time. While the conditions of the business environment changed, the legal department and its leadership stayed the same. There was a mismatch between the new customer dynamics and the old leadership response.

The legal department in the competitor's organization evolved to become business partners with their executives. Their customers needed the IP faster and at a reasonable price and the executives and legal worked together and co-created value for them. The competition was demonstrating customer leadership.

The end of the story is that significant structural and leadership changes were implemented in the legal department to make it more focused on their external customers.

THE PUBLIC AND PRIVATE SECTOR CUSTOMER

The concept of a public sector customer is quite different from that of a private sector customer. Public sector organizations include governments, hospitals, nonprofit agencies, etc. Public policy analysts know there is a difference between the "interest of the public" and the "public interest." Essentially, the interest of the public means that whatever the public wants, the public gets (the private sector model of the "customer"). The proper approach to public policy is to focus on the "public interest," which refers to what is in the long-term public good. Public policy analysts weigh different "interests of the public" regularly and then attempt to make astute choices that are in the long-term "public interest" of society.

The following example of a common public sector customer error illustrates the important difference between the private and public sector customer.

Many educational institutions have embraced private sector language and speak of customer satisfaction as their highest strategic objective. In one academic institution, the professors were advised not to fail any students unless they had a foolproof case against them. They were told that they needed to have the same level of verifiable data required to fire an employee for "cause." One professor decided to fail a student who did not attend class and who handed in mid-term and final papers that were inadequate. The student complained that she paid a great deal of money to attend the university, and the professor had no right to fail her. She was a dissatisfied customer, and the university needed to respond. The professor was required to defend her position and had to review every mark she gave to her student throughout the year. After an exhausting process, they did fail the student; however, the professor learned that in most cases the effort would not be worth it.

This approach to the customer was based upon the assumption that the student was the customer. The university had to satisfy their customer regardless of the correctness of the professor's decision. The professor became the victim when the student complained, even if the professor won the appeal.

The error in this situation is the university's definition of the customer. They defined "customer" in terms of the "interests of the student"—allowing students to get what they wanted—rather than defining what was in the "students' interest." The university's concern needed to be focused on the long-term good of the student and of the society within which the student would work. The measure of customer satisfaction is not dependent on student course evaluation or student complaints (although these measures should be tracked as one measure). It is dependent on the overall development of its student graduates and their overall contribution to society.

Some industries in the private sector need the "customer's interest" to be thought about over the "interests of the customer." For example, a company that sells alcohol needs to show that it is socially responsible through advertising that encourages people not to drink and drive. A company that produces toxic waste needs to ensure it is concerned about the long-term good of the environment and not just the immediate interests of the customer. The production process may be more expensive because of the safeguards to the environment—but that is in the customer's interest.

Regardless of the need to focus on the "customer's interest," public sector organizations must also deliver quality service like their private sector counterparts. Public sector leaders need to understand the changes in customer dynamics and be able to respond quickly to deliver value in the customers' interest.

FIVE EXPECTATIONS OF CUSTOMER LEADERSHIP

To be successful, holistic leaders need to be attentive to the new customer dynamics and how they affect their organizations. These are the five major expectations of leaders to effectively demonstrate strong customer leadership:

1. *Every leader needs to be able to hear the customer's "voice" in everything they do:* The customer's "voice" refers to the customer's interests, concerns, motivations, etc. The holistic leader actively listens for that voice in a variety of ways, including:

   - Building a liaison with the sales and marketing professionals to understand what the customers are telling them directly.

   - Inviting other business unit leaders into their functional area to understand the holistic perspective of the customer challenges.

   - Ensuring that every leadership team meeting includes a discussion about how value is created for the customer.

- Requiring that each executive member see a customer at a minimum of once a month, so that they hear the voice of the customer regularly.

It is important to note that the challenge to hear the customer's voice in public sector environments is much greater than in the private sector. The leader in the public sector needs to hear the many disparate interests of the public and eventually comprehend the "voice" of the "customers' interest." This elusive voice creates an even greater demand in the public sector for leaders to be alert to their customers' voice. It is important for leaders to talk with their staff constantly about how their work reflects the public interest and how it needs to change over time as the forecast of the public interest evolves.

2. *Leaders who are aware of customer needs should be customer advocates, whether others in the organization are or not:* In one company, the R&D group regularly spoke to physicians, pharmacists and other health care professionals. They had a very good sense of the customer issues but from a different vantage point than the sales and marketing department. This company had an entrenched functional leadership approach that the customer was owned by sales and marketing. However, the sales and marketing professionals rarely solicited their input. No matter where they work within a organization, leaders need to have the internal credibility to be able to speak up for the customer. Holistic leaders do the right thing for the customer in their role as customer advocates.

3. *Leaders need to implement only those changes that are customer driven:* All changes need to be put to the test to determine whether they will deliver enhanced value to the customer. For example, the customers of a food manufacturer are the supermarkets. Any change that is introduced within the food manufacturer's company needs to be connected with an external customer value.

In some cases, the value may even extend beyond the direct customer to the "customer's customer." In the food manufacturer example, the food manufacturer needs to understand the tastes and preferences of their customer's customer (i.e. the consumer). Changes may be driven by consumer needs as well as by the direct customer needs.

An important implication for customer leadership is that if the changes cannot be traced to the delivery of customer value (and it is not a legal requirement), then the change should be questioned and perhaps not made. This expectation is somewhat more challenging for customer leadership in the public sector. Sometimes a change that is contemplated will be in conflict with specific customer segments that are motivated by issues that are in their own interest but not in the overall "public interest." Therefore, public service leaders need exceptional capabilities to manage stakeholder relationships, engage in dialogue and reach consensus among parties with very different viewpoints.

4. *Leaders need to be knowledgeable about the entire value chain of how work is delivered to the customers and ensure that the value chain interdependencies work efficiently and effectively:* Perhaps the best example of a value chain is a team of professional relay racers. Typically, four racers run a prescribed distance with a baton that is handed from one racer to the next as they speed around the track. The difference between the excellent relay racing teams and the other teams is often not the speed of the runners. Rather, the difference is in the hand-off of the baton. The precision of the hand-off makes the difference. It must be done so that the team will not lose any speed. If it is done correctly, the four runners will run as if they are one runner.

The same is true of an excellent organizational value chain. All leaders need to know the entire value chain to deliver customer value, and they must know their role in the value chain. Also, the hand-offs between parts of the value chain must be so smooth that the transfer of work does not slow down or reduce the quality of the value to the customer. Essentially, the vision of the entire organizational value chain is that it operates as if it were one chain without any hand-offs.

Customer leadership emphasizes the need to work with inter-dependent partners exquisitely well. They should work as business partners throughout the value chain. They need to have conversations with other leaders in the value chain from a total organizational perspective and not just from their own functional perspective within the value chain.

5. *All objectives and measures for leaders (and their teams) need to be articulated with a clear connection to the value that the objectives create for the external customer:* Leaders need to explore regularly how their areas deliver value to their customers and how they measure the outcomes. The objectives and measures they develop should have explicit links to the customer value they need to create. For example, a warehousing department receives and ships a certain number of products a day. Their objectives should explicitly identify how the receiving and shipping department ultimately creates external customer value through the department's quality, reliability and collaboration with interdependent partners and customer service.

Of course, the customer needs will continue to change over time. Leaders need to be very aware of changing customer dynamics and their implications for their work, and the objectives for their departments. They need to be flexible as their customers' needs change. They also need to create an organizational culture that will be responsive to customer changes and willingly modify their approach and objectives to meet and exceed customer expectations.

FROM CUSTOMER VALUE TO CUSTOMER LOYALTY

This chapter has described the need for all holistic leaders to focus on delivering customer value. However, in many situations, focusing on customer value is not enough. The new arena for customer leadership is delivering enhanced value and achieving customer loyalty. Customer loyalty is essential in most business sectors in order to retain customers against aggressive competitive forces.

Here is an example of a company that believed they operated as customer leaders and delivered customer value continuously. However, they were surprised unexpectedly by the defection of many key customers who they thought were loyal.

A sales and distribution company executive team was dismayed when they discovered that a number of customers preferred a competitor's products and services. The company regularly conducted customer surveys, and their data indicated that their customers were satisfied. They believed they were in a solid position and that they delivered customer value regularly. The company survey results indicated that over 85 percent of their customers rated them as a "4" or "5" on a five-point scale.

One of the many actions they undertook in order to rectify the situation was to conduct follow-up research with their customers to understand why they were caught unexpectedly by the customer defection. To their surprise, they learned that a rating of "4" meant that the company was providing very good service at a level equal to their competition. However, a "4" rating was not sufficient to achieve customer loyalty if the competition introduced a new innovative way of doing business. Only the customers who rated the company on the scale as a "5" stayed with the company—even in the face of formidable competitive challenges.

The company leadership realized that the way to achieve loyalty and ensure customer retention was to stay ahead of the competition. They also learned that the total percentage score of "5" was a better predictor of customer loyalty than the total percentage of "4s" and "5s." Their total percentage of "5s" was only 28 percent. Only one third of the satisfied customers were loyal.

For leaders to achieve customer loyalty, it is essential that they stay one step ahead of the competition. Also, achieving a rating of "5" (on a "1" to "5" scale of customer satisfaction) can define loyalty in most sectors, whether it is a commodity transaction business or it is a complex outsourcing strategic partnership. It also can be an early warning indicator of financial success or erosion for a company.[2]

Figure 4.2 shows four categories of customer value that are common in supplier-to-customer relations. Each higher category is characterized by enhanced customer value that reflects a closer relationship between the supplier and the customer. In general, a customer loyalty rating of "5" is achievable when an organization is able to provide customer value at least one category higher than the category provided by the competition.

Each category starts with the letter "C" for ease of recall and is described below in detail. The customer values—the 4 Cs—are the following:

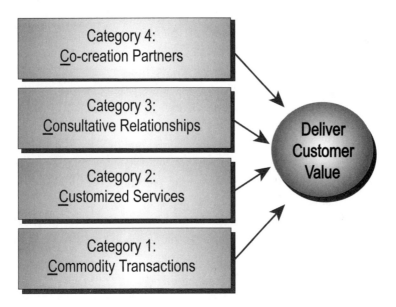

Figure 4.2   *The four categories of customer value*

2. Interestingly, the pattern differs when the same analysis is conducted on employee survey data. The need to increase the number of "5" ratings is important to reflect customer loyalty, but it is an unnecessary standard (to achieve ratings of "5") on employee surveys. The cumulative rating of "4s" and "5s" is sufficient to measure employee engagement.

Category 1: Commodity Transactions

The most common supplier and customer interaction is in commodity product sales. Commodity transaction businesses create shareholder value by selling high-volume products with low margins. Businesses have made many attempts to create new innovations in commodity transactions to generate customer loyalty ("getting to 5"). Most of the innovative approaches involve applying some customization to the commodity transaction.

An important competitive arena in commodity transactions is customization through the use of technology to save time for the customer. Many customers prefer commodity transactions that require little or no human contact, allowing them to make their purchases quickly and painlessly. This pattern is exemplified by customers who are willing to pump their own gas; bus their own trays at fast-food restaurants; and use the telephone, Internet or automatic banking machines to book their own flights and vacations. The technology allows customers to save time and customize the commodity service the way they want it.

The commodity transaction business that generates customer loyalty through the use of technology needs to be operationally excellent.[3] For example, cable and satellite TV companies are becoming a competitive threat to video stores by mass customizing "video on demand" to the home—replacing store-based video purchases. When this service becomes operationally excellent (unlimited choice of movies, ease of access, reasonable price, quality reception, etc.) then it could easily replace the video store as the preferred method of renting videos. Only the very loyal video store customer (the "5") and those without cable and satellite access will remain with the storefront video shop.

The leader in the "commodity transaction" business needs to know how to achieve quality at low cost and reduce any waste that can occur. They also need to understand the business imperatives to find inventive customization strategies to generate customer loyalty.

---

3. Michael Treacy and Fred Wiersema introduced three areas of focus in their work, "The Discipline of Market Leaders," (Perseus Books, 1995). The suggestion is that the discipline of operational excellence will be particularly important for companies that wish to sell commodity products and at the same time provide a customer experience of customization.

Leaders need to ensure that their business strategy includes new customization approaches as an essential part of generating customer loyalty and achieving business success. Leaders also should have the capability to influence others (employees, unions, suppliers, etc.) to understand and accept the ongoing changes needed to customize the commodity experience, to sustain the competitive position of the business and to achieve customer loyalty.

Category 2: Customized Services

Businesses that focus on customized services have a unique set of attributes that they offer to their customers, which serves to position them as superior and preferred suppliers. These businesses often sell less volume of higher-valued products or services and with higher margins than commodity transaction businesses. Customized service providers are characterized by specialized services in a specific niche, often with a deep selection of products and/or services. They are expected to be technical experts with the capability to provide specific answers to customer needs. Their customer service agents are very knowledgeable about their products and services. The agents often are customers for the service as well. For example, the specialized shoe store for young athletes will often hire young athletes as the sales persons, wearing the shoes the customers could buy.

Customer loyalty ("getting to 5") for customized service providers requires service providers to consult with customers to understand their needs.

Here is an example of a "customized services" company that suffered because of a leadership decision that reversed their commitment to consult with the customer.

One health care products organization was striving to generate customer loyalty with their customer groups. They coordinated a global summit in Europe to bring together all of their key customers. The summit would be a celebration of the customer and would include a consultative process to help the company deliver even greater value to their customers.

*One month before the summit, the executives announced a
10 percent cutback on expenses. The marketing group was pressured to consider cancelling the customer summit as a cost-saving
initiative. The climate in their organization did not permit an open
discussion of whether the loss of customer good will (due to the
cancellation) would outweigh the savings from the cancellation.
Eventually, under pressure, the summit was delayed, but the cost
in customer "good will" was high.*

*Ironically, one month later the executives decided to reverse their
decision and allow the customers' summit to be rescheduled—but
many of the customers did not sign up for the event this time. The company learned that when they tried to deepen relationships with
customers, they must follow through or they could lose customer loyalty very quickly.*

In some respects, the leaders in this case failed in their role as advocates for the customer. They needed to present to the organization the
risk of reducing customer loyalty if they cancelled the summit. Also,
the executives failed in customer leadership. They needed to understand
the implications of their decision to choose short-term cost savings over
long-term customer loyalty. They also needed to create a climate in
which the mid-level leaders could openly communicate their concerns.

Leaders who want to create customer loyalty in a customized service business need to focus on the following:

- ***Know and listen intently to the customer:*** Leaders need to be very
  knowledgeable of customer trends. They should stay abreast of the
  trends in many areas, including quality, style, speed, customer intimacy, etc.[4] However, it is not enough to know the industry. The leader
  needs to know their customers' business and listen for the nuances
  that make those customers unique within the industry.

---

4. Often companies that strive to achieve customer loyalty are companies that distinguish themselves by emphasizing customer intimacy as described by Treacy and Weirsema in *The Discipline of
Market Leaders*, (Perseus Books, 1995).

- *Make it easy for customers to give their input, and remember what they say:* The work environment supports mechanisms to enable customers to tell what they want. The leader should have extremely high expectations that employees will welcome their customers' ideas and encourage customer feedback, even when it is negative.

- *Leverage knowledge management to enhance customer focus:* The leader ensures that through a knowledge management system employees share information the customer provides. Consequently, all employees can understand the customers' needs regardless of whether they spoke to the customer directly or not.

Category 3: Consultative Relationships

Consultative relationship businesses create value by the depth of their consultations, the assessment of needs, and the correctness of the proposed solutions. Leaders in these businesses must listen intently, diagnose the problem, and then contribute meaningful ideas and solutions based upon their extensive database and "know-how" to resolve the diagnosed problems. Consultative relationship businesses need to provide explicit descriptions of the solutions they recommend to their customers.

For example, a financial advisory organization wanted to deliver greater customer loyalty as a consultative relationship business. Here is what they did.

The organization realized that they could create greater customer loyalty in their consultations if they restructured how they delivered services to their customers. Most of the competition had mid-level advisors who worked directly with their customers, and the executive leadership were internal mentors for the mid-level advisors. The financial advisory organization decided that they could be more competitive if they put their executive leaders in the field and their mid-level advisors in support positions. The executive leaders were responsible for consultative relationships

*directly with customers. The value these executive leaders creat-
ed through their consultations and assessments of customer
needs surpassed what the competition provided. The result was
that this financial firm secured many more key customers
because they put their best talent in their consultative relationships to assess customer needs and to provide recommended
strategies.*

Astute leaders also know when they are not able to provide immediate value. The trained physician knows when the presenting problem
should be referred to a specialist. In business, there also are times when
leaders do not have the assessment capability or the solution. They need
to involve other professionals. They also need to restrain themselves
and know when not to contribute to a discussion if they have nothing to
say. At times they need to remain silent and seek the support of other
colleagues or other external experts.

Leaders in consultative relationship businesses can achieve customer
loyalty ("getting to 5") if they establish their credibility with the customer that they can provide valuable input even before the problem
arises.

The leaders in consultative relationship businesses need to have a
deep understanding of their customers' business and their needs. Here
are some capabilities effective leaders should possess:

- Be able to anticipate issues for the customer even before the customer
  experiences the problem.

- Have strength of character and an interpersonal style that allows
  them to say things to their customers that may appear critical, but
  customers experience it as helpful and in their best interests.

- Emphasize a broader range of consultations—not just the sales-to-
  buyer interface. These consultative relationships can include
  finance-to-finance, warehouse-to-warehouse, service-to-service
  relationships, etc.

Within the organization, leaders in a consultative relationship business do the following:

- Create an internal environment that is focused passionately on delivering customer loyalty in a manner that both exceeds customer needs and is fiscally responsible.

- Channel all work so that it delivers customer leadership and customer value. Leaders know the voice of the customer and include customer issues in employee discussions and team meetings.

Category 4: Co-creation Partners

Companies that co-create value with customers often hope to have very enduring relationships. Co-creation partners become virtual partners for specific applications, services, and/or products without the legal merger and integration of businesses. Co-creation partnerships may be developed for many reasons:

- To expand geographical reach

- To deliver a broader scope of services to customers

- To optimize intellectual capital between the organizations

- To achieve operational excellence and cost efficiencies

- To expand joint customer lists.

Co-creation partners also enter into the relationship with an assumption that they will have mutual loyalty. Successful co-creation partnerships depend upon the trust of one party for the other. They require more than specialty expertise; they require a full understanding of each other's business and an in-depth understanding of the implications of their joint initiatives on both organizations and their people. Co-creation partnerships ensure that their relevant independent and joint strategies are in alignment. They co-create the development of relevant business strategies and organizational plans from their inception to the achievement of their intended outcome.

Co-creation partner also have the potential to deepen customer loyalty ("getting to 5") by becoming a catalyst for change for their co-creation partner. The "catalyst" category becomes the fifth "C" that can be reached from time to time. It is the level beyond co-creation that can build customer loyalty between the co-creation partners.

For example, one organization had a long-standing co-creation partnership. They knew each other so well that when one party faced a serious challenge, the other co-creation partner stepped in and became the catalyst for change beyond the normal expectation of the partnership. This catalyst provides value that surpasses the expectations of co-creation partners. It expands customer leadership to a level in which the co-creation partners proactively think of each other's interests and help each other change and succeed.

Notwithstanding the benefits of co-creation partnerships, the track record for partnerships of this kind is uneven. The trust expectation between co-creation partners is very high, and the trust is often vulnerable to differing motivations, misunderstandings, personal styles and systemic challenges.

The challenge to retain trust is ongoing. Co-creation partners need a full understanding of the characteristics of trust building and how to avoid the creation of mistrust.

Trust takes forever to build and a moment to destroy.
Mistrust takes a moment to build and forever to destroy.

Trust is similar to a precious diamond that takes a long time to cut perfectly but with one flaw can be damaged permanently. Trust is a continuous challenge; one never arrives at full trust. As soon as one stops working at building trust, it can easily slip away. Mistrust, on the other hand, is easy to create, even unintentionally. However, once mistrust is created, it is very difficult to regain trust once again.

Successful co-creation partnerships are built on three key stages of trust. The categories of commodity transactions, customized services and consultative relationships require a minimum of the first two stages of trust, which are often specified in a contractual document. Co-creation partners need a greater focus on all three stages, which often are documented loosely.

The three stages of trust are:

1. ***Trust in your competence:*** The assumption in every relationship between a customer and supplier is that you have the competence to deliver the product or service. In product businesses, the expectation is that the product works. In service businesses, the expectation is that the person who is assigned the work has the skill to do the work. Also, the person knows when the skill required exceeds his or her capability. Often, contracts are developed or regulators control the competence and quality expectations between suppliers and customers. Co-creation partners may assume and not explicitly articulate the specific competence requirements. The trust of assuming competence without a contract is a higher challenge that must be respected.

2. ***Trust in your honesty:*** The trust element of "honesty" is built on the assumption that there is stage one "competence" already. The question is not whether you are capable of doing the work or producing the product. The trust stage of "honesty" reflects the expectation that you will do what you say you will do. Many times trust is broken on unfulfilled promises to deliver commitments. The three categories of generating customer value—commodity, customized and consultative—often have contractual agreements to confirm that these trust stages will be adhered to. Co-creation partners may have an original contract, but this stage can be broken throughout the relationship by missing commitments and not fulfilling promises.

3. ***Trust that if I am vulnerable you will not hurt me:*** This stage of trust building is perhaps the greatest challenge for any relationship, including co-creation partners. Each party will need to trust that if they share information that could make them vulnerable, the other party will not take advantage of that information. Often, the cus-

tomer will want the co-creation partner to sign non-disclosure agreements (or other such documents). However, there still is the possibility that the trust will falter at the moment one party needs their partner the most.

We have found that if co-creation partners are falling into mistrust, a quick way to recover is to find an opportunity at a time of vulnerability to "be there" for the partner and be a catalyst for change. The partner may still harbor some negative feelings; however, the "being there" response to the partner at a time of need is appreciated usually and will contribute to rebuilding the trust and the partnership.

Leaders—who deliver value to customers as co-creation partners—work with their customers in the following manner:

- *Common focus on the customer's customer:* Co-creation partners are concerned about how their customers can deliver value to their customers. In contrast, the other categories are focused primarily on delivering value to the customer directly (not the customer's customer).

- *Joint development of strategy with the customer:* Co-creation partners work with the customers at the planning phase of strategy development (in areas related to the partnership).

- *Customer access to the organization is fluid:* Co-creation partners are candid and open to discussing issues with their customers with full disclosure.

- *Reciprocal value creation:* Both the co-creation partner and the customer derive value from the co-creation partnership. They are interested equally in being part of the process together and soliciting input from each other.

- *Emphasize cross-business team approaches to address customer needs:* The co-creation partner and the customer's teams are integrated at many levels of the organization to resolve issues for the customer's customer.

Within the organization, leaders need to work with the other leaders to create a work environment and culture that is characterized by the following:

- *Agility to adapt and respond quickly to marketplace opportunities:* Leaders will learn about market developments from the customer at an earlier time and need to respond swiftly.

- *Thinking is broad vs. business/product focused:* Internally, leaders need to think beyond the contract and focus on the broader business relationship and the overall needs of their customer/partners.

- *Reporting lines are typically blurred:* The internal organizational fluidity needs to transcend hierarchy and structure. Employees need to be as comfortable working outside their functional areas as they are working within their function. They also need to be candid within the hierarchy and be able to say what needs to be said to higher levels of management (and the senior management need to be open to that kind of feedback and input).

- *Emphasize internal cross-functional team approaches:* Internally, leaders need to address their external customers' needs with the full force of their capability. This means creating cross-functional teams to maximize the assessments and solutions they provide to their customers. Also, these teams need to have excellent capabilities as participants and leaders of virtual teams with the customer.

- *Reward system supports team success and personal contributions to the team:* The rewards and recognition systems in the organization need to reinforce the co-creation partners business model.

CLOSING COMMENTS

The holistic leadership framework (described in Chapter Three) depicts customer leadership as its centerpiece. It is in that place for a reason—

because it is the centerpiece of all leadership. At all times, the leader needs to look for customer value opportunities and for ways to build loyalty and trust. Customer leadership is the launching pad for business strategy. Achieving customer loyalty functions as a core value that shapes the culture of the organization. It aligns all areas to achieve organizational leadership. It focuses efforts for team and personal leadership.

Quite surprisingly, many leaders need to be reminded of the centrality of the customer to everything they do. Some leaders are deluded by their perception of the importance of their own organization and their own work. Holistic leaders know that their value is created by the perception of the customer and the value the customers attribute to their organization and work. This is true for private sector customers who show their commitment by returning for additional business, and it is true for the public sector organizations (that function in the public interest) by virtue of the public recognition of their value to society.

Customer leadership is the lifeblood of the other components of the holistic leadership framework. All leaders and employees need to strive to deepen customer loyalty.

Business Strategy

The traditional approach to leadership relegates business strategy to the most senior executives of an organization or to a designated group of specialists, such as a strategic planning department. However, the speed of change in the business environment necessitates that all leaders understand business strategy, think strategically to react to changes quickly and align their actions and their teams' direction to the business strategy.

The common approach to business strategy needs to evolve if all leaders are expected to think strategically. Many organizations base their strategic plans on an analysis of the environment, and the result is a long list of strategies and tactics to respond to the challenges. This "shotgun" approach assumes that if enough strategies are sprayed into the market place, one of them is likely to hit its target. It is the easy way to develop strategy because there are few choices that need to be made initially. However, this approach is quite problematic for leaders if they are expected to participate in strategic thinking and to implement the strategy effectively.

The "shotgun" approach generates many problems for organizations and its leadership:

• It often leads to excessive waste, distraction and ineffectiveness as leaders are expected to work on multiple strategies that have mixed value.

- The executives may lose their leadership's confidence as they change their direction searching for the right strategy among their initial long list.

- Lower-level leaders in these organizations are often exhausted and overloaded. They are confused about their priority areas of focus for themselves and their teams, which can lead to chaos and mismanagement.

In almost all cases, the shotgun approach leads to suboptimal results and an inability for all leaders to participate in business strategy effectively.

The alternative is the "laser beam" approach to business strategy. This approach requires focus, precision and accuracy (like a laser beam) as the business strategy is developed. The initial development of strategy is more challenging and time-consuming, but the strategy is much easier for the leaders to evolve and implement once it is deployed. The result of a "laser beam" approach is a business strategy designed to achieve a sustainable advantage against the competition and/or to neutralize a competitor's advantage (i.e., competitive parity). The "laser beam" approach guides leaders at all levels to focus on what is important, to continually make choices to align their direction to the intended strategic outcomes and to achieve results with minimal waste and distraction (that is, lower cost). It also requires all organizational, team and personal leadership activities to be aligned with the business strategy.

This chapter examines the business strategy element in the holistic leadership framework.

There are differing opinions about whether or not leaders need to develop a focused "laser beam" business strategy in a formal manner. One perspective is that leaders need to be strategic thinkers, meaning that their thought process is dynamic—evolving from moment to moment. Their belief is that a formal process for developing strategy is a waste of time. In contrast, others believe that leaders need a structured

Figure 5.1 *The Holistic Leadership Framework*

strategic planning approach, which is based on a stable and linear perception of the world. We will argue that both perspectives are valid and
necessary for building the leadership capacity that is needed in most
businesses.

Here is a case example that illustrates this debate:

*It became clear, after many family deliberations, that the eldest
son and daughter were not interested in running the company
founded by their father. He (the owner) was immensely successful in the healthcare sector, but he could no longer run the entire
company alone. The growth of the company necessitated additional senior leaders for its R&D, manufacturing and sales
divisions. The family also debated whether they needed a business strategy to support the future growth of the company.*

The company's strategy had always been quite simple— employees did what the owner wanted them to do. He created loyalty by knowing most of the managers and employees by name, by giving gifts to employees when they were in need and by distributing bonuses in good and in bad years. He ran the company like one big family, and he was the father of the clan.

The leadership gap was most evident in the company's remote locations. First, the family decided to hire a senior vice president for sales in their southern US operations. The new SVP was recruited from a major healthcare distribution center. Then they hired a new SVP of manufacturing and a new SVP of R&D. Within a brief time, the senior leadership of the company had shifted from a family-dominated team to a group made up of the three family veterans and three strong leaders recruited from other companies.

The new SVPs demanded that a company strategy needed to be developed, but the family resisted. Led by the owner, the family argued that they had been successful until now and that they would continue to be successful in the future. They told the new leaders that strategic planning was a waste of time. They also said that the strategy was quite simple: "First, research it, then make it, and then sell it." But this answer was not enough for the new leaders.

Each of the leaders proceeded to develop their own strategic plans. Each of the plans defined the three- to five-year goals, the core strategies and the associated one-year goals. The leaders grounded the strategy by defining how each of the core strategies would be measured, who would be accountable for them, and how these strategies would be reflected in the performance management objectives for each employee. They then summarized their entire business strategy on a "one pager" for ease in communicating. They also were personally involved as they rolled out the strategy to all their employees in their divisions.

Fortunately, the SVPs were astute enough to collaborate behind the scenes. They all used the same business strategy consultant who brought a consistent approach to business strategy to the divisions. Each SVP also invited the other new SVPs to his or her strategy sessions so that they could all align their outcomes.

However, the SVPs realized their efforts were not sufficient. They needed an overarching strategy. They also felt uncomfortable developing a grassroots strategy without the backing of the owner and his family. The SVPs decided to try one more time to convince them that the separate divisional strategies needed to be rolled up into an overall company strategy. Finally, after many weeks of debate, the family agreed—but reluctantly.

The SVPs proceeded to formulate a written business strategy for the company. The family played along throughout the strategy development process. They even agreed to a set of defined core strategies, a new governance model and accountabilities. However, immediately after the company plan was developed, the family lost interest and continued to manage the business the way they had always run it—by the owner's decree. The executive team had meetings, but nothing was decided unless the owner agreed. No new investment occurred without the owner's signature. The overall strategy for the company was treated as a secret, and no one below the senior executives knew about its contents or used the strategy in any way.

Within the next year, one of the SVPs left the company. The other two SVPs and several other directors were retention risks. They felt they had tried to change the company and had failed. They managed their own mandates effectively, but the company remained disjointed.

DEVELOPING BUSINESS STRATEGY

This case illustrates the debate about the value of engaging in a structured strategic planning process. Owner-operated presidents are often strong believers that a formal process for strategic planning is a waste of time. In most cases, owners built their companies on the basis of their great ideas and customer relationships. In the case example, the owner was an outstanding strategic thinker. He did not need an articulated plan because it was clear to him how to bring his thoughts to reality. He was able to govern his organization by telling others what to do. Excellence in that organization was judged by whether you were a good follower—rather than a good leader. The new SVPs wanted a structured and articulated strategic plan to help define the strategy and to give them the empowerment to lead. It is difficult for owners to understand that new leaders do not have the cultural heritage to be able to operate the way owners do. New leaders need a strategy to galvanize the company.

The failure in the story is the unwillingness of each side to recognize the value in the other's approach. The owner was successful without a clearly articulated strategic plan. Only he knew the strategy that was in his head. The SVPs needed a strategy that was published and that could create a focus for all employees. However, the strategic plan without the owner's strategic thoughts lacked the dynamic and depth that the owner had implicitly set as the standard. Consequently, the owner ignored the strategic plan.

Both methods were important, and both methods independently were not sufficient to meet the current and future needs of the company's business environment. It was unfortunate that the two sides did not collaborate and benefit from the value each could provide.

Our approach to business strategy integrates the individualistic strategic innovations typified by the owner with the managerial systematic approach typified by the SVPs. Strategic planning without the dynamic of strategic thinking is static. However, strategic thinking without a vibrant plan will not be carried out.

Business Strategy Differs According to the Business Context

It is important to note that the approach to business strategy will differ according to the type of business. Here are some types that are worthy of consideration:

- *Owner-operated vs. publicly traded:* Our case example above illustrates some of the dynamics in owner-operated companies. The dynamics are quite different in a publicly traded company. Successful owner-operated companies often excel at strategic thinking and are less effective at formalized strategic planning. Publicly traded companies often excel at the rigor of strategic planning but may lack or even stifle the creativity of those engaging in the strategic thinking process.

- *Private sector vs. public sector:* Private sector organizations are able to focus strategy on achieving advantage against the competition or at least competitive parity. Public sector organizations regard the concept of competitive advantage and competitive parity as distasteful notions. However, public sector organizations do have competitors. They just are not easily identified. Their competitors are not the public who uses their services or the private sector companies that can deliver public services. Rather, the public sector competitors are the global standards, the benchmarks or the stated goals. The strategic challenge to public sector leaders is: "How can the organization achieve sustainable competitive advantage against the global standards, benchmarks and goals?" Their strategic thinking efforts are devoted to discovering the co-creation opportunities with citizens, private sector organizations, other non-profit organizations, other governments, etc., to deliver competitive advantage or competitive parity against specific benchmarks.

- *Independent vs. subsidiary operations:* Independent business leaders engage in the entire business strategy process. In contrast, wholly owned subsidiaries may only have a part of the business strategy to develop and deliver. For example, a home appliance sales and distribution subsidiary developed its strategy. It decided to grow its market through deepening its alliances with builders of condominiums and apartments. The subsidiary also decided to address its excess capacity in warehousing space by turning the warehousing unit into a stand-alone business unit that would sell warehousing space to other companies. However, their headquarters' executives rejected the warehousing strategy as an inappropriate distraction for the subsidiary company. Instead, they instructed the subsidiary to move from the larger warehouse to a smaller warehousing space. The subsidiary leadership learned the limits of subsidiary strategy development. Their strategy needed to be grounded in the vision, mission, values and core strategies of the overall company. The subsidiary had a limited role in developing the strategy and a greater role in deploying the plan and evaluating its outcomes.

THE BUSINESS STRATEGY PROCESS

In the remainder of this chapter, we focus on the business strategy process. Each section explores one of the five phases of business strategy and applies it to related examples. We then identify ways to leverage the phases of business strategy development to both achieve effective business outcomes and to develop high-potential leaders.

To simplify the recall of the five phases of the process, we summarize them with five letters: *ABCDE*, with each letter representing a phase of the business strategy process. Leaders need to develop excellence in each of these five phases (illustrated below in Figure 5.2) to succeed at the business strategy element of the holistic leadership framework.

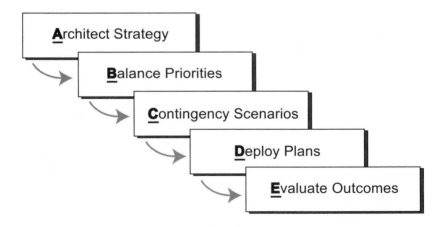

Figure 5.2 *The Business Strategy Process*

ARCHITECT STRATEGY

Leaders who are able to architect a business strategy rely heavily on their own and their teams' ability to think strategically. "Strategic thinking" refers to the ongoing thought process that leads to the co-creation of value with customers, stakeholders and business partners. Here are some characteristics of effective strategic thinkers:

- Strategic thinkers start with the assumption that strategy does not require your organization to win at the expense of the suppliers or the customers. Having better quality and quicker response time does not have to cost more.

- Strategic thinkers are always looking for opportunities to focus their organizations on delivering excellence, achieving competitive advantage and building enduring relationships with customers and suppliers.

- Strategic thinkers also focus on finding efficiencies through driving costs out of the system, reducing response time and leveraging economies of scale.

Research-Based Environmental Analyses

In order for leaders to architect a strategy, first they need to conduct research to understand the evolution of the business environment. Three environmental research analyses are important for developing a strategy:

- *Customer value analysis:* Customer value analysis identifies the major external customers' values in product and service delivery and assesses the organizational performance with each customer.[1] It also compares the customer findings with the findings of the customers of the competition. The analysis generates an overall customer measurement of company performance compared to the competition and identifies business opportunities and gaps. The analysis yields recommendations that result in suggested customer value enhancements.

---

1. See Bradley Gale, "Managing Customer Value," *The Free Press*, 1994.

- *Competitive analysis:* Competitive analysis focuses on the competitive dynamics that are important in the analysis of how to achieve sustainable competitive advantage or competitive parity. It explores a number of elements, including the industry competitive structure, innovations that can replace the company's products/services, and customer and supplier initiatives that can reduce the organization's part of the value chain from development to delivery.

- *SWOT (_S_trengths, _W_eaknesses, _O_pportunities, _T_hreats) analysis:* We approach the SWOT analysis by first exploring those external opportunities the company should focus on to achieve success and the external threats that will block the company from being successful. The leaders then need to identify the implications of the opportunities and threats for the development of strategy.

The analysis of the internal strengths and weaknesses is done after the completion of the customer value analysis, the competitive analysis and the business opportunities and threats. The focus is on the strengths and weakness that are relevant to the new environmental context. The internal strengths and weaknesses analysis are determined by answering the following questions:

- What are the internal strengths that can be leveraged to capitalize on the customer value, competitive analysis and business opportunities, and also mitigate the threats?

- What are the internal weaknesses that may jeopardize the potential to capitalize on the customer value, competitive analysis, and business opportunities and allow the threats to appear?

Architecting the Strategy

Once the future environmental context is understood, the leaders are able to develop the strategy. Figure 5.3 shows how a strategic plan cascades down from vision to strategic initiatives (S) to specific goals (G) and finally to deployable business plans and performance accountabilities.

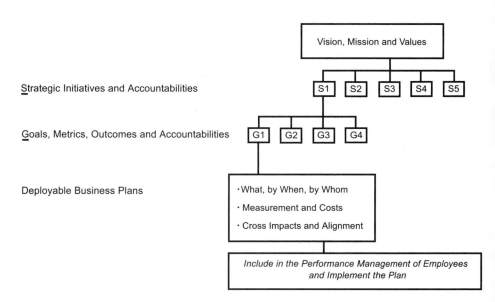

Figure 5.3 *Cascading the strategy from vision to implementation*

The leader who is an architect of strategy requires an *inductive* thought process (characterized by strategic thinking) to identify the innovative thoughts and ideas for the co-creation of value with customers and others. Subsequently, the architect of strategy requires a *deductive* thought process to reduce the macro "big picture" visions and core strategies into workable goals, metrics, outcomes and accountabilities.

The inductive thought process begins with the leaders studying the business customer and the characteristics of the current and future competitive environment. They then use inductive reasoning to develop the business vision (the preferred future reality), its mission (what it does on an ongoing basis to achieve the vision), and its core values (what is important as it strives for the vision).

The inductive analysis helps the leaders identify the strategic initiatives to respond to the anticipated future business environment. We recommend that businesses identify a maximum of five strategic initiatives that will deliver competitive advantage and/or competitive parity.

The number five is not a magic number; it's simply that most people cannot focus on or remember more than five strategic initiatives at one time.

Most businesses include an initiative that focuses on their people and/or leadership as one of the top five strategic initiatives. This strategic initiative should focus on the area of risk associated with its people or leadership that needs to be mitigated. Some examples of people/leadership strategic initiatives are "build leadership capacity," "create competitive advantage through employees" and "create a workplace of distinction." Each one of these strategic initiatives was chosen to respond to current and anticipated business deficiencies that needed attention for the organization to succeed in the future. One of the main purposes of this book is to provide the road map that will enable organizations to respond to the strategic initiative to "build leadership capacity."

Some businesses also include a "capability development strategy" among the five strategic initiatives. This strategy focuses on building the competency and capacity that the business deems essential for the future. For example, one company's executive team realized that they needed to develop the capacity to build alliances to be able to compete globally. They decided to include in their business strategy a two-year "capability development strategy" to develop the capacity to identify global alliance partners, negotiate cross-culturally and achieve mutually beneficial outcomes.

Exceptional seniors leaders set themselves apart when they can think inductively and deductively. Leadership development should provide leaders with the opportunity to build inductive and deductive reasoning skills. However, if leaders are not able to develop these skills, they will need to find the complementary leadership talent to provide them.

BALANCE PRIORITIES

One of the primary challenges in developing a business strategy is to balance the forces for growth with the forces for efficiency and economies of scale. Executive teams rarely revisit priorities and remove goals and projects from their strategies. In most organizations, new priorities are just added to the business plans. Over time, the overabundance of priorities overwhelms employees and distracts them. (If everything is important, how does the employee know what is *really* important?)

For example, in one company the CEO never abandoned any goal or project. The company had fourteen strategic initiatives. The directors expressed significant concern, so the executive team went away to "really focus on the real priorities." They returned with five strategic initiatives. Upon close examination, they had just reshuffled the 14 strategic priorities (actually adding a few more) and bundled them under five broader strategic initiatives. They believed they provided greater clarity by reducing the number of strategic initiatives, but they actually continued to confuse and distract people. Because each strategic initiative was so large, people had a hard time figuring out where they should focus their attention.

Balance Priorities Through Work Optimization

Leaders need to reduce their investments in lower-priority work and reinvest in the areas that develop strategic growth. Most executives would prefer to have unlimited funds to grow strategically and retain what they have. However, throwing more money at new strategic initiatives and goals is no longer a viable option. Leaders need to balance their priorities to manage costs and, at the same time, implement new business strategies. Porter reflected on the need to balance priorities and make trade-offs. He wrote: "Strategy is making trade-offs, in competing. The essence of strategy is choosing what *not* to do. Without trade-offs, there would be no need for choice and thus no need for strategy."[2]

---

2. Michael E. Porter, "What is Strategy?" *Harvard Business Review*, 1996.

> **Leaders need to know what not to do**
> **in order to be free to focus on what needs to be done.**

The need to balance priorities has led many organizations to develop a reinvestment strategy in which the growth investment is balanced with ways to save money through work optimization. One company was experiencing this challenge to balance priorities in order to achieve business growth in a climate of constraint. The executives decided to issue an edict that no division was authorized to add any FTEs (full time equivalents) to their workforce during the current fiscal year. However, they were still required to meet their growth targets. One regional sales group was in a market that was performing well and required additional sales representatives to sell more. However, in the climate of constraint, they were not authorized to hire more sales people.

They needed to analyze how to optimize work so they could hire more sales people and retain the same number of FTEs. The first choice was to identify allocated vacancies that were not filled. They were able to remove several of the vacancies and turn those allocated resources into new hires in sales. They then explored how to realign their sales force and move sales people from old legacy products to the new products that created the business opportunity. However, it was not enough. They needed to explore other ways of work optimization.

Figure 5.4 shows eight ways leaders can balance their priorities through strategic work optimization:

- *Reallocate resources through vacancy analyses, redeployment of underutilized resources and FTE realignment (Items 1, 2 and 3):* Reallocating existing resources is the most direct way to balance priorities. In the previous case example, the company approached the problem by removing allocated vacancies and reassigning sales people to the more profitable product lines. They also could have shifted underused resources.

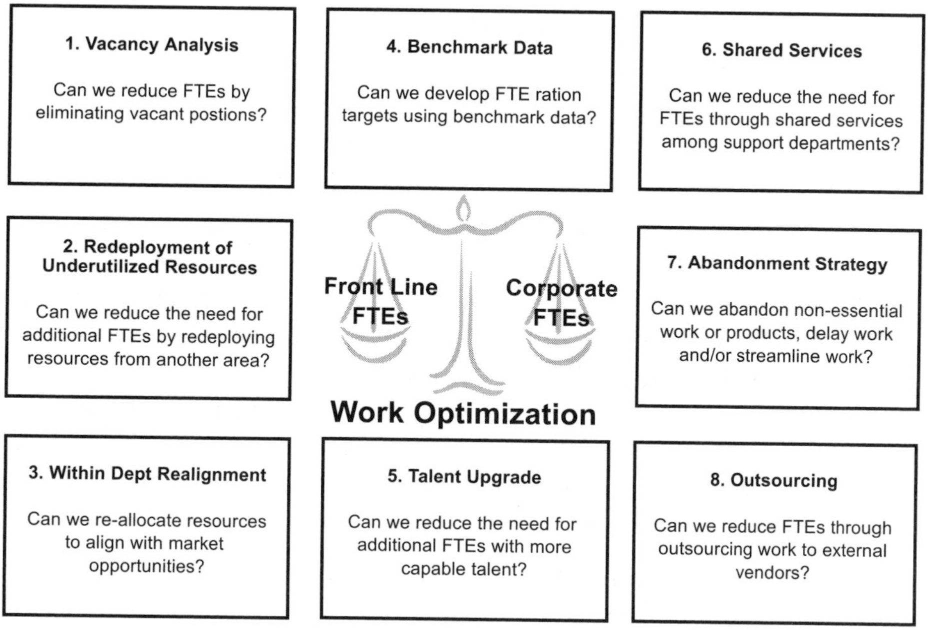

Figure 5.4 *Balance priorities through work optimization*

- *Establish standards through benchmarking (Item 4):* Some organizations find they do not know how many people are required to perform a certain area of responsibility well. For example, one organization discovered, through benchmark analysis, that it employed a very high ratio of planning staff compared to its competition. The benchmarks created a compelling argument to reduce planning staff and reallocate those people to other roles.

- *Reduce the total FTEs by talent upgrades and/or by creating shared services (Items 5 and 6):* Some areas of an organization may require a higher number of employees because their current employees are underperforming. If the employees' skills are upgraded or if the standards are raised, then (theoretically) fewer employees could achieve the results required. Also, shared services can be created to deliver more efficiency, leverage the best talent in one department and also reduce the total number of employees required to do the work. Shared services are created frequently for parts of support functions such as HR, IT, finance, communications and real estate.

- *Reduce the total FTEs by abandoning, delaying or streamlining non-essential work (Item 7):* The challenge to *not* do work that is done currently often meets great resistance. Employees and leaders become attached to their work. They often lack the perspective to balance the priorities between work they are doing and other work that needs to be done. Nevertheless, the abandonment of work in a disciplined manner is an important strategic capability that leaders need to have. There are four methods of abandoning work, each starting with the letter "D."[3]

  - *Dump:* Stop doing the work. Most work that can be "dumped" is work that is duplicated elsewhere (e.g., tracking on paper and electronically) and unnecessary work (e.g., underperforming products, responding to unsolicited resumes, eliminating underutilized metrics and reports).

  - *Delay:* If the work does not require immediate attention do not do it now (e.g., upgrading to a system that is working well, launching a high-risk service).

  - *Distribute:* The right person is not doing the work. If someone else does the work then it would create efficiencies (e.g., consolidate planning, metrics management, data warehousing).

  - *Diminish:* Streamline the work and simplify it (e.g., process simplification, lean thinking, simplify complex reports, reduce multiple signatures, tackle e-mail overload).

---

3. See David S. Weiss, *High Performance HR: Leveraging Human Resources For Competitive Advantage* (John Wiley & Sons Canada, Ltd., 2000). Chapter 3 focuses on the discipline of abandonment, which provides much more detail on how to proceed with an abandonment process.

The questions in the table below are extremely effective in helping leaders discover how their work can be abandoned and more effectively optimized.

1. **Value to customers:** If you had to choose the work that was most strategic in nature and had to be kept on your plate, what would it be? What kind of work may be of lower value to customers? What alternative ways may this work get done even though it is removed from your plate?

2. **Time invested:** What kind of work consumes most of your time? Could that work be done in less time if it were done differently, less intensively, more efficiently, etc.

3. **Work the internal client can do:** What work (if any) are you doing that internal clients can do equally well (within reason)? Is there work that you are doing that can be done by the internal client reasonably well if they learned how to do it?

4. **Work satisfaction:** What is the work that you least enjoy or derive little satisfaction? For which role (or for whom) would this work be more satisfying?

5. **Underutilizing your talents:** What areas of your work are not leveraging your knowledge, skills and capabilities? How else can that work be done?

6. **Work your direct reports can do:** What work should your direct reports do that you are doing instead?

7. **Summary of your work to optimize:** Overall, in assessing your current work priorities and overall workload, what areas may be optimized (where are there potential inefficiencies)?

- *Change the balance of FTEs within and outside the organization through outsourcing (Item 8):*
  Some jobs in an organization can be performed more effectively and at less cost for modernizing if they are done by external outsourced service providers rather than by internal resources. For example, many companies outsource non-core services such as food services, security, custodial services. Outsourcing also is used for core services, such as sales, service and information technology.

  Two important key success factors in outsourcing are:

  - The return on investment for a company that decides to outsource work is much higher if the work that is outsourced is functioning well and is optimized for efficiency purposes prior to outsourcing. The benefits of optimizing the work prior to outsourcing are twofold: (1) the way the work is optimized will be consistent with the way your organization needs it to operate, and (2) the out-sourced company will not be able to extract a premium for optimizing the service on your behalf.

  - The company should identify a skilled vendor manager who will be accountable as the manager of the outsourcing relationship and the service contract.

CONTINGENCY SCENARIOS

It is important to distinguish between the phases of the business strategy process that we describe as "balancing priorities" and "contingency scenarios."

- *Balancing priorities* focuses on how to grow in a climate of constraint.

- *Contingency scenarios* involves planning for the worst and knowing how to respond to those scenarios if they occur.

  Airline pilots are trained aggressively using contingency scenarios. Part of their training involves sessions in a simulated cockpit in which they are bombarded with one contingency crisis after another. The hope is that none of the crises will ever occur. However, if they do, the pilots will be able to respond quickly, professionally and calmly. A similar, but less dramatic approach occurs in the contingency scenarios phase of business strategy. Here is an example of an innovative contingency scenarios process.

> *One executive annually challenged his senior directors to a scenario-based contingency planning exercise. His commitment was that the resources the senior directors secured during strategic planning and their financial targets would remain untouched regardless of the solutions they identified to the scenarios. He gave each leader a disaster scenario to contemplate. The leaders had to develop their strategy for responding. Some of the leaders solved the problem by reallocating resources that they had elsewhere. They obviously had some room to maneuver that they were not disclosing when they first developed the strategic plan. Others did not have extra resources, and they had to discover innovative ways to respond to the challenge.*

The exercise was very useful for three reasons:

- It gave the executive the assurance that each one of his senior directors had a "plan B" strategy. If a contingency plan was required during the year, the leaders would be able to respond without delay and would even be able to discover ways to leverage the side benefits of a crisis.

- It gave them more confidence in their original "Plan A" knowing that they had a strong "Plan B".

- The exercise addressed an aspect of the leadership gap in the area of thinking strategically, and it developed the senior directors' capacity to think strategically and to manage crises.

Often, executives avoid contingency scenario planning. Some avoid contingency planning because of the disheartening scenarios that it presents. Others do contingency planning on mundane issues and do not address business-threatening scenarios. These executives are avoiding the primary purpose of contingency scenario planning, which is to anticipate problems before they occur. Executives may not want to create undue pessimism in the organization by speaking about the contingency scenarios, but there is no excuse for the executives to avoid the contingency analyses themselves.

One useful source of contingency scenario planning is the "threats" that are identified in the SWOT analysis. Consider what the response would be if multiple threats occur simultaneously. How should the strategic thinking leader respond to that challenge? An organizational measurement "dashboard" can then track these threats regularly. The dashboard indicators give early warning signals to the executives to track the threat and determine whether or not a preemptive response would be appropriate.

For instance, one pharmaceutical company was facing the threat of losing their patents on a number of major drugs in the next few years. They engaged in strategic planning, but no one mentioned that 30 percent of the company's revenue was about to disappear when the company no longer owned the patents. There was a remote chance that the patent protection for these drugs could be extended, but it was unlikely. The conversation about these drugs and the implications for the company should have been central to the strategic plan. At minimum, it should have been a key scenario to consider in a contingency planning process. However, the obvious contingency scenario was avoided.

As one leader said: "Hope is not a strategy." Strategic plans that are developed carefully will still face numerous obstacles during the duration of the plan. The more uncertain the environment and the competitive arena, the more essential the contingency scenario planning process. The effective leader is expected to anticipate and respond to the contingency challenges quickly and professionally.

DEPLOY PLANS

One president said at the outset of a strategic planning process that he could fit a tissue paper between his company's strategies and those of his competitors. All the presidents were reading the same books and listening to the same gurus. The difference between his company and his competitors was in the implementation. The company that uses the innovative ideas will win the competitive challenge.

Deploying the strategic plan is not done in a static moment in time after the completion of the planning. The strategy deployment is a continuous process that should be discussed as you architect the business plan, when it is completed and announced, and on an ongoing basis afterwards to ensure it is implemented effectively. The leader who engages in business strategy and then does not give equal focus to deployment is missing the essential purpose of the strategy development process.

The Leadership Communications Challenge

One major challenge in the "deploy plans" phase of business strategy is the communication of the strategy.

Many executives spend a great deal of time developing strategy and little time on communicating it.

Not surprisingly, these executives are perplexed when their employee survey results indicate that their employees do not understand the strategy. The executives wonder what they should do differently to ensure that all employees understand the strategic direction.

We have found three key success factors in the leadership communications of strategy. These are:

1. *Write and communicate the strategy from the vantage point of the receiver of the information rather than the sender of the information:*

In one situation, the president rolled out a strategy and spent most of the presentation explaining EBIDTA, gross margins and earnings per share. However, that was a reality that was foreign to most employees. The strategy was well articulated but it was not understood. The executive needed to translate the strategy into language that the employees could grasp. In contrast, another company's president committed to communicating in this manner. He regularly brought in a group of frontline supervisors to listen to a final draft of his presentation. The frontline supervisors' quizzical looks were very helpful to the president to revise the presentation by translating the message into a language that the "receivers" understood.

2. *Local leaders communicate the message directly to their functional areas, and the president's message validates the local leaders' message:* A common error in the deployment of a strategy is to rely on the CEO to deliver the initial message that describes the strategy. Employees often are unable to absorb the plan when they hear it for the first time, even if it is communicated to them in language they understand. Most employees want to hear the strategy directly from their department or business unit leader, the person to whom they report or at least someone with whom they work closely. In these sessions, the local leaders speak candidly with their direct reports about the strategy, its implications and the employees' role in its implementation. They also discuss how the strategy will be tracked and evaluated. Employees then can ask questions with less concern that they may appear foolish. The CEO does have an important role in communicating the plan, but it is as the executive who validates the plan after the employees have heard it more informally.

3. *Ongoing dialogue about the strategy with employees:* Employees need to hear about a new strategy repeatedly to internalize the message of the new direction. Many effective leaders use their staff meetings as an opportunity to help employees internalize the strategic direction and to discuss how new business ventures align with the business strategy. Also, they invite executives from outside their departmental area to discuss their work on architecting strategy,

balancing priorities and work optimization. The employees will benefit from the deeper and broader understanding of the strategy. This understanding will help them align their independent decisions and actions to the overall strategic direction.

Other Effective Deployment Leadership Tactics

Here are five additional leadership tactics to increase the probability of effective deployment of strategy:

1. *For each business unit, develop mini strategies that align with the overall strategic plan:* This process provides an opportunity for the leaders to develop strategy in a local environment and to ensure that the local strategy is aligned with the overall business direction.

2. *Ensure that employees know the strategic direction and have individual performance accountabilities that are directly linked to the strategic plans:* The individual employee accountabilities can be identified when the local leader convenes a session to define the mini-strategy for his or her function. The remainder of the individual accountabilities are developed in private performance management and coaching sessions.

3. *Implement a set of metric indicators to track progress on the strategies:* Govern the strategic plans through metrics and indicators of success. The indicators should track progress on both growth initiatives and efficiencies. They also should track the potential development of problems that may block achievement of the strategic objectives and that may require a contingency planning response.

4. *Remove any barriers that can limit the effectiveness of the plan:* Leaders need to watch for problematic systems and processes that can slow down the deployment of strategy or impede its effectiveness.

5. *Be prepared to modify the plan, if required, as environmental conditions change:* The strategic plan cannot be a static document that

is put in a drawer and not looked at until the next year. It needs to be vibrant and tracked to determine if the intended course still makes sense.

EVALUATE OUTCOMES

An executive team spent four hours with their "dashboard committee" evaluating outcomes on the measures for each of their company divisions. Each indicator on the "dashboard" was assigned a color of red (below target), yellow (vulnerable to missing the target), green (at target), or blue (exceeding the target). The team diligently reviewed the long list of goals and measures for each division. Also, the divisional representatives on the dashboard committee requested changes for many of the yellow- and red-rated goals to increase the probability that their group would reach its targets.

Subsequently, the executive team debriefed the lengthy session. They were concerned about the committee's approach to evaluating outcomes through the dashboard measurement. First, the level of detail of the goals and metrics bothered them. It was as if every performance management objective were rolled up into the company dashboard. Second, there were too many change requests. They concluded that the motivation behind the change requests was the employees' pay for performance process, which was dependent on achieving the expected results on the dashboard.

The team realized something was fundamentally wrong with their approach. They explored the purpose of the dashboard and identified two alternative questions:

- *Is it a "roll-up" of each unit's performance goals to create a coordinated list of objectives for the entire company?*
  The benefit of this approach is that it exposes progress on individual objectives throughout the year. The weakness is that the executives are micro-managing every person's individual performance.

- *Is it a "roll-down" business dashboard that provides early indicators of the probability of delivering customer value and profitability?*
  Many companies are driven by their financial results (the requirement to deliver shareholder value) and the desire to achieve customer loyalty. However, financial results and customer loyalty are "lagging" measures, evident only after the fact. Kaplan and Norton developed the balanced scorecard to introduce early warning indicators of the financial outcomes.[4] The business dashboard metrics provide an indicator that the business may be off course, and may not achieve its financial targets or its customer value proposition.

  The executives, in the example above, realized that the measurement they had developed was a "roll-up" list of objectives that was overly detailed and had limited usefulness from a business strategy perspective. They needed a "roll-down" business dashboard to function as an early warning indicator. Figure 5.5 illustrates the difference between roll-up and roll-down methods of evaluating outcomes:

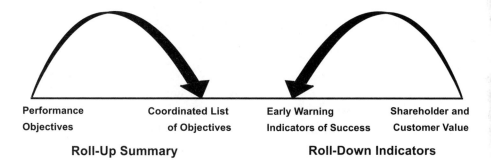

| Performance | Coordinated List | Early Warning | Shareholder and |
| Objectives | of Objectives | Indicators of Success | Customer Value |

Roll-Up Summary   **Roll-Down Indicators**

Figure 5.5 *Dashboard metrics are early indicators for shareholder and customer value*

4. Robert Kaplan and David Norton, "The Balanced Scorecard," *Harvard Business School Press*, 1996.

The team concluded that they needed to change their dashboard approach to reflect the roll-down performance indicators approach. They also agreed that changes to the dashboard indicators could occur only under the following conditions:

- If the change in the measure resulted in changes in the overall metrics associated with shareholder value and/or customer loyalty.

- If the change in the measure had nothing to do with shareholder value and customer loyalty (e.g., changes due to a metric that is measuring the wrong thing, a poorly constructed metric that needs to be modified, or an unnecessary metric).

The challenge for many leaders is to develop the capacity to rise above the micro measures that govern their day-to-day performance management objectives. They need to understand the big picture business strategy expectations and heed the early warning indicators.

LEVERAGE BUSINESS STRATEGY TO DEVELOP HIGH-POTENTIAL LEADERS

The process of strategy development should serve the dual purpose of producing a deployable plan and further developing the strategic thinking capabilities of the high-potential leaders. High-potential leaders need to be developed so that they can succeed at their next level of challenge. Unfortunately, few organizations do this. Here are some implications of not developing the holistic business strategy capability of high-potential leaders:

- High-potential leaders will have a limited understanding of the broader organizational challenges.

- They may make decisions that have negative side effects for the organization without the knowledge to forecast those organizational implications.

- They may complain when other areas seem to receive preferential treatment.

- Their candidacy for executive positions can be limited because they do not understand the interdependencies between various areas of the business.

A common strategy to address this learning need is to send high-potential leaders to external executive development programs. Although these programs can help high-potential leaders develop their strategic thinking capabilities, it is unlikely that they will help people comprehend their own organization-wide challenges.

An innovative approach is to use the internal strategic-planning process to expand the holistic perspective of high-potential leaders. Unfortunately, many executives do not leverage strategic planning as a development process. The executives either believe that strategic planning is a secretive process that includes only a select few people or they simply have not considered the idea that it can be used as a development process.

It is a lost opportunity if executives fail to use this process to achieve a secondary gain of educating high-potential leaders and developing their talents. The long-term sustainability of an organization often depends upon the strength of its high-potential leaders.

Here are three best-practice examples of organizations that used strategic planning to broaden the perspectives of high-potential leaders with great success. The three examples are presented from the "most to least" implications for the traditional "executive only" strategic planning process.

1. *Include high potentials in strategic planning to give greater "voice" to the customer.*
   An executive group was concerned about their strategic planning process because it focused more on internal challenges than on how they could deliver enhanced customer value and grow the business. Upon reflection, they realized that the problem had to do with the functional and staff representation on the executive team. This executive team had eight members, and only three—the President, VP Sales and VP Marketing—knew the "voice" of the customer.

They decided to expand the strategic planning team to include the high-potential leaders from sales and marketing to give the customer greater "voice" in strategic planning. They also realized it would provide an excellent learning opportunity for the high-potential leaders. The strategic planning proceeded with a total of fourteen members (including six high-potential leaders).

The result was a strategic plan that focused more on value to the customer and sustainable competitive advantage. Also, the high-potential leaders were delighted to be part of this process. It increased their understanding of the company-wide challenges and enhanced their readiness to be future leaders.

2. *Involve high-potential leaders as shadow strategic planners.*
   This executive team decided to introduce an innovative approach to their annual strategic planning process. Typically, the executives attended three days of meetings during which time the various divisions of the company presented their current and future state analyses and recommended strategies. About four weeks later, the executives attended a two-day offsite to develop the strategic plan for the next three years and the business plans for the next year.

   This year they decided to create a shadow strategic planning team. Seven high-potential leaders from across the company were nominated and selected to develop a "shadow" strategic plan. They also included a "sunset clause" which meant that after the high-potential leaders made their presentations, their role in the process was over. This "sunset clause" was a great relief for the high-potential leaders. Many had experienced situations in the past in which a temporary assignment became a permanent expectation above and beyond their full-time job. The "sunset clause" removed that concern for them.

   The seven high-potential leaders sat in a gallery and observed the three days of presentations by each of the divisions on the current and future state of the business. They then spent the next three weeks together with a facilitator and developed their proposed "shadow" strategic plan for the company. They presented their plan on the first morning of the executives' two-day strategic planning session. After some discussion, the shadow strategic planners left the session.

The company executives saw great value in this process both in the precision of thought for the strategy and in the engagement of its leaders. The high-potential leaders appreciated the opportunity to contribute their ideas to shape the future of the company, and it helped them understand strategic challenges outside their own areas of expertise. Within two years, two members of the shadow strategic planning groups were promoted to positions of greater responsibility, and one person was promoted to the executive team.

3. *Solicit high-potential leaders' input and share information.*
Another company decided to assign three high-potential leaders to each of their eight executives as part of strategic planning. Each executive contacted his or her list of high-potential leaders after each stage of their strategy development and simultaneously educated the leaders on the business strategy. When the strategy finally was deployed, the 24 high-potential leaders were the key communicators of the strategy and took the lead in the implementation of the new direction.

Each case example yielded impressive results (and perhaps in combination, the benefits would be even greater). However, each innovative approach does require a willingness by executives to be inclusive rather than exclusive as they develop strategy. The benefits are worth it. The high-potential leaders will develop their capabilities in strategic thinking and gain an organization-wide perspective; at the same time, the executives will develop a more thorough and deployable business strategy with greater involvement and acceptance of their high-potential leaders. There is very little risk and potentially great benefit when executives involve high-potential leaders in strategic planning.

CLOSING COMMENTS

To become holistic leaders, executives need to know how to participate in all of the phases of business strategy. They also must ensure that the customer focus and business strategies are implemented in a manner that aligns and engages all employees.

Also, the business strategy process should be leveraged as another opportunity for a learning experience for high-potential leaders. The exposure to strategic issues is very beneficial for leadership development. It also provides a fresh strategic perspective for the executives and increases the probability that the organization will have the leadership capacity to meet its future leadership challenges.

Culture and Values

The culture of ancient Greece has had an enduring influence throughout the ages. This culture was founded on a set of core ideas. One such idea was "paideia," which was seen as a complete course of study necessary to produce well-rounded and fully educated citizens.[1] Paideia was a process of education to realize the inherent potential in men and women. It was a striving to develop whole beings—the sum of their intellectual, moral, aesthetic and physical qualities.[2] Paideia was also an ideal, in that it represented an aspiration of the ancient Greek society. It thereby guided the behaviors of that society through their pursuit of excellence in all endeavors.

The ancient Greek culture also was represented through its architecture. For example, one of the best-known structures is the Parthenon, high on the Acropolis in Athens. The Parthenon still stands today as an icon of ancient Greek culture, what it stood for, and what its citizens accomplished thousands of years ago.

As in ancient Greece, culture and values in organizations can represent an enduring and integrating force—an ideal and an aspiration that an organization is striving to reach. Culture and values also have the potential to establish a common environment that guides behavior,

1. Richard Tarnas, *The Passion of the Western Mind*, (New York: Random House, 1991).

2. E.G. Castle, *Ancient Education and Today*, (London: Penguin, 1961).

serves to distinguish an organization and communicate its unique identity to employees, customers and stakeholders. Leadership is critical to culture and values because it is the leaders of the organization who can create, manage and change an organization's culture.[3] As a result, holistic leaders must realize the potential that culture and values can play in building successful organizations.

This chapter examines the culture and values element in the Holistic Leadership Framework.

Figure 6.1   *The Holistic Leadership Framework*

We define *culture* as the distinguishing features of an organization—the customs and ways of doing things that are unique to one organization over another.

Values represent what is fundamentally important to an organization; they guide behavior and decision-making. Thus, values determine what is important in an organization, and they help employees set priorities.

---

3. Edgar H. Schein, *Organizational Culture and Leadership*, (San Francisco: Jossey-Bass, 1985).

This chapter will explore three pillars necessary to vibrant and enduring organizational cultures and values. The three pillars of success are:

1. Lead culture change,

2. Integrate values into the organization,

3. Drive employee engagement with the culture and values.

Figure 6.2 presents the three pillars in a form that borrows from the majestic structures of ancient Greece.

Figure 6.2 *Culture and Values—The Pillars of Success*

PILLAR 1–LEAD CULTURE CHANGE

Organizations have recently recognized the important role of culture in driving high performance. In their quest for competitive advantage, many organizations have turned to culture because it represents an enduring strategy for differentiation. Many organizations have succeeded exceptionally well. Many others unfortunately have not. In these cases, culture is seen merely as a set of words that rarely inspire employees and in many cases sound similar to an organization's most ardent competitors.

Several well-researched studies have examined the strategic role of culture in contributing to a company's financial performance. Collectively, these studies suggest that organizations that understand the strategic role of culture and manage it well consistently outperform competitors in the marketplace.[4] Research conducted among companies from *Fortune's* Most Admired List revealed that these companies took their culture and values very seriously, and integrated them deeply into organizational processes and programs.[5]

In response to the growing strategic importance of culture, many organizations embarked on becoming "employers of choice." This means that an organization attempts to make itself the most appealing employer in its field. As a result, "Best Companies to Work For" lists have become a global phenomenon.[6] Overall this has been a positive trend, for it has emphasized the importance of culture to organizational success.

Through our experience, we have found that the focus on the "best organizations" lists has also generated a superficial understanding of the strategic role of organizational culture. For example, a recent issue of a national magazine was devoted to the best 100 organizations in the country. On the front cover of the magazine was the following picture: in the foreground were three casually dressed employees playing billiards. Watching the employees was a well-dressed male. One assumes he is the CEO. In the background were two other employees, standing

---

4. John Kotter & James Heskett, *Corporate Culture and Performance*, (Free Press 1992) found that companies that intentionally manage their cultures well outperformed similar organizations that did not over a 10-year period. Collins, J. *Good to Great*, (New York: Harper Business, 2001). Visionary companies had a timeless ideology founded on a culture of values, strong purpose and adaptive business tactics. These companies outperformed the general stock market and comparable companies in their industries.

5. Melvin J Stark, "Five Years of Insight into the World's Most Admired Companies," *Journal of Organizational Excellence*, Wiley Periodicals Inc., Winter 2002.

6. The Great Place to Work® Institute has done extensive work on the global best companies to work for lists. http://www.greatplacetowork.com

around a ping-pong table, giving each other a "high five" slap. The picture successfully captured the culture of this organization as being characterized by a casual, fun and team-based environment.[7]

The danger with these images at times is that they can lead to a faulty assumption about building cultures in organizations. The faulty assumption is that this is an easy process, and one that merely involves bringing ping-pong tables into an organization. Consider the following example of an organization that believed it could transform its culture by changing superficial elements of its environment:

A large and well-known automobile dealership was located for many years in an old part of a city. Their facility was outdated and in need of repair. When customers went to the dealership to service their car, they could often see mechanics and service technicians openly arguing with one another. The culture in the dealership was extremely adversarial. Customers were uncomfortable with this culture, but they had little choice of going elsewhere, because this was the only dealership in town for their particular brand of automobile. Customers complained, but the owners of the dealership could not change the behavior. Customers essentially put up with the old building and negative work climate because they wanted that particular car.

To remain competitive with other dealerships in town, the owners decided to build a new facility in the suburbs. They believed (or hoped) that the new facility would create a new culture. To their credit, they built an extremely beautiful building. It had an indoor atrium featuring natural light, plants, and appealing artwork. It was a captivating backdrop to the new cars that were displayed in the atrium showroom. The customer service area also received a significant makeover. The customer waiting area now had leather sofas, a color television set, a European coffee machine dispensing cappuccinos and café lattes. The service technicians and mechanics also received a makeover. Each was given brand-new uniforms.

7. Maclean's Magazine. October 28, 2002.

> *At first, the customers were overwhelmed and pleased by the change. However, in the course of one year, things began to deteriorate. The coffee machine broke down and the dealership failed to replace it. The television set was removed, leaving only the bare TV stand. And the service technicians and mechanics were once again openly arguing and fighting with one another in front of customers.*

The leadership of this organization implemented only superficial cultural changes and failed to appreciate the deeper changes required to transform a culture.

The Leading Culture Change Formula

Holistic leaders need to know how to lead culture change—for several reasons. First, sustained organizational success is based on an organization's ability to respond to changes in the business environment.

Second, more and more organizations are experiencing mergers, acquisitions and restructuring. Leading culture change is a critical success factor in these situations. For example, research estimates that up to 85 percent of failed acquisitions can be attributed to the mismanagement of culture issues.[8]

In our experience, we have found that effective culture change is a function of three variables represented in the leading culture change formula in Figure 6.3.

$$\text{Culture Change} = f(\underline{M}\text{indset}, \underline{S}\text{tructure}, \underline{R}\text{ewards})$$

Figure 6.3   *The Leading Culture Change Formula*

Leaders need to explore and determine the most effective way to introduce and sustain a new culture that is required to make an

---

8. Roger Miller, "How Culture Affects Mergers and Acquisitions," *Industrial Management* September-October 2000.

organization successful. They need to pay attention to all three variables in the leading change formula:

- *Mindset:* Mindset is the common understanding among members of the organization of the sense of urgency for the culture change. It is the first step to generate commitment and engagement for the culture change to take place.

- *Structure:* Effective cultural change also requires some formal "hardwiring" of the change into some structure. *Structure* includes the design of the organization that is needed to enable the new culture to firmly take hold. Leaders create the necessary structure by redesigning reporting relationships, roles, and accountabilities. The structure helps employees work more effectively together in bringing about the new culture.

- *Rewards:* Rewards are defined as the incentives and consequences that are put in place to provide ongoing reinforcement of the new culture.

If the organization is weak in any one of the three variables, culture change will be difficult. In our experience, the variable that is frequently underestimated by leaders is mindset. Leaders often have a tendency to focus too quickly on the structure variable and consequences, without taking time to ensure that leaders and employees have had conversations to create shared meaning and a sense of urgency for the culture change.

A Culture Change Case Example

Consider the following example of an organization that needed a significant cultural change. The case is somewhat unusual. Most organizations that undertake culture change want a more innovative and empowering work environment—that is, to help employees be more creative and show more initiative.

The organization in this case example needed to change the culture in the opposite direction. This case is particularly instructive because it is counterintuitive for most leaders. The leaders in this case needed to

create a more restrictive and compliant work environment. Here is the
background to their story.

> *A manufacturing facility's executive team was struggling with a
> recent announcement that would affect the future of the organiza-
> tion. In the past, they had researched new products to develop for
> their R&D division. Their primary focus was on innovative devel-
> opment and experimentation, not on standards and procedures.
> They learned that their facility would no longer be a research facil-
> ity, but would instead become a commercial manufacturing site
> for the European marketplace. Their facility would have to trans-
> form. It would have to mass-produce products, meet commercial
> standards, and always be compliant with regulatory require-
> ments. In essence, the change would involve a transformation
> from an innovative culture to a compliance culture.*
>
> *Senior leadership of the company quickly learned that the
> capability to transform their organization to support the culture
> change was far more challenging than it was to shift its manufac-
> turing methods to mass-produce product. They found that the
> most difficult part of the culture change was the resistance to
> operating in a compliance-based facility that would require lead-
> ers and employees to adhere carefully to the rules.*

The process of cultural change in this manufacturing facility was
challenging. The leaders were unsure how to create a positive message
from a more restrictive cultural environment. They decided that they
needed to engage the leaders and have them take ownership of the
change. Here is what they did.

> *The executives recognized that they had to engage their leaders
> first in the process of cultural transformation. They decided to
> engage a small group of leaders in a benchmarking process,
> examining other facilities in the company to determine how they
> could operate most efficiently and also deliver customer value for*

their new customers in Europe. They also explored and identified what leadership needed to do to be successful in the new commercial manufacturing environment. The result of this benchmark process was that some of the leaders began to embrace the new ideas. They became helpers in the transformation, and a few became champions of the process. However, a critical mass of leaders only observed from the sidelines to see how this change would unfold. They still needed to adjust to the new cultural expectations.

This initiative was a good beginning—but not enough to make meaningful change. It had the positive effect of helping some key influencers in the facility to understand the importance of creating a culture of compliance, but they needed to involve more people before the culture change would take hold. And the employees needed more information.

The team decided to invite the Vice President of Operations in Europe to speak to all of the leadership in the facility. He told the leaders that he was struggling to deliver product to his marketplace. The various regulatory controls in European countries made the job challenging—at times, impossible. They explored many options and decided that they needed a dedicated manufacturing facility specifically focused on the European needs. The VP Operations proposed that he needed the most creative talent in the manufacturing organization—those who could meet the complex needs of multiple customers in various countries in one continent. They also believed that it would be much easier to train leaders to be compliant than it would be to train leaders to be flexible. They needed a combination of both; an odd mixture that the VP Operations referred to as "compliant flexibility." The change would be challenging, but the intent was to retain the spirit of innovation and to balance it with the requirement to be compliant.

Many employees began to understand why the culture of compliance was necessary. However, many still were waiting to see if anything real would occur. Would there be any meaningful changes or was all the talk just words.

The executives then understood the importance of hardwiring the new culture into the structure. They decided to send a signal that this change was for real.

The executives in the facility decided to change the structure and hire new leadership talent. They hired two new directors: a director of commercial relations (to liaise with the European VP Operations), and a director for compliance. They also promoted a high-potential manager to the position of director of safety. These three positions were areas in which this manufacturing facility needed focused leadership talent. The facility also responded quickly to compliance and safety issues to reinforce the message of the importance of compliance and safety as the new leadership standard.

The new hires did send a message to the workforce that something was happening. But the new leaders were slow to show any impact. They needed to adjust to the new work environment themselves as new employees and leaders in the organization.

Shortly after the new leadership changes, an unfortunate accident occurred. An employee who was not wearing safety goggles removed a gasket that blew off its valve, nearly blinding him. The new director of health and safety conducted a detailed and highly visible root cause analysis that showed that this was not the first time a gasket had blown off—it was just the first time an employee had been hurt. The employees and the department supervisor knew about the problem, but no one had spoken about it, and the safety hazard had remained. The company had procedures of how to deal with safety incidents and the employees involved in those events. However, the company had never held the leadership responsible for negligence in the workplace.

This unplanned accident became the pivot point to demonstrate that the executives were serious about a culture of compliance. The executives realized that a key would be to ensure that there were rewards for appropriate behaviors and consequences for inappropriate actions.

They decided to use this situation to demonstrate the consequences for leaders who overlooked safety hazards and non-compliance. They terminated one supervisor and promoted one of the high-potential employees who worked in that area.

The executives needed to communicate why they had chosen to do what they did. They needed to talk to all employees to make sure they understood the intentions of their actions and to further reinforce the consequences and rewards associated with the new culture of compliance. They also needed to give the employees some hope that they could work effectively in a culture of compliance. The incident was used to build a culture of compliance. Safety was of great importance to employees and leaders, and the accident made it even more urgent. They decided to call an all-employees meeting.

All the employees and leaders were called into the lunchroom to discuss the accident. The leaders and employees got the message that the culture of compliance needed to be implemented, especially in the area of worker safety. They also began the process of removing barriers to effective leadership and promoting and hiring new talent who were prepared to work in the new manner that was required.

They also launched a SafetyFIRST program that put safety above all other areas of compliance. Employees welcomed greater control and precision in the area of safety. A leadership session helped them explore how to make the workplace safer and to define the expectations of leadership in that process.

A large follow-up group session, which involved all 100 supervisors, managers, and directors, explored ways to make this plant the safest plant in the company's network of manufacturing facilities. Numerous SafetyFIRST programs were promoted and launched, safety was publicly tracked, and whistleblowers

> *on safety hazards were recognized and rewarded. The focus on safety helped all leaders and employees to start accepting the need for a more compliant work environment and a leadership capacity that would ensure that "compliant flexibility" would occur.*

In this case example, the senior leadership succeeded at leading culture change, because they understood the importance of all three variables in culture change—mindset, structure and rewards. They realized early on that they needed to engage their leaders and employees in the process. They paid attention to the human element of change by helping people understand the need for change.[9] They also provided opportunities for people to learn new behaviors and assume ownership through the benchmarking process. From a structure standpoint, the executives put in place three new roles to support the culture change effort. They also effectively used the gasket accident as an opportunity to demonstrate that there were consequences for breaking the new cultural norms. Finally, they established the SafetyFIRST program, which gave employees an exciting initiative on which to focus their attentions. It was also used to institute rewards to promote workplace safety and the change to a compliance culture.

PILLAR 2—INTEGRATE VALUES INTO THE ORGANIZATION

It is important to begin this section by distinguishing between values and ethics.

- *Values:* As described earlier, "values" are what is important in the organization; they guide priority setting and decision-making. The challenge with values is distinguishing between situations when values conflict. Essentially, the challenge of values is helping

---

9. David S. Weiss, *High Performance HR: Leveraging Human Resources For Competitive Advantage.* (Toronto, ON: John Wiley & Sons Canada, Ltd., 2000).

employees make the proper choices between values—that is, between "right versus right."[10]

- **Ethics:** Ethics are the standards of acceptable and unacceptable behavior. There is a right and a wrong ethical answer. For example, "don't cheat on your expense submissions" is an ethical issue not a values issue. Ethics (as well as the law) give clear guidance to determine between right and wrong.

We assume that all employees will operate ethically and if they do not there are clear consequences for their behavior. Our concern in this section is with the more complex challenge of integrating values into the organization. Here is an example of a values clash that is common in organizations.

> A service organization had a set of values that was well established with their employees. However, they regularly had internal conflicts in the application of two of the values - quality and innovation. Both values were considered to be very important and the "right" things to do, so they often struggled with which value was more important. One group chose to promote a culture of free thinkers in their department. However, this approach sometimes compromised the quality of the service. In contrast, another group invested time solely in quality services and service standards, which resulted in high standards but less innovation.

This example illustrates a normal dilemma. The leaders fail in their leadership role if they see the values dispute as dysfunctional and attempt to adjudicate which department has the right approach. In reality, both departments are right. The leader needs to see the dispute as an opportunity for a meaningful conversation to explore the two values and the ongoing choices that need to be made. The "quality vs. innovation" dispute is not a problem; it is an opportunity to discuss when one

---

10. Joseph L. Badaracco Jr., *Refining Moments: When Managers Must Choose Between Right and Right* (Harvard Business School Press, 1997).

of the values is more important than the other, and when both values are required simultaneously.

Integrate the Values Into Organizational Practices

It is important for holistic leaders to integrate the values into organizational practices. Here are some suggested approaches:

- *Integrate values into enterprise-wide practices:* Leaders can integrate the values into the business strategic framework of the organization. They can be linked into business processes. Often the highly leveraged approach is to make the values part of HR systems, such as recruitment and selection, orientation, training, succession planning, rewards and recognition and performance management.

- *Integrate values into teams:* Leaders can use the values to develop team behavioral commitments that guide how team members will behave. They can recognize team accomplishments that are consistent with the culture and values of the organization.

- *Integrate values into employee processes:* From an employee perspective leaders can develop recognition award programs to motivate desired behavior. The also can conduct an individual 360-degree feedback process based on the culture, values and behaviors.

Select, Develop and Promote Leaders
Who Live the Values

Admired leaders represent a key driver of engagement. As a result, organizations must select, develop and promote leaders who are able to model the values. Below are some ideas to consider.

- *Be mindful when bringing an employee into a managerial role for the first time:* Typically, organizations promote individuals into managerial roles, largely because of their strong technical competence. These can yield strong functional managers, but poor leaders of people. Organizations who build inspiring workplaces understand the importance of moving the right individuals into managerial roles. They promote individuals with strong people skills who can build strong teams and inspiring workplaces.

- *Support managers as they assume "bigger" leadership roles:* As managers assume more senior roles, each step places greater expectations and demands on the individual. Organizations must be aware of this, and support these managers during these times to ensure they succeed in the transition to their bigger leadership role.

- *Make leaders accountable for living the organization's values:* Leaders need to be held accountable for living the organization's values and fostering its culture. Organizations that do this well also have the courage to weed out managers who fail to lead in accordance to the values. These organizations recognize that leaders who live the culture and values are critical to ensuring that employees in turn also live the culture and values.

Use the Values to Create a Compelling Place to Work

Holistic leaders need to create a compelling workplace that will motivate employees to contribute and commit to the organization. We choose the word "compelling" deliberately because it means arousing strong interest, conviction and commitment. Here are ways to leverage the values to create a compelling place to work.

- *Create an inspiring workplace:* Many CEOs see the need to create an inspiring workplace as a significant aspect of the current leadership gap in organizations.[11] The ability to inspire employees is built on a strong commitment and adherence to the core values of the organization.

- *Establish a sense of community:* Employees have a closer connection to their organizations if they feel that their workplace also provides a sense of community. The community can be reinforced through

---

11. Benimadhu & Gibson, *Leadership for Tomorrow.*

telling organizational stories—stories describing how the organization was started, its successes, challenges and how it has been guided by its core values.

- *Create an open and supportive environment:* Leaders can reinforce the core values of the organization by fostering working relationships that are open and supportive. These organizations have accessible leaders, open communications, and information shared across the organization. These workplaces also have a sense of fun where everyone works hard, but also infuses the workplace with humor and laughter.

- *Celebrate achievements:* Leaders can instill the values in their workplaces by taking the time to celebrate organizational milestones and accomplishments. All too often, leaders fail to take the time to recognize employee successes, and this serves to undermine the integration of values in an organization. Consider for example the experience of the IT department in a financial services organization. During the large blackout that occurred in August of 2003, power was cut across a large section of North America. This power failure created havoc for many companies. The IT department in one financial services organization managed to "keep the lights on" during the blackout, and customers were not inconvenienced in any way. The members of the IT department essentially lived at their organization during the blackout, accomplishing astonishing feats of teamwork and ingenuity to solve the many problems they were encountering. After the event, the CEO dismissed this significant accomplishment, stating that the IT staff had only done what was expected. This disengaged the IT staff. The CEO missed a real opportunity to celebrate this accomplishment, acknowledge the effort of his employees, and reinforce the values of the organization.

- *Create a climate of continuous learning:* Employees experience workplaces that foster continuous learning as values-driven organizations. Organizations need to support employees to expand their competencies and their understanding of the organization through formal and informal learning opportunities. Organizations can also give employees the tools and information they need to manage their careers within the organization.

PILLAR 3–DRIVE EMPLOYEE ENGAGEMENT WITH THE CULTURE AND VALUES

One of the reasons culture and values have gained prominence in organizations is because of the desirable outcome of creating an engaged workforce, which ultimately contributes to organizational performance.[12] In the past, progressive organizations invested considerably in ensuring that employees were satisfied. However, they soon learned that employee satisfaction was insufficient to create sustained high performance cultures. Organizations do not only need satisfied employees; they need "engaged" employees.

We define "engagement" as the extent that employees are personally invested in their roles and in their organizations. We choose the term "personal investment" purposely because it describes a phenomenon that takes place daily as employees enter their workplaces. Employees come into their organizations on a daily basis and ask themselves, "How much of myself do I give this place, and how much do I withhold?" In some cases, the choice is simple because the organization is not a good place to work. Employees show up and perform their jobs to the bare minimum standards and rarely give more. They may even purposely withhold their best ideas and creativity. This group of employees would be referred to as being disengaged. Several large-scale research studies from around the world estimate that at any given time, approximately 15 to 20 percent of employees in organizations are in this disengaged state.

For another group of employees, their personal investment choice involves an active struggle. These individuals are only moderately engaged. They are more personally invested than the disengaged employees, but are still distracted because some element of the work

12. Anthony Ricci, Steve Kirn, & Richard Quinn, "The Employee-Customer Profit Chain at Sears," *Harvard Business Review*, 1997, pp. 82-97.

environment (such as a difficult boss, extreme work pressures, poor working relationships) is preventing them from investing fully. Research[13] estimates that approximately 55 to 60 percent of all employees are only moderately engaged. The good news is that under the right conditions and with the right leadership, these employees can be inspired to become more engaged in their work. Finally, researchers estimate that approximately 25 percent of all employees are fully engaged. They give of their passion, creativity and ingenuity. They do not withhold their best ideas. In the words of Daniel Yankelovich, they expend their "discretionary effort," or an effort above the minimum they need to maintain their jobs within their organizations.[14] Personally invested employees are not distracted; they do not engage in the struggle to decide how much to give and how much to withhold.

Leaders miss a tremendous opportunity to drive the performance of their organizations, because they are often unaware of the factors that drive employee engagement. To illustrate this concept, here is a scenario in which fifty high-potential leaders were attending a meeting within their sales organization.

The high-potential leaders were taking part in a development program. At the end of the program, there was an open dialogue session. One key theme that emerged in the discussion was that the individuals were struggling to lead balanced lives because of the increasing pressures they were facing in their jobs. The discussion continued for some time, and the tension in the room began to escalate. The facilitator then asked two important questions: first, she asked, "How many of you feel overworked and feel you really can't do any more if asked by your organization?" Virtually every hand in the room was raised. Clearly this group was feeling overworked. Then came the second question: "How many of you feel there is a part of

---

13. Several large-scale studies from around the world have been conducted looking at employee engagement. These include: Curt Coffman & Gabriel Gonzalez-Molina, *Follow This Path*, (New York: The Gallup Organization, 2002); Walker Information Inc. *Commitment in the Workplace: The 2000 Global Employee Relationship Benchmark Report*. 2001; Towers Perrin, *Understanding What Drives Employee Engagement*. The Towers Perrin 2003 Talent Report, 2003.

14. Daniel Yankelovich, "Got to Give to Get," Mother Jones, July – August, 1997.

you—your creativity, passion, ingenuity—that is sitting, untapped by this organization?" Virtually all the same hands were raised.

This scenario strikes at the heart of the engagement challenge facing leaders in today's organizations. On the one hand, here was a group of high-performing employees feeling completely overworked, under tremendous job pressure and somewhat disengaged. At the same time, the same individuals felt there was more in terms of their passion, creativity and ingenuity that they could be giving to their organizations. There was tremendous discretionary effort being withheld from the organization. Sometimes organizations think about culture as a vehicle to get the "most" out of their employees. This can lead to disengaged and exhausted employees. Organizations need to develop cultures as a vehicle to get the "best" from their employees.

Here is a simple question to consider:

> **Does your current organizational culture try to get the most out of your employees, or does it try to get the best from your employees?**

Getting the "best" from employees can only come from creating inspiring workplaces that truly engage employees to give their best to the organization. Leaders need to have an intimate knowledge of where their employees stand in terms of engagement.

Reflect for a moment on your own direct reports and ask yourself the following questions:

- How many employees are disengaged?

- How many are moderately engaged?

- How many are fully engaged and personally invested in their roles?

The Six Factors That Drive Employee Engagement

The third pillar of success stresses the need for leaders to be continually thinking about the extent that their employees are personally invested and engaged with the culture and values. Leaders must also understand the factors that drive employee engagement.

Over the past few years, our firm, Knightsbridge, has conducted focus groups with hundreds of employees at all levels and in a cross-section of sectors. We have found some striking similarities in the factors that drive engagement and the personal investment that employees make to their organizations. These are summarized in the following table:

THE SIX FACTORS THAT DRIVE EMPLOYEE ENGAGEMENT

1. **Being part of a winning organization.**
2. **Working for admired leaders.**
3. **Having positive working relationships.**
4. **Doing meaningful work.**
5. **Recognition and appreciation.**
6. **Living a balanced life.**

---

1. *Being part of a winning organization:* Employees want to know they are part of a winning organization. This could mean the organization is financially successful, or that it is recognized as a thought leader among customers, or that the organization has an ambitious vision, core purpose and well-articulated business strategy in place.

   A strong organizational brand is also a powerful contributor to feeling like part of a winning team. A strong brand can be derived through a respected reputation within an industry, through an aspiring vision, and through being a consistent provider of innovative products and services for customers.

2. *Working for admired leaders:* Admired leaders are another driver of engagement that must exist throughout the organization and at all levels—one of the most important non-monetary drivers of

performance.[15] The sense of loyalty that employees can demonstrate to their admired leaders is often remarkable. A related factor is the confidence that employees have in the senior executive team of their organization. If confidence is low, this translates into a low level of belief in the ability of an organization to succeed in the future.

3. *Having positive working relationships:* Employees value positive working relationships with high-caliber and professional colleagues. Employees describe being excited about the thought of coming to work with these colleagues. An important part of positive working relationships is an environment that is relatively free from politics. Employees today do not want to play the political game. They do not have time for it. They are too busy trying to balance their work and active personal lives for organizational politics. We predict that in the future, the leaders and organizations that can create work environments that de-emphasize traditional corporate politics will do a better job of attracting and retaining top talent.

4. *Doing meaningful work:* Meaningful work is often defined as work that makes a difference or has an impact to the organization. Employees often want to see how their work impacts the organization's vision and strategy. They also want to know that the organization's customers are "touched" by their work. As one individual stated in a focus group, "In the end, you want to know you've made a difference. Not just in your job, but a difference with your life. I want to make sure I can do this through my job."

5. *Recognition and appreciation:* Recognition is another important driver of employee engagement. Recognition may mean monetary rewards and compensation, but it also can refer to the appreciation and direct feedback that employees receive from managers. This recognition and appreciation demonstrates that employees are valued and that their contribution is acknowledged by the organization. Recognition also means that leaders notice

15. Corporate Leadership Council, *Crafting a "Compelling Offer": Overview Of Results From Primary Research Into The Career Decisions Of High Value Employees*, (Washington DC: Corporate Executive Board, 1998).

the often-unnoticed things that employees do to make their organizations successful.

6. *Living a balanced life:* For many employees work-life balance is an important factor that drives their engagement. Organizations that create cultures that value balance, and assist employees to achieve life balance, will be rewarded with highly engaged employees. Work/life balance does not mean that employees are not loyal, not committed to their organizations; it means that employees want to lead whole lives, not lives solely centered on work.

Seven Ways Organizations Typically Fail at Culture and Values

Below we identify seven ways that organizations fail at culture and values:

1. *Believing culture and values are soft business issues:* In some instances, senior leaders may devalue the importance of culture and values because they are seen as being "soft," and consequently take a back seat to "hard" business issues.

2. *Delegating culture and values to HR:* Many organizations see culture and values as an HR initiative, rather than a core business driver. Culture and values must be owned by leaders in all lines of business, and especially owned by the executive team.

3. *Treating culture and values as a project:* Some leaders treat culture and values as a project with a specific start and end date. Once the laminated cards are distributed to all employees, leaders assume their work is done. Culture and values are iterative—there is no start or end date. Leaders must be constantly working on strengthening their organization's culture. Culture can be fragile and eroded quickly.

4. *Failure to develop shared values:* In many companies, the executives develop the values with little input or participation by other employees. These same executives are often disappointed with the

rollout of the values because response from employees is lukewarm at best. In our experience, when executives and employees work together in generating shared values, there is a greater response because it increases the probability that values will be internalized and lived.

5. *Not integrating the values into organizational practices:* Culture and values need to be integrated into an organization by becoming part of organizational practices. For example, they can be part of how an organization creates its business strategy, recruits staff, and handles performance management.

6. *Leaders who fail to live the culture and values:* A critical factor that contributes to failure is the inability of leaders to live an organization's culture and values. In these instances, the leaders assume that the culture and values are for everyone else in the organization but themselves. They also falsely assume that employees do not notice when leaders fail to live the culture and values. Employees are extremely good at detecting the gaps in leadership behavior.

7. *Copying the culture and values of other organizations:* Some organizations believe that they can merely copy what other successful organizations do in order to build their own culture. Leaders must understand that culture and values are unique to an organization. Outside practices will only be relevant if they are meaningful to the organization's employees. If not, then the efforts to change culture will only collect dust.

MEASURE AND TRACK PROGRESS ON THE CULTURE AND VALUES

Leaders should commit to measuring culture and values. The measures of culture and values can become a part of the organization's dashboard and core metrics (as part of the business strategy "Evaluate Outcomes" phase).

There are a number of ways in which leaders can measure the culture and values. For example:

- *Culture and values surveys:* Leaders can conduct culture surveys that determine the strength of the culture and the extent that values are being lived in the organization. They can use the data to identify problem areas, and implement solutions that improve the workplace for employees.

- *Focus groups:* The culture and values surveys can have a follow-up process that includes focus groups to define the factors that drive engagement among employees.

- *Exit interviews:* Leaders can conduct exit interviews to identify issues that might reflect cultural and values problems within the organization. This data also may be used to address the issues and thereby strengthen the culture.

- *Culture organizational audits:* The organization can engage an external reviewer to compare their approach with best practices in culture building and integrating values in an organization. The audit would also assess the extent to which the leadership has avoided the ways that organizations typically fail at culture and values.

Collectively, these approaches to measuring culture and values send a strong message to the organization—that its leaders are committed to its culture and values.

CLOSING COMMENTS

Culture and values represent a living, vibrant force that distinguishes one organization from another. Organizations with enduring culture and values are more successful than those that neglect or ignore their strategic importance. Leaders must apply the three pillars of success to lead culture change, integrate the values into the organization, and drive engagement with the culture and values.

Culture is fragile. Even among organizations that have built strong cultures, leaders must be vigilant in always working to strengthen their cultures by implementing the three pillars of success.

CHAPTER SEVEN

Organizational Leadership

Organizations that are successful in the new business environment are able to respond quickly and effectively to evolving customer needs. They are nimble and flexible. They are able to share with everyone in the organization the information that affects timely responsiveness to their customers. Their human capital, technology and business processes continuously create new value for their customers. Achieving this level of responsiveness is challenging and difficult. It is dependent on effective organizational leadership—the ability of leaders to lead their organizations as a whole enterprise.

We have found that of the six elements in the Holistic Leadership Framework, organizational leadership is one of the most difficult to achieve. This is primarily because the functional leadership mindset prevalent today (discussed in Chapter 3) has created a tendency for leaders to have a strong vertical view of organizations. In contrast, holistic leaders are able to lead their departmental functions and also lead across functional boundaries, effectively leading the organization as a whole.

Figure 7.1   *The Holistic Leadership Framework*

ORGANIZATIONAL LEADERSHIP–LEADING FOR ALIGNMENT AND ENGAGEMENT

In Chapter 4 (Customer Leadership) and Chapter 5 (Business Strategy) we explored the importance of aligning leaders and employees toward a successful business outcome. In Chapter 6 (Culture and Values), we discussed the need to engage employees with the organizational purpose—its reason for being.

Successful holistic leaders can integrate both the alignment and engagement of employees (their "heads" and "hearts"). Let's consider in more detail what we mean by alignment and engagement.

- *Alignment* reflects the degree to which business units, departments and teams in an organization are able to work together efficiently to implement the business strategy and drive customer leadership. When an organization is aligned, its processes, design and performance measures are in accord with one another. Everyone in the organization is moving in the same direction. Organizational leaders ensure that all employees understand the business strategy and how their part in the strategy drives customer leadership for the organization.

- **Engagement** reflects the degree to which everyone in the organization is deeply committed and personally invested in the success of the entire enterprise. Organizational leaders ensure that everyone behaves in a way that is consistent with the culture and values of the organization.

Figure 7.2 shows the four kinds of organizations that result from both effective and ineffective integration of alignment and engagement: the low-performance organization, the passionate organization, the driven organization, and the high-performance organization.

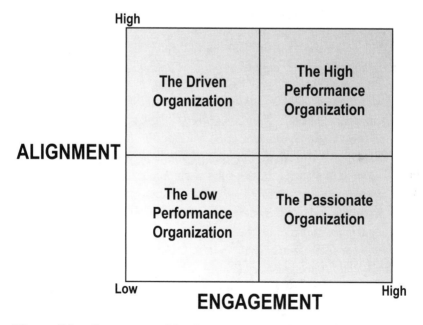

Figure 7.2 *Organizational Leadership—Leading for Alignment and Engagement*

Let's look closely at each of these organizations.

The Low-Performance Organization

The low-performance organization is deficient in both alignment and engagement. Employees have no sense of direction or a strong commitment to the organization. They come to work and perform their jobs but aren't clear about how they impact the organization. Functional units often work at cross-purposes. The result is a high degree of duplication of effort and gaps in processes as the units try to deliver value to customers.

Frequently, large bureaucratic organizations are low-performance organizations. They often have well-entrenched and rigid business processes. They also tend to have ingrained historical grievances that make their organizations very resistant to change. Unless something drastic is done to turn these low-performing organizations around, their current and future value will be limited.

The following "real-life" analogy illustrates the low-performance organization.

Imagine you live in a major metropolitan area. Every day you leave home at about 7:30 a.m., buy a newspaper and then travel on the subway to work. You usually stand in the crowded train throughout the rush-hour ride—about thirty minutes. Every morning, you arrive at your subway station at 8 a.m. The door of the train opens, and you walk with throngs of people from the train car onto the subway platform. The massive flow of people leaving the trains to exit the station moves reasonably well. This is because most of the commuters know where they are going (alignment) and are personally invested (engagement) in arriving at work on time. The flow of traffic also is facilitated by a number of clearly marked stairways, escalators and exits.

Now imagine what happens one morning when this flow of traffic becomes misaligned. During the peak of rush hour, several of the stairwells and escalators are blocked, and one of the major exits is closed due to construction. Commuters are forced to take alternate routes to exit the station and to transfer to the second subway line in the station.

You are not aware of this when you arrive that morning at the train station on time. You unassumingly walk with the crowd of people to your station exit—and then you notice the sign, "Exit Closed." There are no signs indicating where you should exit instead. You look around, and it appears that no one really knows where to go. You continue walking with the hope that the person in front of you has some information about which exits are open—but why would that person know any more than you do?

You finally reach the escalators to the second exit, but they are blocked due to repairs. Bottlenecks and confusion emerge. What was once a freely moving flow of traffic has been replaced by confusion and bedlam. Many commuters seem to still be engaged with getting to work, but the misalignment in the station is stopping them from achieving this.

Let's add a little disengagement to the mix. As you turn around to find another exit, you notice a large group of people with cameras and open maps, wondering how to leave the station. It's obvious they are tourists. Some stop to look at the posters on the subway walls. Others stand in the middle of the platform and begin taking pictures of the frustrated travelers. You can't believe how this day is starting—there is no way you will get to work on time today. So you give up. You call your office and say you will be late for work. You find a bench, read your newspaper and wait until the chaos dissipates.

The low-performance organization is a lot like this story. It needs leaders to make sure that there is alignment in the organization, with clearly marked exits, stairs and walkways that are open when you need them to be open. It also needs engaged employees who are both motivated and confident in their ability to get where they are going.

The Passionate Organization

In the passionate organization, engagement is very high; however, alignment is deficient. There are two kinds of passionate organizations: those that are passionate for the entire organization and those that are passionate for the work of their unit. A different organizational leadership intervention is required for each.

- *Passionate and engaged with the entire organization, but the overall organization lacks clear direction and alignment:* This type of organization invests considerably in its employees. The culture is very people-focused. It's the type of organization where employee birthdays are celebrated, where people join the company's sports teams, where people socialize at company picnics and company holiday parties. A high degree of cohesiveness exists within the organization as well as within departments and teams. Many of the workplace qualities are very positive, but in the end these organizations are low-performance organizations. The reason is that high engagement and passion exist without alignment to a clear business direction.

  The dot-com companies that emerged in the technology boom of the late 1990s represent good examples of this kind of passionate organization. Many of these companies had extremely high engagement, typified by excitement among employees. These organizations invested millions in innovative television commercials to project a strong company brand. However, this was not enough to help them succeed in the long term.

  The leaders in these organizations need to balance the engagement of employees with the focus on a clear and attainable business direction to which all employees can align their passions. The challenge of organizational leadership starts with the executive team—they must take the lead in architecting a clear direction, as described in Chapter 5.

- *Passionate and engaged to their own work within their specific work unit, but the unit is not aligned with the direction of the overall business:* A passionate work unit can achieve remarkable results within its team. The work unit members often believe that their team is one of the best they've ever worked with. The members describe how they work together closely to overcome adversity and internal resistance from other work units. Unfortunately, organizations with work units like this are unaware that the unit's success often comes at the expense of other work units and can cause damage to the business as a whole.

  In many situations miscommunications and rivalries occupy a tremendous amount of the attention and energy of employees. Classic rivalries tend to exist: sales versus marketing, sales versus production and human resources and finance versus everyone else. In many misaligned organizations, the focus is more on the internal competition with their own peers and less on the external competition in the marketplace. As a result these organizations lose in the marketplace because they are more preoccupied with beating each other than they are with focusing on their competitors and creating value for customers.

  Since it's difficult to convince a passionate work group to redirect its passion, in most cases, organizations break up the groups and/or change their leadership. However, there may be a lost opportunity with this approach. A work unit with intense passion is hard to find. It may be worth the effort to try and salvage the group by working with them to align with the business.

  The current or new leader in this kind of passionate organization needs to provide its work units with a great deal of overall business strategy information and include them in implementing the strategy in a meaningful way. The leader needs to create the urgency for the work unit to align its passion to the overall organization's benefit. Also, the work unit leaders across all functions must work together to minimize the number of internal functional units working at cross-purposes and to communicate regularly so that "the left hand knows what the right hand is doing." It requires vigilance on the part of organizational leaders, who must look continually for ways to refocus work units so that they realign and engage with the entire organization.

The Driven Organization

Driven organizations are very high on alignment but are engagement-deficient. They tend to be very successful from a bottom-line perspective, but they are not strong from a culture and values perspective. Numbers and financial metrics typically rule the day, coupled with a relentless pressure to streamline business processes and practices. Driven organizations are vertically focused. They have strong departmental divisions and use formal power and authority. Driven organizations are often very successful businesses, but this success comes at the price of engagement and passion. Employee morale and retention can become significant business issues, which can put the overall business at risk. Consider the following example:

> A large national law firm with a very strong track record of financial success began to have a retention problem. The problem was particularly serious because the retention issues were greatest among younger lawyers who had invested three to five years with the firm. These individuals were seen as the firm's potential future leaders. The firm was experiencing 40 percent attrition among lawyers in this group. The lawyers were leaving to join other firms or to enter the corporate market.
>
> The firm conducted an employee survey to further explore the issue, which was then complemented by a series of targeted focus groups with the "at risk" lawyer group. The findings revealed that most of these lawyers felt like "workhorses" or "small cogs in a wheel." They felt that the work environment was sterile, and that every aspect of their work was measured by specific metrics such

as utilization rates and billable hours. This created a high-pres-sure environment with an overemphasis on the numbers. The quality of legal work was rarely discussed.

The firm also discovered that the competing large law firms were approaching this group. Lawyers were leaving to join the com-petition because these firms appeared dedicated to creating a more positive work environment. The firm also discovered that their lawyers were being lured into the corporate world because compa-nies were investing in work-life balance initiatives. This was important to the group of lawyers because many had young families.

The survey data and focus groups helped the law firm's partners recognize that as senior leaders they were only paying attention to the alignment dimension of organizational leader-ship. The partners initiated several projects designed to create a more positive work environment. Over time, they were able to address the engagement dimensions and considerably slowed down the exodus of lawyers from the firm.

Leaders in driven organizations must balance the business focus with the need to engage employees. The culture and values pillars pre-sented in Chapter 6 are important principles for the organizational leaders to understand and implement. Leaders may also need to seek expert support to help re-engage the workforce. Employees need to trust that the attempts to create engagement are not merely a trick to increase productivity. The process of changing the culture needs to be implemented slowly and at a pace that employees will accept.

The High-Performance Organization

Exceptional organizational leadership is displayed by true high-per-forming organizations because they take a balanced approach to achieve both high alignment and high engagement. The leaders recognize that the path to long-term, sustained high performance comes from paying attention to both business results and the people.

The high-performance organization is characterized by the following:

- A clear sense of who the customer is and a comprehensible business strategy that drives customer leadership.

- Efficient internal work processes that flow smoothly up and down and across the organization. Departmental silos are not entrenched; work, information and ideas flow freely across organizational boundaries.

- Employees who are engaged with the culture and values in the work environment. The employees understand the big picture and know how their work contributes to the organization's success with customers.

- Performance measures and rewards are aligned to the business strategy and are implemented in an engaging manner.

In the next section of this chapter, we explore three broad organizational leadership tools. These tools are important for holistic leaders as they strive to build aligned and engaged high-performance organizations.

THREE TOOLS TO BUILD HIGH-PERFORMANCE ORGANIZATIONS

As leaders assume more senior roles in their organizations, they also assume greater responsibility for organizational leadership. They become more accountable for leading the entire enterprise versus running their functional departments. The world of organizational leadership is a very different world for many leaders. Power and authority take a back seat to influence and stakeholder management; leaders must see both the big picture *and* the details of the business.

In this section we present three tools that are fundamental to effective organizational leadership:

1. Develop an enterprise-wide perspective and work in the interest of the whole organization.

2. Build relationships and influence key stakeholders.

3. Increase the collaboration and integration across the organization.

TOOL #1: DEVELOP AN ENTERPRISE-WIDE PERSPECTIVE AND WORK IN THE INTEREST OF THE WHOLE ORGANIZATION

The first organizational leadership tool is more of a mindset than an actual behavioral tool—an enterprise-wide perspective. Leaders must develop the ability to understand the whole organization, consider the "ripple effects" of their actions on other parts of the organization and work in the interest of the whole business. It is very consistent with becoming a holistic leader in the work environment.

Unfortunately, developing an enterprise-wide perspective is impeded by an entrenched functional leadership mindset. As we discussed in Chapter 3, this mindset creates intellectual and structural rigidity when leaders struggle to think outside their own areas of expertise or department. It also creates structural rigidity as organizations need to work horizontally and across departmental lines. This results in an "inward looking" approach to leadership, with leaders preoccupied with the inner workings of their department and unable or unwilling to work outside their departmental boundaries.

Consider the following example illustrating how an executive team struggles to develop an enterprise-wide perspective.

An executive team meets monthly primarily to discuss financial performance, to address HR matters and to review progress on new organizational process improvements. Most of the executives comment on issues from their own departmental perspectives rather than from an enterprise-wide perspective. The ideas they propose are usually in their own best interests and not necessarily in the best interest of the whole organization.

During one of their regular monthly meetings, the executive team is once again struggling with a chronic organizational issue. As the discussion unfolds, one member of the team suggests that the issue is not being resolved because each executive is focused primarily on driving their own business results and not the results of the overall business. A hush falls upon the executive team. Someone is finally saying what is obvious but what no one has dared to say. Another executive tries to bail out the group with a suggestion: "Our problem is that we have no common project to work on. If we could find a common initiative that could bring us together, then we would be working more effectively for the entire company." All the members reflect on the suggestion for a moment and then agree that it is a good idea. They decide to jointly sponsor a visit from several politicians who were planning to tour their facility and meet the executives and employees. They then move on to the next topic on the agenda.

Some may read this example and wonder whether there is anything wrong with the solution. Indeed, the executives could benefit from some joint projects. However, joint projects will not resolve the problem that the executives are operating with a functional leadership mindset. They still approach issues from their own individual perspectives and not from an organizational-wide perspective.

It also is surprising how executives do not realize that they do have a common project all the time (and it is not hosting politicians). Their common project is "running the company as a whole enterprise." This basic perspective eludes many executive teams because they think about their organizations as a collection of distinct departments. They fail to grasp the sense of the whole enterprise.

The Need to Balance Vertical and Horizontal Perspectives

Holistic leaders work in the best interests of the organization as a whole when they balance the vertical and horizontal perspectives in their roles. This means they have the ability to see the organization as it exists vertically (as in the traditional organizational chart), and also how it exists horizontally across the many departmental boundaries.

Figure 7.3 presents two images representing the two perspectives. The traditional organizational chart is the image representing the vertical perspective. It represents a hierarchical model where delegation and evaluation are delivered from the top to the bottom of the organization. The horizontal perspective is represented by the geodesic dome. It represents a network of connections where everyone can contribute and everyone can communicate with anybody.

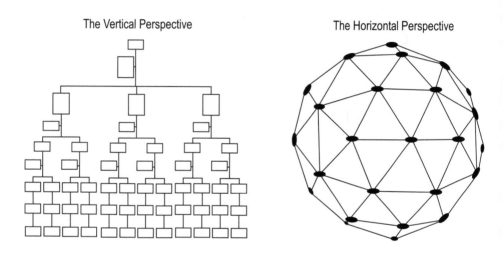

The Vertical Perspective · The Horizontal Perspective

Figure 7.3 *Balancing the Vertical and Horizontal Perspectives*

The vertical perspective has dominated how most organizations have been structured. In this world, leaders lead within their functional areas, departments and business units–primarily within their own "box" on the organizational chart. In the horizontal perspective, leaders do not see a series of discrete boxes or functional areas but rather a series of connections.

In this geodesic dome world, leaders lead by looking outside their departmental and functional silos and becoming aware of how the organization is connected horizontally. It requires looking at the white space between the boxes on the traditional organizational chart as meaningful spaces that need to be filled with connections and communications. We refer to this as "leading outside the box." Both perspectives are important variables of organizational leadership. Leaders must possess a strong vertical perspective to align and engage their own functional areas. They must also have a strong horizontal perspective.

In our experience, we have found that leaders typically do a better job of leading within the box rather than outside the box. It is their own functional area that occupies most of their attention. Reflect on this for yourself: How much time do you spend focused (or preoccupied) with leading inside your functional or business unit box? If you are like most leaders we work with, the bulk of your time is spent leading inside the box. Leaders then must bring more of a horizontal perspective into their roles.

The Need to Work Outside Departmental Boundaries

One leader lamented in a leadership development program regarding his challenge of trying to work outside his departmental boundaries, "I know it is important. But I just don't have the time. I'm so busy focused on my one department, I don't even have time to connect with my colleagues within my department, let alone those across the company." Leaders need to consciously force themselves to go outside the boundaries of their departments.

Consider the challenge faced by a company that held a leadership summit for the top two hundred leaders of their organization.

A company held a two-day event focused on developing stronger organizational leadership capacity and connections across the company. During the opening keynote presentation, the speaker spoke on current trends in leadership development and then discussed organizational leadership. The speaker asked the participants to look at the individuals seated at their tables. He then asked how many participants sat with colleagues outside their own functional areas. It turned out that only a very few participants did so. The vast majority of leaders sat with their own management teams.

The keynote speaker challenged the group of leaders by saying, "How can you ever be effective as organizational leaders, if you can't even get out of your departments and network with your colleagues across the company in a forum like this?" The message was heard loud and clear. The keynote speaker asked participants to get out of their seats and sit with colleagues from other functional areas. This practice was repeated several times during the two-day event.

Like the leaders in this company, all leaders need to challenge themselves to overcome the ingrained behaviors of a functional leadership mindset and start to work outside their functional boundaries.

In another organization a leader (a middle manager in the organization) implemented a simple and effective strategy for doing this. She instituted quarterly "big-picture" lunch meetings where she invited peers from across the company to have lunch and discuss broad business issues. The goal of the meeting was not to solve specific business problems but rather to explore enterprise-wide issues.

The big-picture meetings yielded some very positive results for the organization. First, the group developed an enterprise-wide understanding of the organization. Second, they were able to identify areas where they could work more effectively together. Finally, they began to spearhead initiatives to bring greater alignment and engagement to the organization.

In another organization, a senior leader developed the practice of taking a walk around her office building once a day. Each day she ventured to a different floor and found a colleague to chat with for a few minutes. At first her colleagues did not know how to take this "strange behavior" from someone outside their department. However, the senior leader persisted. During the conversations, she talked about what her colleagues were working on currently, the challenges they were facing and the possible ways they could work together. The practice was personally beneficial to this senior leader because she developed a very good understanding of how the organization operated as a whole. It also helped her to lead her own division more effectively with the interest of the entire organization at heart.

The key to leaders going outside the departmental and functional boundaries is merely one of making the commitment to learn about the various parts of their organization. Once leaders do so, they learn how their organization operates as a whole entity and very quickly develop an enterprise-wide perspective.

The Need to Break Down Organizational Silos

Organizational leadership also occurs when leaders actively work together to break down organizational silos and increase the effectiveness of the organization. Consider the following example:

A technology company had a large product development organization supporting over fifteen software products. The products were "bundled" into five groups, and the department was organized around the five units. Rarely did the engineers and developers from the various units talk to each other. Alignment and engagement did not occur until customers started to complain loudly and clearly. Customers said the current product offerings made it difficult for them to use the software products together. They repeatedly demanded that the company integrate their products into a seamless suite.

The head of the product development unit led an initiative to get the employees from the five units to talk to one another. Very quickly, as the silos came down, a number of innovative solutions emerged on how the company could leverage software bundling to customers. An interesting insight surfaced. It turned out that the software developers and engineers already were discussing these issues within their business units, but the silos prevented the ideas from working across the department and being implemented in a meaningful manner. Eventually, this situation led the department to reorganize their software products to more of an integrated suite of products focused on meeting customer expectations.

This example points out the inverse relationship that exists between organizational silos and innovation. The greater the number of silos in an organization, the lower the innovation; the fewer the silos, the greater the innovation. Leaders must actively look for ways to break down silos to increase the flow of information and ideas. Organizations today and in the future will need leaders who actively breakdown silos and barriers, instead of building them.

TOOL #2: BUILD RELATIONSHIPS WITH AND INFLUENCE KEY STAKEHOLDERS

Effective organizational leadership is based on the ability of leaders to build relationships with key stakeholders across and outside the organization. We define a stakeholder as an individual, department or organization with a common interest or stake in the success of an organization. Stakeholders can influence the outcomes either directly or indirectly. As a result, it is important to build relationships with them.

In the past, when organizations were structured more vertically, leadership decisions were largely a result of exercising formal power and authority. However, in the new world of organizational leadership, leaders more frequently find themselves leading without formal authority. When leaders work across organizational boundaries, they are confronted with a different set of challenges than those they found when working within their functional department. Their success is dependent on their ability to build strong relationships across and outside the organization through an effective key stakeholder management process. Leaders work in partnership with stakeholders who have the common interest of seeing the organization succeed.

> **Effective organizational leadership emerges when leaders choose to collaborate or partner with a variety of stakeholders such as fellow leaders, employees, suppliers, advocacy groups and regulators.**

Stakeholder management is fundamentally about building win-win relationships that enable the organization to achieve greater degrees of alignment and engagement and thereby become high-performance organizations. Relationships based on an adversarial or competitive approach do not lead to success in the long term.

Stakeholder management yields many benefits for leaders:

- Leaders develop a network of contacts whose expertise they can access across the organization.

- Leaders find it easier to get most things done in organizations because a positive relationship has already been established, and stakeholders genuinely want to help.

- Change initiatives are often implemented more smoothly because key stakeholders have been involved in the development process.

- Leaders develop a high degree of personal credibility with key stakeholders in the organization.

Here is a case example of an organization that benefited from a stakeholder management process.

A Canadian division was part of a large global auto parts manufacturer. It competed with companies located in other divisions for contracts to produce products for the global marketplace. Unfortunately, the division had lost out on the last three significant opportunities and not necessarily to the other divisions with the largest manufacturing sites. Upon further exploration, the Canadian division realized that key decision makers and influencers had misconceptions about the division's ability to produce quality products. These misconceptions were based largely on past problems. Even though the problems had been corrected, the misconceptions still lingered in the stakeholders' minds.

The division's management team decided to align around a stakeholder management process. They began by defining all of their key stakeholders. They then defined who on their team had existing relationships with the various stakeholders. They also conducted an assessment of the current status for each relationship. This was an honest assessment based on their beliefs of the strengths and weaknesses of the relationship. They then hired an outside consulting firm to conduct a series of stakeholder interviews. This approach was adopted for a dual purpose: (1) to uncover the stakeholders' perceptions, and (2) to begin educating stakeholders about the capabilities of the division.

The data revealed that even though the corporate decision-making body consisted of ten individuals, there were four key individuals at the corporate head office that had the most influence. Furthermore, they validated that the misconceptions about their division's ability to produce high-quality products were still affecting the decisions made by the corporate group.

Armed with this information, the management team created a common message and communications strategy. Any time a member of the management team went to the corporate head office, the same message was communicated to the global players. Over time, the strategy worked. The plant began to secure more significant projects.

Leaders often underestimate the need for a stakeholder management strategy. It tends to take a back seat to more pressing business issues. In the above case example, the management team began the process only after they realized their division was losing contracts to other divisions. Leaders need to continually invest time to build relationships with key stakeholders. They do not need to wait for problems to arise, but rather, they should make stakeholder management a daily part of their leadership roles.

Many leaders find stakeholder management challenging for a number of reasons:

- ***Stakeholder management takes time:*** Busy leaders often find stakeholder management to be time-consuming and without immediate benefits and results. A critical success factor of effective stakeholder management is a long-term perspective. It does take time, but time will be saved in the future because it will become easier to get things done across the organization.

- *Stakeholder management is not valued:* The Vice President of Research and Development of a global company introduced the concept of stakeholder management to her management team. One director immediately resisted the idea by saying, "I don't even know why we have to do this. We do a really good job and that should be enough. Why do we need to go around telling everyone that we do a good job?" Effective organizational leadership requires an understanding of the stakeholders' interests, the ability to do a good job to meet their interests and the ability to communicate what you have done for them.

- *Stakeholder management requires credibility and trust that may be absent:* Strained relationships can exist between departments, which can lead to low trust. The remedy is to repair the reputation, building it on enduring credibility. Credibility also exists at a team, business unit and departmental level. For example, in a production facility, the human resources department developed a reputation as the "police" of the organization. They believed their job was to enforce the organization's policies. One senior HR manager made it his life's mission to monitor the employee parking lot on a daily basis to see that employees parked where they were instructed to do so. Those that did not were caught and dealt with swiftly by the HR manager. This department's reputation was so bad that even senior managers and executives dreaded the thought of walking down the hallway to visit them to discuss business issues. In this case there was little trust of the HR department. Also, the department did not understand or appreciate how their internal clients and stakeholders perceived their collective behavior, so they were largely ignored on corporate initiatives. Other departments developed as many "work arounds" as possible, just to avoid dealing with members of the HR team. This is a good example of how not to demonstrate strong organizational leadership.

- *Stakeholders do not want to play:* In a public sector organization, the new director of the policy department embarked on a process to build relationships with internal clients. She immediately encountered resistance. It appeared the other departments did not want to play the stakeholder management game. Part of the reason was that the policy department did not have a good reputation within the organization. The new director realized that she first needed to establish her personal credibility coupled with stakeholder management. Over time, the policy department's reputation within the organization improved, and the department encountered less resistance.

Leaders will encounter challenges when implementing stakeholder management, but they must persist. Here are recommended work steps that leaders can use to build stakeholder relationships and eventually high-performance organizations.

Step 1: Identify Key Stakeholders

Organizations, departments and business units must make stakeholder management a priority, and it begins by identifying a list of key stakeholders. Often, we find that just creating this common list is helpful. It forces departments and business units to look outside their boundaries and consider how their success is dependent on the strength of these relationships.

Step 2: Assess The Status Of Each Relationship

Once the stakeholders are identified, it is important to conduct an honest assessment of each relationship. This establishes a baseline, which is helpful in determining approaches to strengthen the relationships.

Step 3: Determine Stakeholder Interests

Leaders must determine the interests of their stakeholders. One senior leader developed this practice every time she began a new role in her organization. She did not assume she knew her stakeholders' interests.

Rather she met with each stakeholder and stakeholder group to define their interests and determine how her department could work more effectively with them. Leaders also must attempt to balance the interests and needs of various stakeholders.

Step 4: Develop a Common Message

It is important to communicate with stakeholders and let them know what you are doing and what you have achieved. Here is an example of a finance department that realized they needed to develop and communicate a common message.

> *The management team of a finance department was engaged in a process of developing its stakeholder relationship strategy. After identifying their stakeholders' interests, they realized they needed to do a better job of communicating the value the department provided to the organization. They had always had this information, but they had never shared it with their stakeholders. For instance, the department was the most successful finance department in the global company based on several performance measurements. They recognized they needed to communicate to their stakeholders in a dignified way that the finance department was delivering significant value.*

Step 5: Use Both Formal and Informal Ways of Remaining in Contact With Stakeholders and Building Relationships

Once a common message is developed, it must be communicated on a regular basis to stakeholders. A dual strategy combining formal and informal tactics is required. Every opportunity is a chance to communicate the message to stakeholders and build the relationship.

In *The 7 Habits of Highly Effective People*, Stephen Covey provides a useful analogy of the Emotional Bank Account.[1] He states that

---

1. Stephen Covey, *The 7 Habits of Highly Effective People*, (Simon & Schuster: New York. 1989) p. 188.

relationships can be seen as a bank account. Daily actions either act as withdrawals (actions that weaken the relationship) or deposits (actions that strengthen the relationship). The analogy of a bank account also is appropriate in stakeholder management. Some leaders do not value stakeholder management and have not even opened up a bank account. For those that have, effective stakeholder management is about building strong stakeholder relationships by making several daily deposits that grow the bank account. The daily deposits are based on the personal and departmental credibility. Leaders who value stakeholder management are effective organizational leaders because they have many stakeholder "bank accounts" across the organization with very healthy balances.

TOOL #3: INCREASE THE COLLABORATION AND INTEGRATION ACROSS THE ORGANIZATION

The final tool for increasing the organizational leadership capacity to create high-performance organizations is to increase the collaboration and integration across the enterprise. Here are the five levels of collaboration and integration that increase organizational leadership:[2]

1. Shared learnings among departments

2. Joint planning and problem solving

3. Common processes

4. Collaboration on specific cross-functional initiatives

5. Structural integration.

1. *Shared learnings among departments:* Shared learning among departments is an effective way to increase collaboration and create greater integration across organizations. Separate departments,

---

2. The five levels of collaboration and integration are based upon the final chapter of David S. Weiss, *High Performance HR: Leveraging Human Resources For Competitive Advantage* (John Wiley & Sons Canada, Ltd., 2000). That chapter focuses on the levels of integration between internal service functions such as HR, Finance, and IT.

divisions or business units come together to better understand what each other does and how they can work more effectively together in a more aligned and engaged manner. The outcome of this practice is better working relationships, reduced duplication of effort and better use of organizational resources. Many times, simple approaches are the most effective ways to share learnings among departments. For example, the marketing department in a packaged goods company allocated fifteen minutes during each monthly product managers' meeting to hear a presentation from a guest speaker from another part of the company. Departments also can apply more formalized approaches by using technology for knowledge sharing and knowledge management. Job shadowing and job rotations are another effective strategy for shared learnings among departments.

2. *Joint planning and project management:* The human resources and finance departments of a public sector organization met to explore how they could work together more effectively. They discovered that their internal practices were misaligned and resulted in frustration among their common internal clients. The two departments, working independently of one another, had implemented several organization-wide initiatives that were working at cross-purposes. For example, the two departments realized that the organization's performance review process and budget planning process took place within the same three-week period each year. This placed a considerable strain on the organization's managers. Yet both departments, working in isolation from one another, had failed to realize the impact. Once the departments started to conduct joint planning sessions, they discovered more effective ways to plan their work, manage their projects and thereby align their processes more effectively. This ultimately led to greater engagement and compliance among the organization's managers.

3. *Establish common processes:* Different departments and business units from across the organization need to establish common processes—common approaches to strategic planning, business planning, implementing change, financial reporting and service level agreements. Common processes lead to efficiencies because the organization utilizes its internal resources more. The issue is not what needs to be done—it's how it is done. In many cases, departments continue to operate independently, but they operate more effectively because they use a common business process.

Here is an example of how common processes helped a corporate services division deliver more value to the other divisions in their organization:

The corporate services division of a municipal sector organization consisted of a broad mix of independent departments, including IT, Finance, HR, Legal, Real Estate and Communications. Many of these departments were placed under corporate services because they did not "fit" in any of the other four divisions in the municipality. The leader of the corporate services division recognized that the departments were distinct from one another and that they could continue to work independently—and they did. However, the divisional leader wanted to project a stronger image of corporate services within the organization. From her perspective, there were many common processes across the departments to simplify relationships with the other divisional leaders. Over a period of time, she began to work with the other divisions and began to identify some common processes that would make the other division leaders' lives simpler. One of the most successful was the development of a common service level agreement process that her entire division could use when working with internal clients. So even though the departments remained distinct, this process helped them become more aligned and project a more professional image within the organization.

4. ***Collaboration on specific cross-functional initiatives:*** Leaders can also increase organizational alignment and engagement by initiating collaboration for specific cross-functional initiatives. Here is an example of an organization that discovered a way to integrate initiatives effectively:

A large financial organization discovered they could generate increased collaboration among several enterprise-wide initiatives by introducing what they referred to as "integrator roles." This organization often had several large-scale initiatives taking place at the same time. What they found was that little integration took place among these projects. While each project had its own project manager, it often focused only on managing its own initiative. Project managers were given integrator roles with the sole purpose of working across the organization. These project managers looked across at all the large-scale initiatives and uncovered the opportunities for collaboration and integration. The organization discovered that the integrator roles were invaluable in keeping all project managers aware of the ways the projects were linked. These roles also enabled the organization to utilize resources more effectively as employees were moved from initiative to initiative and as the projects' demand for resources varied over time.

5. ***Structural integration:*** Sometimes organizations drive greater alignment and engagement through structural integration. Essentially, the organization looks at its structural design, breaks up silos and reconfigures them to increase the degree of alignment and engagement to the organization's business strategy. One example of structural integration is shared services, increasing the collaboration and integration among the transactional components of internal services (e.g., HR, Finance and IT). This strategy can lead to economies of scale and better use of internal resources. In some cases, the departments that had excellent external service providers

may believe that the requirement to use internal shared services will reduce their standard of service. However, at the same time, departments that received poor service in the past often benefit from the greater value of service delivered by the shared services.

CLOSING COMMENTS

At a recent gathering of a hundred high-potential leaders, a seasoned CEO reflected on the issue of organizational leadership. He said to his audience, "I've come to learn that leadership is largely about alignment and engagement. Any manager can get people to do things. But real leaders align work and engage people to the company's future direction and energize their people to that direction. This is what alignment and engagement means. This is what is at the core of leadership."

In this chapter we explored how holistic leaders can lead for alignment and engagement and thereby build high-performance organizations. In the next chapter, we explore the element of team leadership and discuss how leaders build leadership capacity through strong teams.

Team Leadership

Most great accomplishments within organizations are the result of strong teams, and strong teams require effective team leadership. However, team leadership is not as well understood as other aspects of leadership and as a result has been elusive. Bennis observes that personal leadership has been one of the most researched and examined topics in business, while the area of team or group leadership has been largely ignored.[1]

The purpose of this chapter is to enable leaders to lead teams successfully.

We define team leadership as the ability of leaders to leverage the potential of the individual team members to create something greater. In other words, the goal of team leadership is to create a whole that is greater than the sum of its parts.

TEAM LEADERSHIP— EVEN MORE IMPORTANT TODAY

Team leadership has always been important to the success of organizations, but it has taken on greater significance because the external business environment is more complex than ever before. Organizations can no longer rely on a few minds at the top to make business decisions. In order to effectively resolve complex challenges, organizations need to bring many perspectives together to tap teams' collective intelligence.

---

1. Warren Bennis, "The Secrets of Great Groups" *Leader to Leader No. 3*, Winter 1997.

Research conducted by our Knightsbridge organization confirms the increasing importance of team leadership.[2] We have found a clear shift in the expectations expressed by boards of directors and organizations when they have been recruiting senior leaders. One of the central capabilities that organizations look for in leaders is team leadership capability. More specifically, they are searching for leaders who can exercise strong team leadership by:

- Aligning and engaging senior management teams to a common strategic direction

- Defining success for the whole company, rather than just themselves

- Creating open communication through dialogue

- Enabling teams to deal with ambiguity, uncertainty and conflict

- Building collective leadership in an organization rather than being self-absorbed with their own personal agendas and egos.

The purpose of this chapter is to explore the element of team leadership that is part of the Holistic Leadership Framework.

Figure 8.1 *The Holistic Leadership Framework*

---

2. These research findings have been provided by Brad Beveridge, Managing Director of Knightsbridge Executive Search 2004.

The chapter examines the four types of teams that exist in organizations to give leaders an understanding of the scope of team leadership. We then explore a case example of how to build team leadership. Finally, we provide eight tactics to enable leaders to strengthen team leadership capacity.

THE FOUR TYPES OF TEAMS

Essentially four types of teams exist in organizations today: 1) traditional and virtual teams, 2) self-directed teams, 3) cross-functional teams and 4) communities of interest.[3] Each represents an important way for groups of employees to come together to work on common issues and drive organizational success. The four types of teams are shown in Figure 8.2. The differences among the teams can be described by two factors:

- The extent to which the teams are led by a team leader (either Leader led or Leader Less)

- The extent to which the team members work in the same functional areas (functional or cross-functional).

	Functional	Cross-Functional
Leader Led	**Traditional Teams**	**Cross-Functional Teams**
Leader Less	**Self Directed Teams**	**Communities of Interest Teams**

Figure 8.2 *The Four Types of Teams*

3. Etienne Wenger, & William M. Snyder, "Communities of Practice: The Organizational Frontier," *Harvard Business Review*, January-February 2000, pp. 139-145.

1. Traditional Teams

Through the years, traditional teams have been characterized by the following:

- All team members report to one team manager.

- Team members are relatively constant.

- Team members tend to work in a common location and thereby have many opportunities to meet face to face.

- Team members also have clear and documented responsibilities for themselves, their team and their function.

- The managers have power and authority based on their position as the team leaders.

- The manager's role is to plan, organize, control and evaluate the performance of the team. This power is mainly derived from the manager's position in the hierarchy given to him or her by someone other than the team members (usually the person to whom the team manager reports).

The challenges for traditional teams tend to involve issues such as lack of direction, low morale, internal conflict and failure to deliver results.

Traditional teams are not very traditional anymore. Modern "traditional" team leaders are expected to manage their teams whether all the members are located on one floor in an office or are scattered in different cities or even countries. If team members are located remotely, the team leaders have to rely heavily on their influence skills. They also must have the skills to empower those team members so that they can take independent action in alignment with the overall expectations of the team. The membership of the traditional team is not static. It can change based on the needs of the team, although most members stay with the team on a consistent basis.

The evolution of the traditional team to include virtual members and multiple locations is advantageous for several reasons:

- Virtual teams can put people on a team for a temporary period when specific input is required—thereby enhancing an organization's ability to tap its internal expertise.

- Virtual teams can maximize the use of employees' intellectual capital, no matter where they are in the world, and can reuse ideas across the organization once they are developed for multiple virtual teams.

- Virtual teams can contribute to employee retention. Employees are usually exposed to many virtual teams, which expands their knowledge base and provides them with personal development opportunities.

- Virtual teams provide employees with more opportunities for career development since employees do not have to move to a specific location in order to receive interesting work assignments and promotions.

Sustaining virtual teams also involves challenges. For example:

- Inadequate communication among virtual team members and with the virtual team leader can occur. Communication is very important for virtual teams, and through the use of technology, teams can stay connected. However, virtual teams do need to meet face to face on occasion in order to build their relationships.

- Rewards and recognition sometimes need to be aligned within the virtual team. It is essential to establish clear deliverables so that all can focus on the same end point.

- Virtual teams must develop clear accountabilities for themselves and the members, specify the metrics for the accountabilities and evaluate the performance of both the team and each member of the team.

2. Self-Directed Teams

In an attempt to be more nimble and responsive, self-directed teams began to arise within organizations. Some of the characteristics of self-directed teams are:

- They are similar to traditional teams in that they have constant members within a function; however, the team is autonomous and therefore leaderless.

- Self-directed teams often have relatively clear responsibilities for themselves, the team members and their departments, just as traditional teams do. However, self-directed teams differ in their approach to team leadership. The team members often assign the work and evaluate the members' performance themselves.

- Self-directed teams face the challenge of working well in a shared leadership environment. This becomes especially important when self-directed work teams encounter crises or when they underperform.

- Self-directed work teams tend to be used with groups that have a focused task that needs to be accomplished and where all the members of the team are doing similar work at which they are competent. For example, an experienced team working on a shop floor in a manufacturing setting can work without a leader. They understand their work well and can usually schedule the work that needs to be done efficiently. Direct supervision in those frontline situations may add little value.

Over time, traditional teams and self-directed teams have influenced each other and converged to some extent. Traditional team members have become more empowered—especially in virtual leadership situations. This has made traditional teams function more often as leaderless teams. At the same time, self-directed teams have often introduced some form of governance in order to make decisions and deal with problems. For example, self-directed teams sometimes have rotating "team leads," or elected representatives to help manage the teams, without compromising the empowerment of its members.

3. Cross-Functional Teams

Cross-functional teams are becoming more prominent as a way of ensuring that all stakeholders and functions come together effectively. Two primary characteristics of cross-functional teams are: (1) Cross-functional teams have one leader, and (2) team members are from multiple functions within the organization. For example, many organizations have cross-functional project teams designed to investigate a new strategic initiative or to implement a complex change. In one insurance brokerage company, a cross-functional team was formed to plan a major consolidation of two offices into one location. The membership of the cross-functional team included the new leader of the consolidated office, several members from each of the two offices, an information technology professional, a communications expert, and a specialist in change management. The team needed to work together cross-functionally to consolidate the two offices, and, at the same time, the members had to respond to their local functional pressures to meet their local commitments.

Perhaps the best example of a cross-functional team is an executive team. In many organizations, the executive team is the only cross-functional team that is structured into the organizational charts. From a team leadership perspective, the executive team is the most important cross-functional team in an organization. It's critical because it is the team that sets the organization's strategic direction. The team must excel at utilizing the various team members' perspectives and expertise. Finally, the executive team also is a model to the rest of the organization to show how a team should function.

Executive cross-functional teams have many challenges, including:

- Executive teams often struggle to find the time necessary to build their teams. Typically, team members are so busy running their own functions that little time is left for building a truly effective executive team.

- The president (team leader) may have a difficult time leading team members if dual reporting relationships exist—which is customary in large global companies. Executives report to the president (team leader) but also report to a corporate department executive. In some cases, presidents have direct reports with only a dotted-line reporting relationship to the president.

- Many executive teams underestimate how important it is to model good cross-functional executive leadership for the whole organization. If the senior team is not seen as being the model of an effective leadership team, the confidence of the entire organization can be undermined.

- Executive team members may be located on one floor or they may work virtually from multiple locations. At times, they can be spread out globally and thus have similar characteristics to a virtual team. Like virtual teams they may be challenged in their ability to share information and stay connected with one another.

As a result of these complexities, leading an executive team can be one of the most difficult cross-functional team leadership challenges. That is why many executive teams fail to leverage the executive talent available around the table and, in the end, underperform.

4. Communities of Interest

Communities of interest emerged in organizations to respond to the need for shared expertise and learning across the organization. Some of the characteristics of these teams are:

- Groups of people are informally bound together by shared expertise, a passion for learning and a willingness to take responsibility for a joint enterprise.

- Communities of interest can develop spontaneously within organizations without the need for approval, which makes them distinct from other types of teams.

- The members of a community of interest join the team out of personal interest rather than along functional lines. For example, the female managers in a financial services company formed their own community of interest to share ideas and experiences of how to be a leader in their male-dominated work environment.

- The community of interest team development is organic, in that there is no prescribed approach to evolve the team.

- Finally, since they are fairly informal, these teams are often resistant to traditional forms of team supervision.

One of the challenges with communities of interest is in sustaining their existence. In many organizations, senior leaders must cultivate communities of interest as legitimate team entities. Therefore, executive sponsorship is a critical success factor for creating sustainable communities of interest teams. It also is important to provide community of interest teams with strategic information to help focus their passion, remove obstacles and allocate budgets so they have the resources to sustain themselves in the long term.

ASSESSING TEAM LEADERSHIP

In this section we explore the challanges of team leadership in action through a case example of an executive team of a medical devices manufacturing company.

The CEO of a medical devices company was in his role for two years. During this time he was able to achieve considerable success. He was able to get the company back on track from a growth perspective. The company successfully launched a new diagnostic device for screening prostate cancer; it was well received by the medical community. The CEO worked closely with HR to address low employee morale issues that had plagued the company for some time. Despite these successes, the CEO struggled with his executive team. He felt the individuals around the table were exceptional, but somehow as a team, they were mediocre. The only area where the team seemed to excel was in its ability to respond to crises.

The team consisted of a total of eight members: the CEO and seven Vice Presidents, including the VP Sales and Marketing, the VP Research and Development, the VP Production and Quality Assurance, the VP Legal and Corporate Affairs, the VP HR, the VP Information Technology, and the VP Finance.

There were some obvious issues that were affecting how the team operated. For example, the VP Legal and Corporate Affairs rarely showed up for the monthly executive team meetings. When he did, he was constantly interrupted and called out of the meeting to attend to "pressing legal matters." The VP IT was new in her role and did not seem to contribute actively during meetings. The CEO also struggled with the fact that some team members had a direct reporting relationship to the corporate office and only a dotted-line reporting relationship to him. He found that these executives paid more attention to "pleasing" their corporate bosses than focusing on the priorities of the CEO. Finally, the team had difficulty dealing with conflict. Team members were very cordial and polite with one another during meetings, but after the meetings, the executives would each go to the CEO to complain about their colleagues. Despite these challenges the team did seem to have an ability to work well during a crisis and to respond with quick solutions.

On the counsel of the VP HR, the CEO agreed to meet with an external consultant who was retained to gather some data to better understand the issues going on with the executive team. The plan was that the consultant would interview every member of the team. He would also conduct a set of interviews with a cross-section of directors reporting into the VPs. Once the data collection was completed, the consultant met with the CEO to debrief the findings.

He validated that the team saw itself as being mediocre. The team members expressed that they had had much better previous team experiences in their careers. They each had a sense that the team meetings were a real problem. Some said the meetings were too operational and that they did not focus on broad strategic issues. Others complained that the VP Legal and Corporate Affairs never attended meetings. As one team member stated, "We are all busy, but we know how to delegate our work. This guy is a control freak and hasn't built a strong team around him to deal with his legal issues." Others expressed the issue differently by stating that the CEO was not tough enough and could not hold this individual accountable.

Team members also stated that they really did not know one another well from a personal standpoint. Outside the meetings, they worked with one or two of their colleagues, but beyond that, there wasn't a good sense of the people who sat around the table. This contributed to a fairly polite and reserved team climate. "There are some key issues which we seem to be afraid to talk about openly because they'll be seen as a criticism of someone's department or of the individual themselves. So instead of addressing these issues head-on, we avoid them and keep talking around in circles," explained one executive.

One final team dynamic created the most frustration. Many executives described how significant team decisions were often made outside the monthly meetings. The CEO, VP Sales and Marketing and VP Finance made these decisions on their own. This group was referred to as the "inner circle," and it was creating a rift within the team. This issue was important because the other executives were rarely informed of the decisions and often found out about them through their own staff. This made the executives look bad and also created the impression within the organization that the executive team was not cohesive.

The data emerging from the VPs' direct reports validated the key issues expressed by the executive team members. The directors suggested that each individual executive had developed a high degree of personal credibility, yet the team had not. Many directors saw the executive team as being quite weak. As one director said, "It's strange. The individuals on the team are strong, but put them together, and somehow, the whole team becomes weaker than the individuals are on their own."

Upon hearing this feedback, the CEO became visibly frus-
trated. He was surprised by some of the feedback but felt that the
entire executive team needed to hear it as well. He and the con-
sultant agreed that this would be the next course of action.

This case example illustrates some of the key challenges that organizations face in building strong team leadership. This team was not necessarily a dysfunctional team. They saw themselves as a mediocre executive team that failed to perform to its potential. Often, when teams are mediocre, they do not respond to team issues with a sense of urgency; these teams can operate for quite some time at a low level of effectiveness.

When we examine the team leadership issues, what emerges is a deeper understanding of the team dynamics and areas of focus that can potentially lead to improved executive team performance.

For example, even though the team members believed their team was mediocre overall, the team had a strong competency—they were able to adapt and respond to changes and crises when they surfaced. The team uncovered that they were not able to play to each member's strengths. Furthermore, the team's "inner circle" affected its ability to collectively make business decisions and creatively solve problems as an intact team.

The team members all understood their short- and long-term goals. However, the "team wisdom" was weak. Since the team only came together during the monthly meetings, team members did not know one another very well. This affected the sense of openness, ability to challenge one another and to engage in meaningful cross-functional business discussions during meetings.

The members also did not feel a high degree of cohesion and loyalty to the team. What was particularly troublesome to the team was that others in the company also saw the lack of cohesion. This insight actually served as a common rallying point. They each realized that this affected their credibility. The team members agreed that they needed to become a more cohesive unit and set a positive team example for the benefit of the entire organization.

The team also lacked a shared vision of what they wanted this executive team to be and how it added value to the business. Discussions also revealed that almost half of the team members openly expressed a low level of belief in the team's potential to be outstanding.

Armed with the knowledge about their collective strengths and weaknesses, the executive team implemented the following strategy to increase its team leadership capacity:

- *Agree on what the executive team wants to be:* The executive team focused a planning session on what they believed was the executive team's value that would be missed if it was not there. This process shifted their attention to developing, tracking and evaluating the implementation of the business strategy as their primary value proposition.

- *Develop mutual accountabilities:* They concluded they would become a team if they had mutual accountabilities that they all would own together. They also put the mutual accountabilities into their individual bonus plans and allocated 20 percent of their bonus potential to the achievement of the mutual accountabilities.

- *Acknowledge the inner circle:* The dynamic of the team's "inner circle" was finally acknowledged. The three executives who were part of this inner circle understood the negative impact of their behavior. However, they made clear that their behavior was not motivated to exclude other team members; rather, it was driven by the need to make quick business decisions. They agreed that in the future they would attempt to make decisions with the entire team. When conditions demanded quick decisions outside formal team meetings, they agreed to communicate first to the executive team and then to the rest of the organization.

- *Develop executive team commitments:* The team developed a list of team commitments that defined their behaviors during team meetings. Since these team meetings represented the only time that the team actually came together face to face, it was important for the meetings to be effective. The team committed to ensure meetings were successful and to create an honest environment, where each member could challenge ideas and criticize their colleagues and do so in the knowledge that the comments would be received in a positive way. In addition, the CEO agreed to meet with the VP of Legal and Corporate Affairs so he could understand how important his commitment to attend monthly meetings was to the team's overall success. The team also spent time identifying their mutual expectations of one another. This served as an important strategy to enhance the team's wisdom and leverage the team's potential.

- *Get to know each other:* The team realized that because they did not know each other well, the openness within the team was affected. To increase their "bonding" competence, the team decided to explore common projects to work on together. They also decided to get to know each other through a series of social events to be held throughout the year. Furthermore, members were encouraged to take the initiative to have lunch meetings with their counterparts.

After implementing these strategies, the team felt an immediate boost in their performance as a team. However, as time progressed, they also recognized that they began to slip into old behaviors. The process of building strong cross-functional team leadership requires ongoing attention and focus. They discussed considering regular "health checks" on their team to continually develop the executive team leadership.

HOW TO BUILD STRONG TEAM LEADERSHIP

In the beginning of this chapter we defined team leadership as the ability of leaders to leverage the potential of the team's individual members to create something greater. We also discussed that the goal of team leadership is to create a whole that is greater than the sum of its parts—where the team's potential is realized for the benefit of the team and the organization.

Strong team leadership is often elusive and organizations squander the potential of teams.

Consider a typical scenario. A team begins to experience conflict. Trust is low, and infighting is high. At some point the situation becomes unbearable. At a meeting someone blurts out, "We need a team-building session!" Soon the team finds itself in the woods. A nervous team member is standing on top of a forty-foot pole in a safety harness. Below the pole is a facilitator who yells, "Jump! Your team members will catch you!" The nervous team member looks down, and given the lack of trust and amount of infighting with her team members, she realizes her chances of survival would be greater if she jumped into a pool filled with piranhas.

This scenario is how organizations have often treated team leadership. When issues become unbearable, there is often some form of "team-building" session that fails to effectively resolve the team issues. Leaders must understand that team leadership cannot be neglected. Furthermore, the typical approach of addressing team issues only when conditions become unbearable does not work.

Building strong team leadership is a lot like maintaining proper oral hygiene. It is common knowledge that healthy oral hygiene comes from daily brushing and flossing and regular dental checkups. The typical approach to team leadership is to avoid proper maintenance. But then when tooth decay sets in, the only intervention is to fill the cavity—or, worse, get a root canal. Leadership teams that require "root canals" often end up with different members on the team.

Below we present the eight tactics that leaders can implement on a daily basis to build strong team leadership.

THE EIGHT TACTICS THAT BUILD STRONG TEAM LEADERSHIP

1. Enhance the team's knowledge of itself

2. Allow teams to gel

3. Measure the team against collective goals

4. Create team commitments

5. Establish a clear decision-making process

6. Identify mutual expectations and interdependencies

7. Use coaching to drive team performance

8. Manage team conflict

1. Enhance the team's knowledge of itself

A team needs to be knowledgeable about its fundamental task as a team, who the team members are, their strengths and weaknesses and the environmental issues they are contending with. The team also needs to enhance its team knowledge continually. One important tactic to ensure this happens is for the team leader to make "the team" a regular agenda item at team meetings.

2. Allow teams to gel

Exceptional team leadership emerges when members both get along well with one another and deliver results. It is harder for team leaders to use power and authority to encourage team members to get along with one another than it is for them to use their power and authority to drive the attainment of business results. A leader cannot just proclaim to the team members, "Okay, everyone, like each other!" Team leaders must first recognize that teams need time to "gel" and that allowing time for this to happen contributes to strong team leadership. Team leaders often undervalue the importance of allowing teams to gel, focusing instead on the results teams must attain. Allowing teams to gel ensures that negative team dynamics do not impede team success. Often, the most effective strategies are informal, with teams getting together for social events, people making the effort to meet outside of team meetings, and the leader making team relationships a fundamental critical success factor.

3. Measure the team against collective goals

Often in teams the members are measured against individual performance goals. This can create tension and conflict, because members may work toward individual success over the team's success. The alternative is for team leaders to create collective goals for the team (in addition to individual goals) and to use these collective goals to guide the team's focus and energy.

4. Create team commitments

Team commitments reflect a series of behavioral statements that govern how the team members will behave and relate to one another. Team leadership is enhanced when teams take the time to create team commitments. However, there is a tendency for teams to avoid this tactic. Below are a few suggestions for creating team commitments:

- *Commitments must be team generated.* Team commitments must be generated by the team members and not by the team leader alone. The process of collectively identifying team commitments is an important strategy for building the team.

- *Use the organization's core values as a foundation.* Teams should use their organization's core values as a springboard to develop their team commitments. They can do this by taking each value and defining a behavioral statement that describes how the value would be evident in the team's behavior on a day-to-day basis.

- *Make the list easy to remember.* Long lists of commitments with too many words and sentences are easily forgotten and difficult to implement. We have found that teams often develop lists that contain five to seven short team commitment statements. One executive team created a poster with a short list that they each signed. The team referred to the list after each meeting to determine how successful they were in living the team commitments.

- *Discuss the consequences.* Once a team has defined its list of commitments, members should discuss the consequences for individual team members who do not uphold those commitments. The team becomes self-regulating, and team members hold one another accountable for applying the team commitments on a daily basis.

- *Review the team's progress.* It is important periodically for teams to review their success and progress in upholding the team's commitments.

- *Update the team commitment list.* Since the composition of team members often changes, it is helpful to update the commitment list from time to time.

5. Establish a clear decision-making process

A clear decision-making process reduces confusion and ensures that decisions get made.

For example, one executive team of a technology company realized that a gap in its decision-making process was the absence of a pre-consultation phase on key initiatives. The executive team struggled continually because it took too long for them to make decisions. Executives came to their monthly meetings and proposed ideas for immediate implementation. Since this was often the first time that the other team members had heard of these ideas, they would be inclined to slow the progress of the ideas because they needed more information. Therefore, the team kept deferring decisions on key issues. This in turn created a high degree of frustration within the team and the organization.

After further analysis, the executive team realized that they needed a pre-consultation phase as part of their decision-making process. They decided that any executive who wished to propose an idea for implementation on an enterprise-wide initiative would have to first consult with members of the executive team either individually or in executive team meetings. The goal would be to provide information and get input on their proposed idea. This simple change significantly improved the team's decision-making ability because when executives came to propose ideas, everyone around the table had already been made aware of it and had had an opportunity to provide thoughtful input.

6. Identify mutual expectations and interdependencies

At times, in spite of the best intentions, team members can work at cross-purposes. It is important for team members to clarify their mutual expectations —what team members expect from each other or their respective departments. It also is important for team members to define their interdependencies, i.e., where they are dependent on each other for their own success.

Consider the example of a cross-functional senior management team of a public sector organization leading a major change initiative. Their project was not going well; ongoing hurdles emerged to thwart the team's momentum. The team members became very frustrated with one another, and conflict began to surface during team meetings. The team decided to bring in an independent perspective by asking a senior HR manager to attend their next meeting. Upon listening to the team's struggles, the HR manager quickly realized that the team did not spend time upfront identifying mutual expectations and interdependencies. Instead, each team member was making assumptions about what other team members were expected to do. Over the course of several meetings, the HR manager facilitated a process that enabled the team members to articulate their mutual expectations and define their interdependencies. These became the most positive meetings that the team had experienced. They immediately found value in the process, as the project began to attain some momentum and minor wins. Over time, the team was able to sustain a more positive climate and was able to get back on track.

7. Use coaching to drive team performance

Team leadership also is strengthened when leaders apply coaching as a method to enhance their personal and collective performance. Our five-step coaching model is based on the acronym DRIVE.

- *Define coaching needs.* Leaders of teams will typically encounter five coaching needs.

  - *Competence:* Coaching may be required to address a performance issue that is a result of lack of competence on the part of the team member.

  - *Career:* Coaching conversations can focus on career concerns where leaders assist their team members to understand their future career paths within the organization.

- *Conflict:* Team leaders may coach to help team members deal with conflict situations.

- *Context:* Changes to the business environment demand changes to how teams function. Leaders use coaching to help teams understand these changes and the implications for team performance.

- *Confidential:* Leaders can coach team members on their confidential or personal concerns. The critical role for a leader in these situations is to be a concerned listener and sounding board, and refer to the appropriate resources as needed.

- *Review business results.* Leaders recognize where coaching is helpful as they focus on business results that the team is attempting to achieve. This is an important way to ensure coaching aligns and engages the team to the organization's business strategy.

- *Initiate coaching conversations.* Leaders take a proactive approach to coaching by initiating good coaching conversations. These conversations are often mutual and interactive, with give and take, questioning and sharing of information and ideas. All parties are fully involved. The conversations are also concrete. This means that leaders use language that is specific and focuses on what can be done, what can be learned, what can be improved. Good coaching conversations are logical. The conversation develops and flows in a clean and straightforward manner. The coach keeps the conversation focused on its purpose. Finally, coaching conversations are respectful. The leader avoids behaviors that communicate that the other person is inferior or that ridicules, belittles or judges an individual.

- *Verify action plan.* Leaders end coaching conversations by checking for understanding and verifying the action plan emerging from the discussion.

- *Evaluate progress.* Leaders also make a commitment to evaluate the team members' progress in implementing the action plan through follow-up conversations and meetings.

In addition to coaching responsibilities, a good team leader also realizes that the team collectively may benefit from external coaching as well. It is very difficult for a team leader to both attend to team dynamics and also be the observer of team process. Teams need to be self-aware, and they often need collective coaching to help them get there. For example, in one company, the executive team coach attended every executive team meeting and provided feedback at the midpoint and at the conclusion of the meetings. The reflections were about the group process and whether they were able to optimize their collective decision-making to "create something greater." Also, comments were offered about whether the executive team was dealing with the right kinds of issues at the appropriate level of complexity.

8. Manage team conflict

Conflict is a reality of organizational life. Strong team leaders understand that conflict is inevitable the moment a group of highly talented and passionate individuals become a team. When conflict is managed effectively, it acts as a mechanism to strengthen relationships, to address issues openly and to make better business decisions.

Conflict without contempt is a helpful form of conflict that can generate new ideas and solutions. Conflict with contempt is a problem that needs to be avoided.

The key task is to manage the emotional aspects of conflict so that its destructive potential is minimized and the constructive potential is maximized.

Leaders need to know how to manage destructive team conflict. Here are some ways for leaders to manage conflict with contempt:

- *Respond early:* When significant team conflict arises, team leaders must deal with it, rather than avoid the situation. The faster the leader can address the conflict issue, the easier it will be to resolve it.

- *Depersonalize the conflict:* Often when conflict surfaces, issues can become personal. Team leaders must help their teams understand the various sources of conflict and move the discussion away from the personalities involved.

- *Apply process skills before problem resolution skills:* At times, team leaders may intervene, but they then may jump into solving the problem too early. Leaders must first apply process skills, such as effective dialogue and good listening, to encourage the team to openly discuss and understand conflict in a healthy way. Once this has taken place, the leader can then work with the team to generate solutions.

- *Let teams self-diagnose conflict:* Team members need the skills to manage conflict and assume the accountability for it. By helping team members to self-diagnose conflict, leaders are able to help their teams effectively deal with future conflicts.

- *Respect team commitments and norms:* When conflicts escalate, team commitments and norms may be violated. In these cases, it is important for team leaders to stop and deal with the violation of the norm. They need to also ensure that it does not continue.

CLOSING COMMENTS

The four types of teams and the eight tactics to build strong leadership teams are the basic building blocks of effective team leadership. All leaders need to be effective team leaders, from the frontline employee to the president. In addition, all team leaders need to know how to be effective participants on a team when they are not the leaders. The exceptional leader knows when to lead and when to follow to build a team that can leverage the potential of the individual members to create something greater.

Personal Leadership

Leadership in today's organizations is fast. Leaders must attend to multiple priorities and make quick business decisions. Operating in this climate can be a personal challenge. Leaders rarely have the time to sit back and approach their practice of leadership in a more strategic, deliberate and thoughtful manner. This can impede the personal effectiveness of leaders and deteriorate the overall leadership capacity of an organization.

This book's premise is that organizations need a more holistic understanding of leadership. The Holistic Leadership Framework that we have been exploring provides a complete and comprehensive view of leadership, identifying the key elements for sustaining organizations' competitive advantage. In the previous five chapters we have explored the elements of the Holistic Leadership Framework:

- *Customer leadership:* How leaders create value for customers

- *Business strategy:* How leaders develop a comprehensive business strategy that drives customer leadership

- *Culture and values:* How leaders lead culture change, create inspiring workplaces and drive employee engagement

- *Organizational leadership:* How leaders create high-performance organizations through aligning and engaging internal work, processes and stakeholders

- *Team leadership:* How leaders build strong team capacity in their organizations.

Figure 9.1   *The Holistic Leadership Framework*

The final element of the Holistic Leadership Framework is personal leadership, which we define as the ability of leaders to lead in a more reflective and conscious manner. Personal leadership means slowing down and becoming more deliberate in the practice of leadership. Success in the other elements of leadership (customer leadership, business strategy, culture and values, organizational leadership, team leadership) is dependent on effective personal leadership.

In this chapter we discuss what holistic leaders must do to build inner strength so that their customer, organization and team leadership are effective and so that they are able to create successful business strategy, culture and values.

THE PERSONAL FACTORS
THAT CAN DERAIL LEADERS

Some leaders may derail or fail in their leadership roles, placing an organization at risk. In recent years, several studies have examined why leaders fail in their careers.[1] Some of the top "derailers" typically cited in the research include:

- *Personal arrogance:* Behavior that is pompous and/or conceited. Many leaders are highly egocentric and self-absorbed by their own personal agendas. These individuals frequently have low credibility within their organizations and fail to develop strong working relationships with colleagues.

- *Emotional incompetence:* Behavior that demonstrates impulsiveness, insensitivity towards others and a lack of emotional maturity. Many leaders with this behavior have difficulty leading others and struggle under stressful situations. They are often unable to inspire and engage their staff.

- *Domineering leadership styles:* Behavior that demonstrates a style of leading that is over-controlling and impatient. Leaders are often extreme micromanagers who have difficulty letting go and delegating work to direct reports.

- *Conflict avoidance:* Behavior that shows a reluctance to deal with difficult people issues because of conflict avoidance. This behavior undermines leaders' credibility and creates a poor working climate, as poor performers are not dealt with effectively.

- *Risk aversion:* Behavior that demonstrates a hesitancy to take calculated business risks. When leaders play it safe, they may fail to achieve performance breakthroughs.

Consider the following case example that illustrates the derailment of one leader who aspired to be promoted to more senior levels in his organization.

---

1. Barrett & Beeson, *Developing Business Leaders for 2010*; See also David L. Doltich, & Peter C. Cairo, Why CEOs Fail, (New York: Jossey-Bass, 2003).

Roger, a senior director of marketing for a food services compa-ny, received feedback from an executive coach working with his company. The coach gathered the feedback from several of Roger's peers, and it suggested that Roger was seen as being an overly aggressive, self-absorbed leader, who was concerned only with his own personal agenda. He was known to treat his staff harshly and would often "fly off the handle," yelling at his staff when they failed to deliver on projects. He failed to recog-nize the need to get things done by influencing others rather than by bullying them. Though seen as having exceptional mar-keting savvy, Roger lacked the ability to build positive working relationships with other executives and as a result did not pos-sess a high degree of credibility with them.

The feedback provided by the executive coach surprised Roger. Part of the reason was that when he joined the company as a marketing manager, he was touted as the "golden boy" who had the potential to become an executive in the company. He was quickly promoted into the director ranks. Roger saw himself as a driver, one who had the ability to deliver business results. Nonetheless, Roger did acknowledge that he was not the easiest person to work with. He was extremely demanding of his staff; but he stressed that he also was demanding of himself. He would put in long hours, often at the expense of his family life. What Roger did not realize was that the shine on his golden boy image was beginning to diminish.

The event that triggered Roger's derailment on his journey to the top was the considerable fallout that emerged after he did a presentation with two peers to the company's board of direc-tors. They were updating the board on a large-scale project. They had one hour on the meeting's agenda, and they decided that each would take twenty minutes for their presentations. Roger was first to present, and his presentation was going well. The members of the board began to ask him many questions, and Roger responded to each one. He became so absorbed in his presentation that he took forty-five minutes instead of the allot-ted twenty. He realized he went overtime but dismissed it because the board kept asking him questions. Unfortunately, his two colleagues were forced to race through their parts of the presentation in the remaining time. During their presentations, Roger was visibly detached. He was replaying his own presenta-tion in his mind and basking in his own success. After the presentations, his two colleagues rushed out of the meeting without giving Roger a word.

Later that week Roger's manager asked to meet with him. He discussed what had transpired at the board meeting and told Roger that his credibility among the senior executive team was severely damaged. Roger's manager then said that if Roger did not demonstrate significant change in his leadership style his career aspirations for executive positions would be jeopardized.

If we explore the reasons for Roger's derailment, several person-al leadership issues are evident. While Roger possessed strong marketing expertise and had a track record of delivering results, this was not enough to ensure his success as an executive in the company. The harsh way he dealt with his employees, his tendency to be pre-occupied with his own personal agenda and his inability to appreciate the need to build strong relationships with his peers, all served to slow down, if not completely stop, his journey to the top. Roger was largely unaware of how his behavior and leadership style affected those around him.

When Roger first joined his company, he appeared to have it all and was well on his way to the top. Expectations for him were high within the organization, but he derailed, and his career was in jeop-ardy. Despite the setback Roger was given one more opportunity to turn things around. This challenge was one of the toughest Roger ever had to confront. It was a challenge that we refer to as becoming a CAPABLE personal leader.

CAPABLE PERSONAL LEADERSHIP

Effective personal leadership is based on the capability of leaders to lead in a more conscious and reflective manner. When this is done well, leaders are better able to focus and integrate the other elements of the Holistic Leadership Framework. In this section we present the "CAPABLE Personal Leadership Model," which uses the CAPABLE acronym to describe the actions that lead to effective personal leadership. The *CAPABLE* Personal Leadership Model is presented below in Figure 9.2.

Cultivate Credibility
Achive Results
Practice Humility
Acquire Perspective
Build Leaders
Leverage Conversations
Exercise Balance

Figure 9.2   *The CAPABLE Personal Leadership Model*

The seven letters of the acronym *"CAPABLE"* represent actions that characterize effective—or "capable"—personal leadership. Here is a list of questions to assess the extent to which you (the reader) are a CAPABLE leader. Then read on to understand what these seven CAPABLE personal leadership actions mean in greater detail. After you read the chapter, reassess your responses to the seven questions to determine which actions you need to develop further to be a CAPABLE leader.

CAPABLE Personal Leadership	Almost Never	Sometimes	Frequently	Almost Always
Do You Cultivate Personal Credibility?	1	2	3	4
Do You Achieve Results?	1	2	3	4
Do You Practice Humility?	1	2	3	4
Do You Acquire a Broad Perspective?	1	2	3	4
Do You Build Others Into Leaders?	1	2	3	4
Do You Leverage Employee Conversations?	1	2	3	4
Do You Exercise Work-Life Balance?	1	2	3	4

Cultivate Credibility

CAPABLE leaders cultivate credibility. They are believable and are believed by their peers and followers. Belief is an important variable in leadership. Consider, for example, the following case of a new plant manager hired by a manufacturing company that had a long tradition of providing high-end technical products to global customers:

The new plant manager was brought in from outside the industry. He had limited high-end manufacturing and engineering experience, but he believed his abilities as an operations expert and business strategist would compensate for this. His objective was to turn his plant into the number one manufacturing facility in the company. After looking at the growth prospects, he realized that a new business model was needed. The model he introduced involved reducing the plant's fixed costs and pursuing projects staffed by external engineers who would be retained on contract. This meant the role of the internal engineering staff would change. Instead of doing the work and applying their expertise, engineers would be sourcing contractors and managing projects. Without consulting anyone the plant manager decided to announce the change to bring about his new business model in the facility.

Unfortunately, the proposed change did not go over well with employees. There was a high degree of resistance, even among members of the senior management team. Interestingly, the resistance was not to the idea but rather to the lack of belief in the new plant manager. His lack of industry experience was seen as a weakness. The employees believed he did not know the business and so believed his proposed changes were not based on substance. Employees also were concerned that the shift to the new business model would hurt the company's quality reputation with existing customers. The plant manager believed he could introduce the new business model because of the authority of his position. In reality, his credibility was a bigger factor than his title.

Leaders need to be mindful of their personal credibility and understand the importance it plays in their ability to influence employees, stakeholders, customers, shareholders and the general business community.

Below are several tactics for cultivating one's personal credibility.

Cultivate Credibility Tactics

1. Be congruent between what you say and what you do.

2. Speak truthfully.

3. Accept failure and apologize when mistakes are made.

4. Behave ethically.

---

1. ***Be congruent between what you say and what you do:*** Credibility is cultivated when words and actions are congruent, so that what you say and what you do are closely connected.[2] CAPABLE leaders take their personal credibility very seriously and work to ensure their words and actions are congruent. As one leader said,

---
2. The tactic of credibility also is reflected in the second stage of trust described in the last section of Chapter 4 ("Customer Leadership").

"At the end of the day, all you have as a leader is your credibility. You have to cultivate it and constantly work at it. If you ignore it or assume it is not important—then don't even bother to lead because you will not be effective."

2. *Speak truthfully:* It is important for leaders to set a positive tone in their organizations. Yet, in some instances, when the message is always delivered in this manner, receivers of the message begin to distrust it or assume that what the leaders are communicating is not true. This is known as the "spin factor." For example, in one manufacturing company, the senior executives were constantly upbeat about the business. Even though the economy was experiencing a downturn, the executives kept projecting an upbeat message so as not to discourage employees. On the production floor a different story was unfolding. Employees saw excess inventory and a slowdown in production, signaling to them that problems were occurring in the marketplace. The two stories—those from the senior managers and those from the employees' direct experience—did not match. Leaders clearly must be positive, but they need to avoid "spinning" stories that are not based on truth because this will erode their credibility.

3. *Accept failure and apologize when mistakes are made:* Recent high-profile corporate and political scandals have been very instructive from a credibility standpoint. In many instances the leaders involved in these scandals rarely have apologized for their actions; in many cases they have not accepted responsibility for their mistakes, choosing instead to behave in a self-righteous manner. Credibility is not only damaged in these circumstances—it is completely destroyed. CAPABLE leaders understand that there will be times when they will fail. During these difficult moments, an acknowledgment of failure, combined with a sincere apology, can go a long way toward maintaining one's credibility.

4. ***Behave ethically:*** Credibility is also cultivated when leaders are the standard of strong, ethical behavior in their organizations. Ethics (as we defined them in Chapter 6) represent standards of acceptable behavior in organizations. Ethics define what is right and what is wrong. Leaders need to be beyond reproach in their own ethical behavior and in the ethical guidance they give to others.

Achieve Results

CAPABLE leaders are committed to and achieve results. They understand that a key leadership accountability is to drive results for the organization, its customers, employees and shareholders. Consider this example of a telecommunications company that emphasized the personal leadership action of "achieve results."

> *The VP Sales repeatedly used a simple three-word "mantra" to establish a single point of focus for employees—"line of sight." He told his employees that "line of sight" meant that at any moment they must be able to make a direct connection between what they were doing and how it was connected to one of the company's strategic initiatives. If they could not make a direct link, then they were empowered to stop performing that task. The three-word "mantra," as the VP Sales referred to it, instantly gave everyone in the organization a single point of focus on results.*

Below we describe tactics that CAPABLE leaders use to achieve results.

Achieve Results Tactics

1. Provide direction.

2. Reinforce the values.

3. Eliminate distraction.

4. Define what is not important.

---

1. *Provide direction:* A primary way that CAPABLE leaders achieve results is by providing direction for their organizations. Providing direction does not stop once a leader has created a vision or developed a business strategy. Instead, it is an ongoing process of giving the organization signals that tell the company where it is going and what is important for success.

2. *Reinforce the values:* Leaders achieve results by reinforcing the organization's values. As we discussed in Chapter 6, values define what is important to the organization and how results are to be accomplished. In some organizations the "end justifies the means" and "results are accomplished at all costs." However, results that are inconsistent with an organization's values are difficult to sustain over time. CAPABLE leaders recognize that results must be attained in a manner that reflects the organization's core values.

3. *Eliminate distraction:* In many organizations, employees are distracted because of what we believe is "a battle for brain cells" taking place in organizations. People are overwhelmed by the vast amount of information they receive daily and struggle to make sense of the ever-increasing demands and priorities affecting their workloads. Their brain cells become "saturated" and, in turn, they become distracted. The price of distraction is often intangible, but considerable. Distractions can lead to ongoing misinformation among employees, wrong conclusions and faulty business decisions, rework on projects and missed deadlines. Collectively, these will lead to a failure to achieve desired business results.

4. *Define what is not important:* Leaders also help their organizations achieve results by clearly articulating what is not important to the organization. For example, an employee survey conducted in a public sector organization revealed that middle managers believed the organization did not have an overall sense of direction. This was due to the fact that the organization had too many

priorities, and managers were unclear which results to achieve. Once the senior management team began to look at the issue, they realized that they kept adding priorities but never took any away. Consequently, the organization spent considerable time completing "legacy projects" that no longer delivered value.

Practice Humility

CAPABLE personal leaders practice humility in the way they relate to others in their organizations. Yet, the dominant image of the "heroic leader" is far from being humble. In many cases leaders are brash, arrogant and overconfident. While confidence is critical to a leader's success, overconfidence that borders on personal arrogance can lead to ineffectiveness and potential derailment. In his book *Good to Great*, Collins found that many of the presidents of the companies he researched were not the charismatic, flamboyant and arrogant leaders often projected in the media.[3] Instead, the leaders of great companies displayed a combination of humility and determination. These leaders were self-effacing, quiet, reserved and even shy. They were highly ambitious, but their ambition was first and foremost for the success of the company rather than for their own riches and personal renown. They practiced humility through a "compelling modesty." They typically attributed success to others and assumed full responsibility for poor results, rather than blaming external circumstances.

Consider this example of a leader who was successful, in part, because she practiced humility.

> *A new supervisor was promoted to a senior manager position within a large manufacturing organization. The culture in this unionized environment was not as positive as it could be. Essentially, employees came to work, did their jobs and went home. The employees performed adequately but did not demonstrate a high degree of commitment to the organization. Part of the*

---

3. Jim Collins, *Good to Great*, (New York: Harper Business, 2001).

reason was that the employees saw the management team as a group of "bureaucrats" who were more interested in jockeying for their next career move than they were in creating an inspiring place to work.

The new senior manager was a very quiet individual. Over time she began to work her magic. She first identified a few young employees who seemed to have a "glimmer in their eye" and who had a desire to do something more than just their regular jobs. The senior manager set up a committee designed to make the workplace more inspiring. At first only a handful of employees took part. However, as employees began to see this senior manager in action, they realized she was a different kind of leader. She demonstrated a genuine desire to improve the organization. She was deeply committed to customers and to the employees. However, she also was a humble leader who preferred to lead from behind the scenes. She did not put herself forward, choosing instead to raise the profile of her people.

One day in a meeting, a group of employees were discussing how to introduce a new computer system into the organization. The room was fairly quiet because employees were typically afraid of speaking their mind. The ideas that were generated were not innovative. But the senior manager remained calm, and she began slowly to challenge the group to come up with more inventive ideas. Then, a relatively new and very young employee presented an off-the-wall idea. She said, "Instead of implementing this technology in the way we usually do things, why don't we have fun with this? Why don't we do something like an Olympic event?" The idea sparked something in the group. Suddenly, a sense of energy emerged that had not been evident in this organization. The team developed an innovative implementation plan for the computer system. It involved running an Olympic-type event to introduce the change to all employees.

When the idea was presented to the senior management team, they immediately pushed back and frowned on the idea. The senior manager stood up and talked passionately about the employees' *creativity and the importance of letting them run with this. The senior management team reluctantly agreed. After the meeting the general manager took the senior manager aside and told her that "her head would roll" if this project failed. The project did not fail. It was a tremendous success, and the new computer system was implemented in the region more effectively than in any other place in the organization. Through the process employees became engaged in their organization. The culture was alive for the first time in many years. Through it all, the senior manager led quietly always looking for ways to provide opportunities for others to lead.*

Below are several tactics which CAPABLE leaders can apply when practicing humility.

Practice Humility Tactics

1. Be altruistic.

2. Give credit to others.

3. Act in the best interest of your organization.

4. Give back to society.

---

1. ***Be altruistic:*** Arrogance is the flipside of humility. It is characterized by leaders with large egos, who are predominately focused on themselves and who act primarily out of self-interest. CAPABLE leaders practice humility by being altruistic. They demonstrate an unselfish regard for the welfare of others rather than being preoccupied with their own self-interests. Yet, within many places in our society today, genuine altruistic behavior is lacking among leaders. The recent corporate scandals that have occurred globally reveal many examples of senior leaders who have behaved out of self-interest rather than out of collective interest. Robert Greenleaf defined leadership in altruistic ways in his book *Servant Leadership*.[4] *Servant leadership* is based on a conscious effort to put the needs,

---

4. Robert K. Greenleaf, *Servant Leadership: A Journey Into The Nature Of Legitimate Power And Greatness*, (New York: Paulist Press, 1977).

aspirations and goals of others above one's own. At times, the line between self-interest and collective interest can be a fine one. CAPABLE leaders consistently walk the line that leads to collective interest.

2. *Give credit to others:* CAPABLE leaders practice humility when they give credit for success to others. As the case of the senior manager described above, she constantly gave credit for her personal success to her employees. She went out of her way to raise the profile of her direct reports. She never felt threatened by their performance. As a result, her employees were extremely loyal to her.

3. *Act in the best interest of your organization:* CAPABLE leaders are mindful when they are tempted to operate out of self-interest. It is not that operating out of self-interest should be avoided at all costs, but if it becomes the only way that leaders operate, then it can lead to personal derailment. In one organization, a president became quite frustrated with the degree of "entitlement" that he perceived among the employees. He created a company that was, in his eyes, very generous towards employees in terms of compensation and benefits. However, the president believed that the employees took advantage of this generosity and failed to appreciate it. This sense of entitlement perceived by the president may have been true, and yet at the same time, the president did not seem to be aware of the sense of entitlement displayed by himself and his own executive team. For example, it was customary for the executive team to have quarterly meetings at extremely lavish resorts. They went to very expensive restaurants and ordered $500 bottles of wine with dinner. The discussion during these dinners often focused on the company cars and other perks. The executives genuinely believed they were entitled to these perks because they were the senior leaders of the company. To a large extent, the leaders were not leading in the best interest of the organization. They were leading out of self-interest and were setting a poor example for the employees.

4. *Give back to society:* A founder and owner of a large retail operation was always one who gave back generously to his local community. He had a genuine sense of gratitude for his customers and believed they made him successful. He, therefore, gave back to his community and society, not because it was good for business but because he had an obligation to do this. He often told his employees, "This community has been very good to us, and we have an obligation to give back in kind." CAPABLE leaders give back to their communities and to the greater society. They not only give back through traditional modes of philanthropy and donations but also by giving their time. They also encourage their employees to give back to society.

Acquire Perspective

CAPABLE leaders acquire perspective so that they can effectively lead in ever-changing business environments. Perspective comes from a commitment to learning and to constantly seeing the world in new and different ways.

Here is an example of a CEO who was committed to acquiring different perspectives:

The CEO of an electronics manufacturing company had a reputation for being an avid learner. He realized that his success was largely dependent on his ability to be exposed continually to new ideas and new ways of thinking. He had built a very profitable company and was very successful—so some might say he had no reason to be committed to new perspectives. Yet, this CEO's motto was, "Learning never stops." One of the ways he exposed himself to new ideas was to be involved actively in the company's New Employee Orientation program. The young employees coming into the organization personally energized the CEO. He often commented, "These young people have an energy and a way of seeing the world that is completely different from my own. As new employees, they also have a set of fresh eyes on the company. They can see things that are no longer apparent to everyone else in the organization."

Too often, very successful leaders assume they no longer need to learn and gain new ideas. CAPABLE leaders commit to their ongoing learning and to acquiring perspective.

Below are some tactics that CAPABLE personal leaders use to acquire perspective.

<u>A</u>cquire Perspective Tactics

1. Broaden your knowledge base to force you to think creatively and shift your perspective.

2. Be accessible.

3. Never be too comfortable with your approach—because it will become obsolete quickly if you do not continue to evolve.

4. Be an observer.

5. Develop personal insight.

---

1. ***Broaden your knowledge base to force you to think creatively and shift your perspective:*** The complexity of the business world today demands that leaders have broad perspectives, which come from an expansive knowledge base. Leaders need to be eclectic thinkers and learn outside their areas of expertise. One senior manager developed a simple way to broaden her knowledge base. She realized that every time she entered a bookstore, she automatically headed towards the business section and then directly to the marketing books. As a marketing professional, she believed this was a good way to stay current in her own field. While this was true, she realized she was keeping her knowledge base fairly narrow. She decided to change her routine so that each time she went to a bookstore, she went to a different section. It did not

matter whether or not she was interested in the section, the exposure to different ideas and different ways of thinking about the world proved to be valuable to her.

2. *Be accessible:* "It is lonely at the top!" That was the refrain of one executive who often complained that his staff rarely came into his office to tell him what was taking place in the organization. What he did not recognize was that he made himself fairly inaccessible. He spent most of his days locked away in his office. He rarely walked through the building or had informal conversations with the staff. He did not have lunch in the staff cafeteria. These behavioral patterns created an impression that he did not want to talk to anyone. CAPABLE leaders are accessible. They demonstrate this accessibility by being approachable—leaving the comfort of their offices and going out into their organizations to meet with employees and learn what is happening on the front lines. By doing this, leaders keep in touch with their organizations and gain valuable perspectives.

3. ***Never be too comfortable with your approach—because it will become obsolete quickly if you do not continue to evolve:*** The VP of Information Technology in a retail organization was unable to solve several ongoing problems plaguing his department. His staff insisted that the solutions he was introducing were outdated and that he did not have a good grasp of how the team's work was done. The VP was frequently overheard saying, "When I was project leader, this is how I used to do things, and it worked." He was right—his approaches did work, but he failed to recognize that the world had changed. His staff was encountering similar problems, but the context and business environment were completely different. Old solutions to new problems often do not work. This leader was too comfortable with his old ways of doing things, and it was affecting his department's ability to succeed.

4. *Be an observer:* Leaders also can acquire perspective by learning to routinely "step outside of themselves" and be observers while they

are engaged in action. In *Leadership Without Easy Answers*, Heifetz suggests that leaders gain this kind of perspective by what he refers to as "getting on the balcony."[5] He asserts that leaders need to be keen observers of themselves in action. Rather than being totally immersed in the action, they need to be able to view patterns as if they were on a balcony. In one of our programs, a senior executive related the following story that effectively demonstrates this ability to be an observer.

The executive was having a fairly heated debate with a colleague. His self-perception was that he was handling the conversation well. At one moment during the debate, his eyes shifted to a wall behind his colleague. The wall was made of a frosted glass panel, and the executive was able to see his own reflection in the wall. Instead of the calm, collected individual, which he thought he was projecting, he saw a tense face and a visibly upset person. The image of himself "stopped him in his tracks." At that instant he realized his physical demeanor was only serving to make the conversation more heated and not helping to resolve the issue. He immediately backed into his chair, composed himself and altered his emotional state. His colleague noticed the difference and also began to calm down. The two continued the discussion and resolved the impasse. With the help of the frosted glass wall, the executive became an observer.

CAPABLE leaders do not get so caught up in the moment that it interferes with their performance. They actively observe themselves in action to gain perspective.

5. ***Develop personal insight:*** CAPABLE leaders acquire perspective through personal insight. This means they have the ability to be aware of their strengths, weaknesses and vulnerabilities. This personal insight leads to perspective because it enables leaders to understand how they would react in certain situations.

---

5. Heifetz, Ronald A., *Leadership Without Easy Answers* (Cambridge: Harvard University Press, 1994).

One senior manager observed that she had a tendency to read documents on her desk whenever she was in a meeting in her office. This was validated by feedback she received from her staff who suggested she never really gave them her full attention. She took the feedback to heart and reorganized the furniture in her office. She brought in a table so that she had a place to meet people free from the distraction of her desk. She learned to put herself through a mental and physical routine before these meetings. She moved to the table and sat with her hands on her lap. She focused on the people with direct eye contact when they spoke. Initially, this felt awkward for her, but over time she found that the meetings were shorter and more productive, and her staff members were increasingly pleased with her leadership style.

Soliciting feedback from trusted colleagues, peers and direct reports is an effective way of knowing more about oneself. Self-awareness also is enhanced through personal reflection. Many leaders use daily practices like journal writing, walking, reading or quiet time to reflect on their role as leaders and to acquire perspective along the way.

Build Leaders

CAPABLE leaders work collectively throughout their organizations to build leaders not just at the top but at all levels, in all areas. The ability to build leaders is emerging as a new expectation of leadership. Noel Tichy writes in *The Leadership Engine* that leaders in winning companies demonstrate a strong capability to teach leadership.[6] In essence, it is a core competency, and he believes great leaders are great teachers. These leaders do not see their organization's leadership development solutions as the only way to build leaders. Instead, they recognize that these solutions are amplified when they make a commitment to building future leaders.

6. Tichy Noel M., *The Leadership Engine*. (New York: Harper Collins Publishers, 1997).

Here is an example of a well-established leader who took the responsibility to develop new leaders very seriously.

This company was growing rapidly. To fill the need, the executives created a new layer of management reporting to the company's directors. The executives were so busy hiring managers that they were unable to devote time and energy to orient them. They decided to give the new managers three to six months to "get their feet wet" and develop their style of leadership in the organization.

After the first year of this initiative, they found that a high percentage of the new managers were failing in their new roles and that the hiring strategy was not working well. However, there was one anomaly—the success rate of the new managers in the marketing department was exceptional. The executives decided to explore why the marketing department was succeeding when all the other departments were not.

They found that the Director of Marketing had a different approach to the orientation of new managers in her department. She believed that the first two weeks of new employees' tenure was a pivotal time to develop them and build relationships with them. For that first two weeks, she had each new manager "shadow" her as she did her daily work and attended meetings. Only afterwards did they take over their managerial responsibilities. The two weeks of job shadowing were very important to the new managers' success. The Director and new managers shared ideas and talked about why the Director took certain actions. The Director also began to understand the way the new managers thought and how they could be developed to maximize their success in the organization. It then was easy for the Director to function as the ongoing mentor for the new managers. The executives attributed the new managers' success rate to this Director's orientation practice.

Below are some tactics that CAPABLE personal leaders use to build leaders.

B̲uild Leaders Tactics

1. Reflect on experience.

2. Help leaders understand their own personal leadership stories.

3. Focus on leadership life cycle transitions.

4. Provide opportunities for leadership.

1. ***Reflect on experience:*** When it comes to building leaders, experience is the best teacher[7]—but only when leaders can reflect on experiences effectively. As a leader stated, "It is hard to get 20/20 insight when you are going at a hundred miles per hour!" It is only through reflection that enduring leadership lessons from their experiences can be learned.

2. ***Help leaders understand their own personal leadership stories:*** Every leader is influenced by what we refer to as his or her "personal leadership story."[8] This means leaders are intimately aware of their past history and the experiences that shaped their approach to leadership. For example, the VP Sales of a global manufacturing organization grew up in Europe during World War II. He and his family lived in poverty. It planted the seeds in his personality and created the motivation for this leader to strive for greatness. He resolved early in his life that he did not want to live in poverty. By understanding the elements of his personal leadership story and sharing it with his colleagues, he became a more effective leader.

---

7. Bennis and Thomas studied 43 leaders and in their book *Geeks to Geezers* (2002—Harvard School Press), they found among the leaders they studied that each had at least one "crucible" life experience that unleashed their abilities and taught them who they were as leaders. Also see Morgan W. McCall, *High Flyers: Developing the Next Generation of Leaders* (Harvard Business School Press: Boston, Mass., 1997), as well as Morgan W. McCall, Michael W. Lombardo, & Ann M. Morrison, *The Lessons of Experience: How Successful Executives Develop on the Job*, (Lexington Mass: Lexington Books, 1998), who demonstrated that when senior leaders are asked to describe the learning events that most contributed to their own development as a leader, the classroom rarely appears on the list. Rather, experience is regarded as the best teacher.

8. The concept of creating stories is further explored in this book in Chapter 11 "Embedding Leadership In The Organization".

His colleagues better understood what motivated him and who he was as a person.

3. *Focus on leadership life cycle transitions:* CAPABLE leaders pay close attention to times when future leaders transition to new roles in their leadership life cycle. There are several key transition moments along the leadership life cycle—for example, when an employee first becomes a manager or when a manager first heads up a division or becomes an executive for the first time. Each transition in role presents new challenges and pressures. To succeed, new leaders need to develop new ways of thinking about their roles. Unfortunately, in many organizations little support is provided for new leaders at these critical junctures in their careers. Many organizations adopt a "sink or swim" attitude, which can lead to the derailment of leaders.[9] CAPABLE leaders, on the other hand, stay close during these transitional times and support new leaders in their evolving roles.

4. *Provide opportunities for leadership:* Domineering and overcontrolling leaders minimize the opportunities for people to lead. CAPABLE leaders try to build leaders at all levels, searching for ways to allow the leadership potential of others to surface. They actively conduct conversations to better understand the career goals and aspirations of their direct reports. A project manager in a technology company made this his primary goal as a leader. Even though he led large corporate-wide projects, he always managed to provide career opportunities for others to lead and grow. He was so successful that employees competed with each other for opportunities to work with this project manager.

Leverage Conversations

In the past, strong leaders were seen as "great communicators," able to communicate to the "masses" and generate motivation among

---

9. See Jay A. Conger and Robert M. Fulmer, "Developing The Leadership Pipeline," *Harvard Business Review*, December 2003 .

employees. Today, effective personal leadership is more a function of being a "great conversationalist." CAPABLE leaders leverage day-to-day conversations as a way to develop shared meaning with employees, peers, key stakeholders and customers about critical business issues. Conversations are used to align and engage people to the direction of their organization. The most effective conversations are mutual and interactive. There is give and take, questioning, sharing of information and ideas, and both parties are fully involved. Good questions enable individuals to discover their own answers, thus developing self-responsibility and ownership for the results. CAPABLE leaders know that in today's organizations there is too much information and not enough understanding. This leads to distraction and ineffectiveness. So they consciously take the time to have meaningful conversations with others. Consider the following example:

> A head nurse in a hospital was known as being a strong leader among her peers. One of the reasons was that she was seen as having an uncanny ability to effectively speak with employees throughout the organization. It would not be uncommon to see this head nurse throughout the office and hospital wards, huddled with individuals or small groups of employees. The conversations were engaging and energizing. Employees looked forward to the conversations because the head nurse was always able to quickly get to the heart of the matter, and help her colleagues think through problems and plan next steps.

Here are some tactics of how CAPABLE leaders leverage employee conversations.

Leverage Conversations Tactics

1. Create the space for dialogue.

2. Hold fireside chats.

3. Conduct skip-level meetings.

4. Hold town hall meetings.

---

1. *Create the space for dialogue:* Leaders leverage conversations by creating the "space" for dialogue to emerge.[10] Through conversations leaders provide the opportunity for a deeper kind of dialogue to take place—one in which 1) people listen to each other rather than think about what they want to say next; 2) suspend judgment and explore differences to achieve understanding; 3) make implicit ideas and beliefs more explicit; and 4) surface the underlying assumptions, issues and concerns.

2. *Hold fireside chats:* "Fireside chats" are informal conversations in which the leader sits almost as if in front of a fireside to have a conversation with groups of employees. One managing director in a professional services firm held an unusual style of fireside chats. She convened breakfast meetings on a monthly basis to celebrate employees' birthdays. Each month, she invited the employees with birthdays during that month to attend the breakfast. She and the employees informally discussed key business issues, and then they sang happy birthday to each other and shared birthday cake.

3. *Conduct skip-level meetings:* This is a conversation a leader has with groups of employees who are at least two levels below that leader. The skip-level meetings allow for a different kind of conversation to occur and often generate a great deal of candor and openness.

4. *Hold town hall meetings:* Many leaders hold town hall meetings in which large groups of employees discuss business and organizational issues. At times there may be a tendency to overcontrol the process. However, the value often comes from the informal nature of the conversation. Employees need to feel free to speak with confidence about what is in their minds and hearts, surface the underlying assumptions and attempt to make what might be implicitly understood, explicitly clear.

---

10. David S. Weiss, *High Performance HR: Leveraging Human Resources For Competitive Advantage.* (John Wiley & Sons Canada, Ltd., 2000). Chapter 7 explores in detail the importance of dialogue and how leaders can demonstrate dialogue effectively.

Exercise Balance

Work/life balance is a fundamental personal leadership challenge. One senior leader described his life this way: "The pressure is relentless. The pressure at work is unbelievable, and it doesn't stop when I get home. The moment I open my front door, my kids rush out to greet me, and my second day begins. By the time I put the kids to sleep, I am usually exhausted. I watch a little TV and then go to sleep, only to wake up six hours later to start it all over again." CAPABLE leaders need to exercise balance because their long-term sustainable success is dependent on it.

The scenario described above by this senior leader is one that is played out currently in the lives of many employees. Working in today's organizations does have its pressures. For one, everything is driven by speed and a constant sense of urgency. In one telecommunications company, the director of finance developed the habit of calling his executives at home late at night to discuss "urgent" business issues. Most people can also give personal examples of e-mails they have sent or received in the wee hours of the morning. Downtime or even "slack" aren't built into organizations, making it virtually impossible for leaders and employees to pause, meaningfully reflect on what they are doing and renew their energy.

Personal balance leads to an emotional and intellectual steadiness. In other words, when leaders exercise balance, they are "steadier" as individuals—less likely to lose their composure. In essence they demonstrate more effective personal leadership.

The consequences of not exercising balance are manifested in many ways. Here is an example of the negative implications of the lack of balance:

One young manager who was a high-potential candidate in his organization was completely absorbed by his work. He spent most of his time, attention and energy focused on work issues. One evening, after several out-of-town trips in a month, he returned home to his five-year-old daughter's hug and comment of "Daddy, I'm so happy you came home for a visit." He was very upset by her innocent remark. He sought out some coaching and told the coach, "I'm consumed by my work. Even when I'm home or at the park playing with my kids, I find myself constantly thinking about work." He made a list of the negative implications that stemmed from his failure to exercise balance. Here was his list:

- *Distant or disconnected personal relationships*
- *Lack of perspective and tolerance*
- *Inability to manage stress*
- *Increased irritability leading to strained work relationships*
- *Difficulty relaxing*
- *An inability to stop thinking about work.*

He then thought about what an older employee said at his retirement party. He talked about the false image of irreplaceable people and concluded, "The graveyards are filled with irreplaceable people." The young manager reflected on that comment and realized he needed to get his priorities and balance right.

Exercising balance is a very personal issue. Part of the problem, though, is that organizations have created a false dichotomy between "work and life" and view the two as being diametrically opposed to one another, when they are not. As we discussed in Chapter 6 on culture and values, employees are demanding greater work/life balance and are seeking leaders and organizations that will help them attain it. As Ciulla expresses in the book *The Working Life*, the challenge for most employees is not work, but rather how to make their lives work in a more balanced and integrated manner.[11]

Below we present some of the tactics that CAPABLE leaders use to exercise balance.

---

11. Joanne Ciulla, *The Working Life*. (New York: Crown Business, 2001).

Exercise Balance Tactics

1. Be a balance role model.

2. Focus on what really matters.

3. Adopt slow leadership.

4. Sustain your personal energy.

5. Grow a healthy support network.

6. Retreat.

1. *Be a balance role model:* Perhaps the most important way that leaders exercise balance is by being effective role models of work/life balance. Many executive teams we work with acknowledge that they are often the worst examples of balance within their organizations.

CAPABLE personal leaders recognize that one of the powerful ways they can demonstrate effective leadership is by personally exercising balance in their lives.

Consider the following example:

A president of a large electronics manufacturer was an extremely successful businessperson. Not only was his company very successful, but it also revolutionized the way the industry did business with customers. The president was highly regarded within his industry and among other business leaders for his strong leadership. Yet, when asked what success in his life he was most proud of, he did not refer to the business empire he built. He cited his wonderful marriage and that he and his wife had raised four children who had each achieved success in their lives. What he learned early in his career was to make balance a priority. He stated, "I realized when I first began my company, that I could work twenty-four hours a day and never get every-

thing done. So I had to make choices about my time. I found that if I worked too much, I was not effective. I found that when I balanced my work with my home life, I was more effective at both. So balance became a key value for me. It is something I inculcated in our culture and encouraged among our employees."

2. ***Focus on what really matters:*** One leader spent his career (actually his life) devoted to his work as a senior project manager. He traveled so frequently that he had only enough time to return home to pick up another suitcase for his next trip. Over time, his work began to provide less and less satisfaction, and his performance began to slip. He realized he also became distant from his family. He said, "It's as if they learned to live without me. They have developed a life of their own, and I'm not part of it." This committed senior leader failed to exercise balance, and it became not only a risk to himself and his family but also a risk to his organization. When people are out of balance, it shows up at work. Leaders need to focus on what really matters to them.

3. ***Adopt "slow-leadership":*** In the book *In Praise of Slow*, author Carl Honoré chronicles the slow movement emerging in many areas around the world.[12] The slow movement had its origins in Rome, Italy. It was established in response to the first McDonald's restaurant that opened in that ancient city. The slow movement attempts to provide an alternative approach to living in our fast world. The same idea applies to leadership. As we discussed earlier in this chapter, leaders operate at lightning speeds. At times this is necessary, but when it becomes the norm, balance is lost. The paradox, as Honoré points out, is that slow does not always mean slow; a slow approach can yield better and faster results. From a leadership standpoint, slow yields more thoughtful and deliberate leadership actions. Slow yields better conversations, better decisions, the right solutions to the right problems, and working at a more reasonable pace. Does everything really need to go so fast in

---

12. Carl Honoré, *In Praise of Slow*, (Toronto, Canada: Knopf Canada, 2004).

our organizations? Some things do, that is a given. But not everything.

4. *Sustain your personal energy:* Leaders need to look for ways to continually manage their personal energy. Small consistent pockets of time devoted to renewing energy can have a long-lasting effect on the ability to lead with balance. For example, in the book *The Power of Full Engagement*, authors Loehr and Schwartz identify the power of positive rituals to renew four sources of energy: mental, emotional, physical, and spiritual.[13] Leaders must remain mentally sharp through continual learning and reflection. They need to work on managing their emotions and their relationships with others. They need to be physically strong to effectively deal with stress. They need to pursue practices that address their spiritual needs.

5. *Grow a healthy support network:* A strong support network of relationships is another important way to exercise balance. A healthy network is invaluable during stressful times and is a key determinant of one's overall health.[14] CAPABLE leaders do not let themselves become so inaccessible or disconnected that they fail to build a network of relationships. Strong relationships are needed with family, relatives, and friends. They also are needed with peers and colleagues.

6. *Retreat:* Increasingly, many leaders exercise balance through personal retreats. They block off uninterrupted time to take a breather and reflect on their work and life. These retreats play an important role in enabling CAPABLE leaders to reconnect with themselves and identify what is truly important. One manager took one day a month to work from home. During the day, she would make herself unavailable and use the time to reflect on her work role, thinking

---

13. Jim Loehr & Tony Schwartz, *The Power of Full Engagement*, (New York: Free Press. 2003).

14. World Health Organization, & Health Education and Promotion Unit, *Health Promotion Glossary*, (Geneva: World Health Organization, 1998). The World Health Organization has identified the importance of relationships and social support as a determinant of one's health and the overall contribution to the social capital of societies.

about strategic issues, and catch up on her reading of trade magazines and business journals. The day was invaluable to generating breakthrough ideas and recharging her batteries. Another leader would take a day each quarter to go hiking. He found the time away from work and family not only made him a better leader, it made him a better person. Personal retreats need to become a valued practice in organizations because they lead to greater long-term effectiveness of leaders.

CLOSING COMMENTS

In today's busy and fast-paced world, organizations need CAPABLE leaders who can effectively practice a slower, more reflective approach to leadership. The capabilities that defined leadership success in the past are giving way to a new set of capabilities that emphasize cultivating credibility, achieving results, practicing humility, acquiring perspective, building future leaders, becoming strong conversationalists and exercising balance. The pressures and pace of the world will always exist. Organizations and leaders must accept joint responsibility to ensure that all leaders and employees are able to effectively deal with this environment.

part three

THE ORGANIZATION'S RESPONSE

Leadership Capacity Implementation: An Overview

Many organizations are waking up to the fact that leadership capacity is a primary driver of their competitive advantage. For example, a survey of more that 750 executives conducted by *Chief Executive* magazine and the Center for Creative Leadership reveals that almost 80 percent of CEOs see leadership capacity as critical for competitive advantage.[1] However, most do not really know what to do about this problem.

Part Two of this book explained the six elements of the Holistic Leadership Framework that leaders need to adopt—but the responsibility for becoming holistic leaders should not reside totally with leaders. Organizations need to do their part and put in place the systems, processes and development needed to implement holistic leadership. Part Three focuses on the organization's role in bridging the leadership capacity gap.

In our experience we have found the struggles in the implementation of leadership capacity stem from a lack of a comprehensive organizational approach. Some organizations do not even have a strategy. Other organizations have a series of practices (such as leadership development programs, key talent management processes or succession planning) that exist in isolation from one another.

What organizations need today is a comprehensive strategy for building leadership capacity. This strategy must be enterprise-wide in nature and integrate four critical success factors. Figure 10.1 provides a graphic representing the four factors.

---

1. Peter Haapaniemi, "Leading Indicators: The Development of Executive Leadership." *Chief Executive*, October 2002.

Figure 10.1   *Leadership Capacity Implementation*

1. ***Embed leadership in the organization:*** Organizations need to focus relentlessly on "embedding leadership." We define this as a process of ensuring that leadership capacity is seen and becomes an integral part of the very fabric of the organization. Consequently, leadership is seen as a primary driver of competitive advantage, and building leadership capacity is done continuously rather than just when a crisis occurs. The three embedding strategies (see Chapter 11) are the foundation on which the subsequent three chapters are built.

2. ***Focus on critical positions and key talent:*** Organizations need to give particular attention to their areas of key leadership strength. They need to remove the risk of any vulnerability that could occur if they cannot fill critical positions or if they cannot retain high-performing talent (see Chapter 12).

3. *Integrated leadership development:* To be successful, organizations need to approach their leadership capacity development from a broad and multi-disciplinary perspective. We refer to this approach as an integrated-solution approach to leadership development (see Chapter 13).

4. *Accountability for leadership capacity:* Organizations need to have clear accountabilities to ensure that leadership capacity stays as one of the top priorities for executives, line managers and HR professionals. Organizations also need to audit their leadership capacity and track their progress at bridging the gap (see Chapter 14).

WHY LEADERSHIP CAPACITY IMPLEMENTATION IS IMPORTANT

The following case example portrays a situation in which the four critical success factors for leadership capacity implementation were absent in varying degrees. The example will be punctuated by explanations of the organization's failure to do its part to bridge the leadership capacity gap.

> The HR Director in a healthcare products company decided to take matters into her own hands. She knew the details of the company's leadership demographics, which she was certain signaled troubling times ahead for the company. The average age of the top leadership was over 50; over 30 percent of the top two levels were eligible to retire with pension within five years.
>
> The HR department began with back-room work, plotting how to build leadership capacity for the company. They decided not to involve the executives at this point. After all, the executives had just rejected HR's request for an annual HR budget increase because of cost-cutting measures they were taking. But that was not going to stop the HR team—they were convinced they knew the right thing to do. They believed that once they presented the problem and provided a solution, the executives would see the overwhelming

value of the business case, and they would have to support the direction suggested.

Perhaps we should pause the description of the case example at this point to explore the HR department's first error of judgment. The compelling argument for the focus on leadership capacity was the high risk of not having the leadership capacity to function in the future, which could threaten the company's competitiveness. Typically, the accountability for strategy needs to originate with the executive group. In this case, the HR professionals decided to implement leadership capacity without involving the executives. In these kinds of situations, it is common that the HR professionals can get so far ahead of the executives that the executives will not be able to catch up with HR's passion and zeal for the effort.

Therefore, the first step the HR Director should have taken was to educate and engage the executives about the compelling need and strategic nature of the leadership capacity problem. They then could have started leadership capacity implementation by working with the executives to embed leadership in the organization (see Chapter 11), as an essential way the organization needed to do its business.

Next, the HR Director assigned one of the HR managers to plan a leadership development program for middle managers (managers and directors) with a focus on high-potential talent. The HR staff believed that the future rested in the organization's current key talent and high-potential talent. After some discussion they decided that if they chose some people for the program as high-potential talent, they would alienate all the others who were not chosen for that group. They also struggled with distinguishing between various managers and directors without input from the executives—and at this point they wanted to proceed alone. As a result they decided to design the program for all the directors in the organization.

The decision to train all the directors is not surprising since HR was unable to identify who should be included and who should not be included in the program. However, if they had involved the executives early in the process to focus on critical positions and key talent (see Chapter 12), they could have created more focus for this leadership development experience.

Their analysis at this point led them to proceed as follows:

The HR manager assigned to the project hired a leadership designer on contract who had success in program design in the automotive sector. The contractor was given the assignment of developing a best-in-class leadership course for the company. The contractor brought in a co-designer who helped him design the program he led in the automotive sector. Their goal was twofold: 1) to design the course based upon systems theory and 2) to analyze balancing and reinforcing factors that can create systemic barriers to efficiency and effectiveness. The contractor argued that systems theory would be helpful for developing the cognitive capacity of the middle managers, preparing them for higher levels of leadership. The HR Director and HR manager accepted the argument.

The leadership program concept presented a design flaw that contributed to the problem in the case example. The design of the program was developed in a vacuum based upon the designers' previous experiences in another sector and did not include input from the executives and participants of the program. This design process was flawed and was a dangerous approach. It could result in a program that did not address successfully the real needs of the participants who dealt with difficult business problems. This process is similar to engineers who create a design without asking for input from the users. The engineers believe it is the right thing to do until reality confronts them and they find out the design does not address the real issues and concerns of the people the design was meant to assist.

The case continues with the decision by the HR Director to add another component to her leadership capacity strategy.

At the same time, the HR Director realized that the leadership program alone was not enough. She decided that they needed to evolve the metrics system to measure leadership capability. As a result she asked one of her managers to prepare an extensive modification to the current performance management system. The plan was to categorize all managers on a performance-by-potential matrix. The managers who were categorized as "high potential" would be asked to attend the leadership course they were developing for directors. Also, the senior leadership would be able to provide coaching and support to the middle managers as they proceeded through the leadership program. The remainder of the managers would not receive any special attention. The HR Director theorized that it would not be a problem, because managers did not receive any attention anyway.

The back-room work proceeded for 10 months. The design of the leadership program progressed slowly but steadily. The design contractor convinced HR that the systems design ideas were the leading edge ideas that should be taught. As a result detailed course designs were developed. The performance management forms also were developed. The HR department contracted a desktop design firm to prepare the look of the materials so that they would be attractive when they were presented to the executives.

The HR Director monitored the progress of the entire process and kept it within budget so that the executives would not notice it. She reported to a VP of Administration who was on the executive group. He was the former Finance Director and had very little understanding or interest in HR matters. He implicitly trusted the HR Director and let her do what she thought was best, as long as she stayed within budget.

Let's take another pause in the case example to analyze what just happened. The HR professionals made a good decision to use more than one approach to implement leadership capacity. Combining the leadership development program with a reinforced performance management process increased the chances that some change in the work environment would occur. However, the multi-solution approach may not have been enough in this case, especially without executive support. HR needed a comprehensive approach to the overall leadership capacity challenge. This approach should have included:

• Multiple methods of learning for leaders

• Targeted learning for key talent

• Expanded work on coaching and mentoring for leaders who were identified as high potential

• A broad-based approach to learning and development for those who were not designated as the key talent and future successors of the organization.

This comprehensive approach is referred to as "integrated leadership development" (See Chapter 13).

Here is what happened when the HR Director finally introduced the executives to the ideas she was developing:

Finally, the time arrived to go public with the idea. The HR Director was convinced that once she showed the executives the compelling need and how it would be addressed, the executives would support this process entirely and immediately. She predicted to her HR team that the executives would enthusiastically support the project and would allocate a special budget to it. She spoke to the VP Administration and requested time on the executive group's monthly meeting agenda to discuss the leadership capacity issue.

The day arrived for the presentation to the executive group. The HR Director thought it would add power to the presentation if she brought the two HR managers with her to the executive group meeting—the manager who coordinated the contractor's work on the course design and the manager who redesigned the performance management process. She decided against bringing the leadership design contractor because the executives were not aware that that contractor had been hired.

She stayed with her two managers in a waiting room until they were called into the executive group meeting. She approached the executives as an executive professional—thinking to herself, "Act like a VP and they'll treat you like a VP." She presented her ideas, involved the HR managers in the discussion and told the story of the 10 months of development that had led them to the conclusion that the time to act was now. The executives sat in silence. When the HR Director was finished she asked for approval and the budget to continue with the project and to launch the pilot leadership development program for a select group of middle managers. After some embarrassing moments of silence, all eyes turned to the VP Administration, who finally said that he thought it was a good idea.

The President and the rest of the executive group were in a difficult position. They had just decided to cut costs by changing the health benefits program to reduce dental and vision care for non-executive employees. They planned to announce the cuts in about six weeks. They also had just decided to delay a new promotional campaign that they were considering. But how could they say "No" to a motivated HR Director and her managers when they were so well prepared and passionate about their presentation? After some brief discussion and questions about the plan, the President said that they could proceed, and he allocated the budget to complete the design and to run the pilot leadership program.

Let's discuss what just happened in the case example. The HR Director presented the pilot project and received the approval from the executives to proceed. However, the influence approach used was faulty and did not create an executive "*accountability for leadership capacity*" (see Chapter 14). Although the VP Administration had little knowledge of HR issues, it would have been a far more effective approach to ensure that he, as the executive sponsor for this project, understood it and could support it wholeheartedly. Also, the HR Director should have foreseen that before she launched into her presentation, she should have provided the President, who was a key stakeholder, with additional discussion. Finally, the entire executive group would have benefited from some staging of the problem and the solution—perhaps presented over two sessions so that they could get used to the idea and start to take personal ownership of the problem and the solution. Instead, the executives agreed reluctantly but didn't take ownership. The HR Director put herself in a highly vulnerable position that had little room for error. The project had to succeed. Here is what happened:

> The HR Director and the managers were delighted when they left the executive meeting. They believed they had the executive support to complete the leadership program design and launch the pilot. Over the next two months, they finalized the program design and completed the revisions to the performance management process.
>
> HR randomly selected twenty directors and invited them to the pilot leadership program. At first the program seemed to be progressing well. The directors were excited about the idea of participating in a leadership program. But then the rumblings started. Some executives called the VP Administration and asked why they were not informed about this program. The executives also said that the timing was terrible; they could not release their directors at this time of year. The VP Administration pleaded for support, and most executives acquiesced. At the same time,

some of the other directors, who were not selected, expressed concern about what it meant that they were not invited to the leadership program. Also, to make matters more complicated, one week before the program's launch date, the reductions to the benefits plan were announced, and the response was not positive.

The VP Administration began the leadership session with a welcoming comment and then left the room. A guest speaker then began talking about the ecosystem and how organizations were similar to the environment that needs to be in balance. The participants did not understand what the presentation had to do with leadership or their work in the company, but it was early in the program. Then the speaker introduced systems' thinking using an analogy of the reinforcing factors that increase population growth and the balancing factors that can offset population growth. The participants were asked to think of a company-specific analogy, and they chose the recently announced cuts to the benefits program. Very quickly, the program regressed to a complaint session against the executives for the reductions in the participants' personal benefits program. The participants were particularly outraged when they found out that the cuts were only for non-executives. The complaints escalated, and all attempts to quiet the group and to proceed with the program were unsuccessful.

After the first day of the three-day program, many of the participants called back to their offices and told whoever would listen that the program was a fiasco. At the beginning of the second day, one well-respected director stood up and said she thought this program was a waste of time and potentially was destructive. Others agreed. The participants decided they would continue with the program in the morning to listen to another guest speaker who was prebooked, and then they would end the program after lunch.

Two days later, the HR Director was called to a meeting with the President and the VP Administration. They spoke to her about trust and commitment. They suggested that the executives really had not wanted to support the program in the first place but that they had felt they had no choice but to fund the initiative. However, now that it was unsuccessful, they would not support any further work on the project.

The HR Director was outraged and argued that it was a harsh response to a pilot program, and she stormed out of the room. The grapevine spread the news rapidly—first about the cancellation of the program and then about the tense interaction with the HR Director. Managers concluded that the company was never really serious about leadership development. They also determined that the company's stated core value of innovation really meant that you could be innovative as long as it worked.

In the case example, the executives appeared to take the accountability for the leadership program by providing the budget for it. Did the executive group forget their commitment to the leadership program? Perhaps the HR Director knew that the executives would not support the project. As a result, she took accountability for leadership capacity without seeking meaningful executive commitment. Part of the problem was the secretive approach to developing the project. Because of the way the HR Director presented the leadership program to the executive group, the executives acquiesced rather than committing to the program. When the program's initial results were not positive, the executives quickly rescinded their support.

If the organization's Board of Directors had required the executive team to focus on leadership capacity, then the initiative would not have been eliminated after a failed pilot program. After the pilot failure, the executives would have held a planning meeting to find an alternative way to deal with the strategic issue of leadership capacity and to repair the damage from the failed program. The executive also would have publicly declared that leadership capacity is a key strategic initiative and that it was fundamental to the success of the company, regardless of the outcome of the pilot.

However, in our case example, the program remained an HR accountability. After the failed pilot program, the executives dispensed with the program, which also meant they rejected the entire strategic issue of leadership capacity. They treated the strategic issue of leadership capacity as nothing more than an embarrassing training program that needed to be cut as soon possible.

CLOSING COMMENTS

Could this outcome in the case example have been avoided? What could the executives have done differently in this case to respond to the leadership capacity challenge in their organization? What could the HR Director have done differently to avoid this kind of outcome?

The answers to these kinds of questions are explored in detail in the next four chapters. The overall answer is a dual response to the leadership gap. Both leaders and organizations need to partner to bridge the gap in leadership capacity. Individual leaders cannot do it alone.

Embedding Leadership in the Organization

Let's consider the situation of a manager who is conscientious about developing his skills as a holistic leader. Does the organization know how to support the manager and his continued development? Many organizations are unfamiliar with or ineffective in the process of bridging the leadership capacity gap.[1]

This chapter explores the first critical success factor for effective leadership capacity implementation—embedding leadership in the organization as shown in the figure below. As discussed in the previous chapter, we use the term "embedded leadership" to mean a process of ensuring that leadership capacity is seen and becomes an integral part of the very fabric of the organization. Consequently, leadership is seen as a primary driver of competitive advantage and building leadership capacity is done continuously rather than just when a crisis occurs.

---

1. The last section of Chapter Two of this book defines the need for the partnership between the individual leader and the organization to bridge the leadership capacity gap. Part Two of the book focuses primarily on the individual leader's areas of responsibility. Part Three focuses primarily on the organization's areas of responsibility.

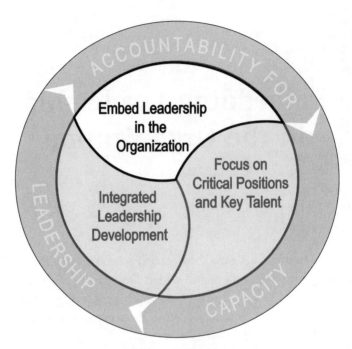

Figure 11.1 *Leadership Capacity Implementation*

It is essential for organizations to embed leadership in order to support leaders who are committed to becoming holistic leaders. This also serves as a motivator for the rest of an organization's employees.

EMBEDDING LEADERSHIP: THE JOURNEY

Embedding leadership is an ongoing challenge that requires a long-term perspective. It needs to be nurtured and fed regularly.

It's like planting a fruit tree. For the first few years of effort, there is little reward. The tree is skinny, gives little or no shade and has no fruit. After three or four years, it starts to blossom and bring forth some fruit. However, the gardener cannot stop there and assume it will take care of itself. Along the way the tree requires nurturing and caring to ensure it continues to grow, bear fruit and give shade. Embedding leadership requires the same level of attention and nurturing.

Best-practice organizations fundamentally believe that building strong leadership is a critical source of sustainable competitive advantage; they see this commitment as a long-term strategy.[2] Organizations that are committed to the long-term journey to build the required leadership capacity have a distinct advantage over their competition. In contrast, organizations that do not commit to the journey often have limited leadership capacity and are at risk.

A focus on leadership capacity has to become part of the organizational culture and needs to be reinforced strongly by senior executives.

It's a journey—and it takes time and effort. Here is a story of a company that had a scattered and unorganized approach to leadership and wanted to commit to the leadership capacity journey.

A large financial institution had an elaborate training infrastructure for its leaders. Most leaders attended at least one program a year that was designed to enhance the leadership competencies of the participants. The VP of Learning and Development conducted a leadership audit and found that very few leaders spoke about leadership in a similar way. They also had no consistent model or approach that was used regularly.

The company explored this dilemma further and discovered that the creation of the problem was of their own making. Their leaders tried to put what they learned in the courses into practice. They even referred to the many models that were taught. The problem was that the executives never took the courses so they emphasized different ideas in leadership. Also, the course trainers were not aligned and taught different models and approaches.

---

2. Robert Gandossy & Marc Effron, *Leading the Way*, (John Wiley & Sons Inc., 2004).

The VP of Learning and Development decided they needed to embed one leadership approach in their organization to reduce the confusion. They started with the executive team, who attended a session that focused on agreeing to a common model and approach to leadership for their company. Eventually, the leadership development programs were modified to reflect the leadership approach they supported.

Embedding a common leadership approach into an organization has substantial benefits. These include:

- Leaders have a clear and usable approach to leading their organizations and to working cross-functionally.

- Leaders can move more easily between functional areas and adjust quickly to their new roles.

- Employees can move between departments and not have to struggle as much with the adjustment to a new leadership approach.

- Senior executives can speak informally with all leaders and have greater confidence that they understand and can utilize the leadership messages they are communicating.

- HR professionals can develop formal and informal learning experiences and processes that can be applied throughout the organization.

THE THREE FOUNDATIONAL STRATEGIES FOR EMBEDDING LEADERSHIP IN AN ORGANIZATION

Our research in this area has uncovered three foundational strategies that contribute to embedding leadership within an organization. The foundational strategies can be viewed as three overlapping circles. Each strategy alone has value, but the greatest value is in the overlapping section.

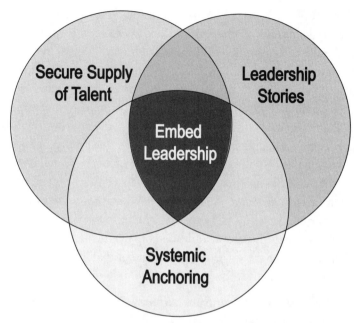

Figure 11.2   *Foundational Strategies for Embedding Leadership*

This chapter explores the three strategies (i.e., secure supply of talent, leadership stories, and systemic anchoring) and how to use these strategies to establish the foundation on which to embed leadership in the organization. We then consider what is lost when one or more of the strategies are absent from the approach to embedding leadership in an organization.

STRATEGY #1: ENSURE A SECURE SUPPLY OF LEADERSHIP TALENT

The term "security-of-supply" is one used in the energy industry to describe the availability of gas or oil products. In a similar way, organizations need to develop a secure supply of leadership talent. The reliability of the supply of leadership talent is a good indicator of the long-term viability of an organization. Traditionally, companies prefer to secure talent from within their talent pool through a variety of leadership development initiatives. However, most recently, the leadership gap described in this book has led many companies to secure additional talent through external hires, outsourcing, strategic alliances, associate relationships, and acquisitions and mergers.

Executives are giving particular attention to ensuring they have a secure supply of leadership talent because of the frailty of their own organizational leadership talent. A president of a major retail chain indicated that selling product was the easy part of the business. The challenge was to motivate the fifty thousand employees who worked in the stores to engage and align to what the business needed to do. The solution rests with the supply of leadership talent.

The following are ways to increase the probability of a secure supply of leadership talent:

- *Develop leadership talent from within:*
  In one company the CEO emphasized that leadership is not strictly the domain of people who have direct reports. Leadership can and should be demonstrated by all employees in their relationships to customers, suppliers, peers and direct reports. When this company conducted leadership development sessions for those who had direct reports, they referred to this group as the "leaders of leaders." The central question in those learning sessions was how could the leaders help their direct reports become leaders and deliver great customer service.

    In a similar manner, all organizations need to nurture and develop leadership from any location and from any level in the hierarchy. All employees need to have both an understanding of the business needs and the opportunity to discuss their interests to develop leadership skills in support of those needs. Unfortunately, many organizations ignore the importance of these discussions with employees. Some leaders, in their "exit" interviews, say that they left their company because they never had a career conversation with a senior leader in their organization. No one ever told them, "We believe in you, and see a future for you in this organization." Often, simple statements like that can do a lot to retain a leader and secure his or her commitment to the organization.

Another way to ensure a steady supply of leadership talent from within the organization is to take the risk of giving people more complex responsibilities to stretch their capabilities. Appointing the right person to a stretch opportunity often is received well. However, sometimes executives make the mistake of promoting someone who does not emulate the organizational values. In one case a company promoted a talented but abusive person whom no one respected. The promotion signaled to the employees that the organizational value of respect for the individual was lacking substance. Eventually, that leader was terminated for continued misbehavior. If they had promoted a high-performing individual who modeled the values, the values would have been reinforced. In addition, the probability that leadership talent would be in supply in the future would have been improved.

- *Focus on high-potential leaders:*
Another strategy for ensuring a steady supply of leadership talent is to focus on high-potential leaders in the organization. The best return on investment in leadership development that businesses can make is to "invest in the best." The high-potential employees know how to use the information they gain and how to put it to use immediately.[3] Barrett and Beeson[4] also found a similar pattern. Best-practice organizations focus their leadership development programs on those leaders they think have the greatest potential to succeed at the executive levels. These organizations invest considerable attention and resources on succession planning by identifying and cultivating high-potential leaders early in their careers. The number of leaders

---

3. David S. Weiss, *High Performance HR: Leveraging Human Resources For Competitive Advantage* (John Wiley & Sons Canada, Ltd., 2000).

4. Ann Barrett and John Beeson, *Developing Business Leaders for 2010.* (The Conference Board: New York, 2001).

targeted as high potentials varies from the top two to fifteen percent, depending on the organization

The focus on high-potential leaders is not without possible shortcomings. Some suggest organizations should not only focus on identifying and developing high-potential leaders but should also look for ways to enhance the leadership potential of all employees.[5] Another possible problem is that efforts to identify high potentials (in contrast to average performers) may be flawed. In the research conducted by Barrett & Beeson, only 34 percent of best-practice companies actually reported being effective in identifying future leaders.[6] The researchers suggest that current approaches, which often rely primarily on executive feedback, can be highly subjective.

Despite these concerns many organizations are not abandoning their high-potential strategy; rather, they are focusing on building leadership capacity throughout the organization and, at the same time, providing specialized development for high-potential talent. As part of this process, a more systematic way of identifying high potentials is needed.

- *Discover new leadership talent externally:*
Many organizations are approaching the employment marketplace more aggressively to discover an alternative source of supply for key leadership talent.

One organization approached the search for leadership talent as a constant expectation of its recruitment function and not as a process undertaken when there was a job opening. For instance, this company's leadership decided that one of their executives would meet annually with a well-regarded, uniquely talented, high-performing individual who worked in a competitor's organization. The relationship was very professional and demonstrated ongoing interest and extreme patience. Eight years after the initial meeting, the high-performing individual called the executive and said her company had just

---

5. Benimadhu & Gibson, *Leadership for Tomorrow.*

6. Barrett and Beeson, *Developing Business Leaders for 2010.*

been acquired, and she was ready to leave. The executive asked her what she wanted in her employment contract, and they reached an agreement by the next day.

Another untapped source of external leadership talent that will emerge over the next few years is older, retired leaders. These individuals are familiar with their former companies' leadership needs, understand the business and often have great credibility. If the leadership gaps persist, companies may see this source of talent as an attractive interim management solution to fill the talent gap until they can develop leadership talent internally.

- *Conduct executive leadership talent reviews:*
  It is common in energy-producing companies to conduct executive meetings to track the security-of-supply of energy products. A similar process is appropriate to track leadership talent as well. Executives emphasize the importance of the leadership talent through a leadership talent review process conducted annually, at minimum. This leadership talent review, to be fair, requires preparation. Each leader who is reviewed is assessed to determine his or her potential and level of current performance. The high-performing and high-potential leaders usually are the individuals who are of the greatest interest to the executives.

  Some more enlightened executive groups review all the high-potential leaders, even if they are not star performers currently; they do not want to lose any potential leaders. For example, a high-potential leader might be performing at a moderate level because s/he recently was assigned to a new role.

- *Conduct board of director reviews of critical leadership talent:*
  Boards of directors are expected to review talent critical to the success of the organization for both risk management purposes and to protect shareholder interests. Most boards of directors are accountable for hiring, reviewing and terminating the president. The president is accountable to manage the organization and deliver the forecasted results.

However, recently, several high-profile financial mismanagement disasters have occurred, and exorbitant bonuses have been paid to executives even as the companies have lost money. Shareholders are demanding that boards demonstrate greater fiscal accountability and manage critical leadership positions and key leadership talent more aggressively. Consequently, many boards are expanding their mandate to conduct critical leadership talent reviews to include a much broader list of critical positions and leadership talent in the organization.

(A more detailed analysis of critical positions, their evaluation and development of candidates for those positions appears in Chapter 12.)

STRATEGY #2: DEVELOP A COMPELLING ORGANIZATION-SPECIFIC LEADERSHIP STORY

Organizations need to have a compelling story that communicates to employees the organization's philosophy and approach to leadership.[7] The story becomes part of the folklore of the organization and creates an expectation of leadership to behave consistently with the story and its message.

An effective leadership story can be very helpful in a number of ways:

- It can be a strong motivator that encourages leaders to model the examples in the leadership story.

- If well publicized, it can be a retention factor for talent.

- It has the potential to draw external talent into the organization.

- It can become one of the foundational strategies to embed a leadership culture in the organization.

An effective leadership story is meaningful and captures the hearts and minds of employees. The story then becomes a living symbol—not one that has to be explained. A symbol that requires explanation is a dead symbol.

---

7. Vince Molinaro, "Filling the Leadership Gap," *Canadian HR Reporter*, December 2, 2002.

It is similar to the power of family stories that are retold to symbol-
ize the virtues of a family member—like this one that became folklore
for a family about the wisdom of a grandfather.

> An elderly grandfather took his adult grandson golfing. The 91-
> year-old grandfather was playing 3-par golf every other day, and
> each shot went 100 yards gracefully down the fairway. The adult
> grandson was taking mighty shots, far exceeding the distance of
> his elderly grandfather, but very often the ball shanked far to the
> right of the hole. The elderly grandfather kept noticing the
> aggressiveness of his grandson and knew that he would never
> succeed that way. Finally, the grandfather decided to tell him
> what he thought—but in story and imagery. He picked up a golf
> ball and walked slowly to the young man. He looked him in the
> eye and said: "My son, remember, the ball is your friend. Stop
> hitting it so hard." The image of the ball as a friend worked—the
> grandson's next shot was far less powerful, but it was straight.[8]

This story symbolizes the grandfather's patience and love for
his grandson. It also sends the message that holding back a bit
can produce a better result. Finally, it reminds the family that
grandpa was a special person and a good golfer into his 90s.

A meaningful leadership story can have the same long-lasting effect.
It can be a motivator and an important factor in the retention of talent
in an organization. There are at least four ways to construct a meaningful leadership story:

1. Build the story around compelling challenges.

2. Personalize the stories to individuals.

3. Reflect the story in a well-delineated leadership model.

4. Carefully craft and communicate the story.

---

8. The grandfather who gave this wise advice is Mickey Lubin who currently lives in Miami,
Florida.

1. Build the Story Around Compelling Challenges

A good story needs drama. It requires a compelling challenge that may appear insurmountable but is overcome successfully. A distribution company embedded a leadership story that reflected a compelling leadership challenge. Here is their story:

> *The executives in a distribution company wanted all employees to take accountability for the quality of their products that leave the warehouse. A new initiative allowed any employee to place a sticker on a truck if he or she believed it was carrying products of an unsatisfactory quality. A packer in the warehouse saw a product leaving the warehouse in a defective state, took initiative and placed the sticker on the truck. The truck was not allowed to move or leave the site. Bedlam broke out. The warehouse supervisor shouted that the shipment had to leave to meet the customers' timelines and that the product was safe. However, after an investigation, it was found that the product was unsafe and the young packer was right. The supervisor was released and the executives decided to appoint the young packer as the new warehouse leader.*

The packer's story became folklore in their organization. It sent the message that every employee should be a leader and take initiative to ensure the safety and quality of the company's products.

2. Personalize the Stories to Individuals

Wonderful leadership stories can be created by relating personal actions associated with individual leaders. Consider the following example:

> *The CEO of this global packaged-goods organization took personal initiative to get to know and develop the future key talent of the organization. He had a special annual event, inviting twelve employees to his cottage to discuss their innovations. The employees could be anywhere in the organization globally and*

at any level. Most were shocked to be contacted, very honored and equally nervous. The group innovations session was an inspiring experience for the participants. They had a chance to spend a few days with the CEO, they met some terrific employees from around the global operations, and they were motivated to push forward their innovations.

The sessions helped create a leadership story within this company and emphasized that innovative leadership can come from anyplace and at any level.

A number of executives have been successful in creating leadership stories by articulating their specific leadership "point of view" that reflects their approach to conducting business and leading an organization. The concept of a "teachable point of view" is explored in *The Leadership Engine.*[9] The author, Noel Tichy, suggests that the leader's point of view is often a set of simple, basic principles; the challenge is for the leader to fully implement (or fully "live") the principles of the leadership story.

While many people may be very interested in reading about heroic leadership stories, there are some potential pitfalls in stories created about heroes:

- **The leadership story can be more about the hero leader and not enough about the organization:** Sometimes a leadership story is fueled by the executive's personal ego, which can distract the organization from its primary focus on customer and stakeholder value. A leadership story needs to endure longer than the tenure of the leader. Effective leadership stories emphasize an individual but send a message about the business, the organization, the employees, and/or its customers.

- *An executive's behavior may send a message that is counterproductive:* A leader who often spoke of his commitment to leadership development was discredited because of his behavior that contradicted what he said. Here is the story that spread throughout his organization:

---

9. Noel Tichy, *The Leadership Engine, How Winning Companies Build Leaders at Every Level.* (New York: Harper Collins Publishers Inc., 1997).

*During a leadership session with his company's directors, the
Vice President of Sales introduced the session and spoke of his
strong commitment to leadership development. He also told the
directors that it was very important that they participate actively
in the session. He then stood up and promptly left the meeting.
The directors were stunned; they had just heard him say that he
thought leadership development was extremely important and
yet he hadn't even stayed for the first part of the session. They
believed that what he did demonstrated his views more than
what he said.*

3. Reflect the Story in a Well-Delineated Leadership Model

An organization-specific leadership model needs to reflect the major
messages of the leadership story. The well-delineated leadership model
should define what leadership means within the organization and help
tell the story of why it is critical to the organization's future success.

One well-known example of a company that has built a specific
leadership model is Johnson & Johnson (J&J). J&J already has a well-
publicized definition of its culture and values that is based on its
Credo. The Credo is probably the most recognized culture and values statement within a company anywhere in the world. The Credo
was the anchor reason that J&J pulled Tylenol off the market after
the brief Tylenol scare.

J&J decided to extend their story directly into the leadership
domain with the development of their "Standards of Leadership"
model. Many line executives participated in developing this model to
reflect the unique leadership approach expected of leaders at Johnson &
Johnson. The J&J Credo and expectation of business results are at the
core of the model. The Standards of Leadership surround these core
elements and define the specific leadership competencies that the company views as key to its success.

4. Carefully Craft and Communicate the Story

A story has its own personality. It describes what makes the organization's history and culture distinct and special. Some ideas to consider in crafting your organization's leadership story include the following:

- *Focus on the most important aspect of the leadership story and why it helps the organization succeed:*
  Make it simple. Complicated stories confuse people and can send a message of disorganization and lack of focus. One effective approach is to tell about the transformation from the former business environment (E1) to the new environmental reality (E2) and how leaders and employees have responded successfully to the environmental changes.

- *Be flexible and keep evolving the story as the organization changes:*
  A leadership story is not static. As an organization changes, the story evolves. For example, in a technology company that had operated in traditional silos, the CEO identified the need for leaders to work in a cross-functional manner. The traditional pattern had to change if the company was going to continue to be successful. The CEO and his executive team began to tell a leadership story that emphasized the need for the organization to work cross-functionally and "organize around customer needs."

  Over time, this leadership story evolved and deepened. The examples that further evolved the original leadership story were very effective because they clearly articulated what success in the new business environment would look like. In addition, the examples helped increase the confidence within the organization because a successful track record was being established.

- *Repeat the key messages of the leadership story:*
  In their communications within their organization, senior leaders should find ways to give messages about their approach to leadership. The frequency of the messages can influence others to adopt the leadership approach that is symbolized by the stories.

- *Communicate the leadership story to current and potential employees:*
  Imagine an organization that has a strong leadership story to tell—one that communicates an enviable track record of developing people and building leadership capacity. Employees need to hear this story to appreciate what their organization does. Also, potential employees will be very attracted to the organization when they hear the story of how the organization has demonstrated commitment to leadership development. Organizations should be known for their leadership stories at least as well as they are known for the stories about their products and services.

STRATEGY #3: ANCHOR TO A WELL-ESTABLISHED ORGANIZATIONAL PROCESS

Perhaps one of the most intriguing discoveries in our research is that organizations do not need to change all of their processes to support leadership capacity explicitly. Rather, they need to find the most entrenched organizational process and anchor leadership capacity to that process.

The challenge is to find the best process on which to anchor. Here are some examples of current processes to which anchoring of leadership capacity has occurred successfully:

- *Anchoring to an employee survey process:*
  One company had a well-established survey process for employees and leaders. Most of the questions focused on how aligned and engaged the employees and leaders were with the company. The company used sampling theory to electronically survey one-fourth of all the employees every quarter. The data were reported throughout the company, and the reports were included in executive quarterly financial and operational reviews.

  The executives realized they could anchor a leadership capacity assessment onto the well-established process of completing and evaluating employee survey reports. They added a few questions to the employee survey to generate sufficient information to assess leadership and provide feedback. This revised survey also sent a clear message to all employees of the importance of leadership to employee alignment and engagement. Also, the frequency of the surveying process further reinforced the message of the importance of leadership capacity to the company.

- *Anchoring to a quality audit process*
  Another company leveraged a different organizational process. This company had a very well-established focus on quality. The company won awards in quality, and most employees were proud of the standards their company set for the industry. However, most of the quality metrics were on product and process quality. There were no questions about leadership quality.

  A team was organized to define "quality leadership," and those metrics were used globally. It had the effect of quickly reinforcing the company's commitment to building and assessing quality leadership.

- *Anchoring to a performance management process*
  One company had a performance management process that had been used for over twenty-five years. The company also was specific about consequences for executives and leaders who did not follow the performance management process. The company decided to leverage the performance management process as their entry point to drive their leadership capacity model.

Three Types of Processes to Consider When Anchoring Leadership Capacity

Essentially, there are three kinds of processes to consider when anchoring leadership capacity in an organization. These are:

1. *Aligned processes*
   Aligned processes are the current organizational processes that can be the anchors for an approach that one wants to embed, such as leadership capacity. The employee survey, the quality audits and the performance management process are examples.

2. *Neutral processes*

These are important processes that do not contradict or necessarily support the approach (i.e., leadership capacity). Neutral processes do not need to be modified to ensure that leadership capacity is anchored. All that is needed is one aligned process for a deeply embedded anchor—all the other processes can be "neutral." For instance, in the example of anchoring leadership capacity to the quality audit process, it is possible that the employee survey and compensation are neutral to a focus on leadership capacity.

3. *Antagonistic processes*

Antagonistic processes are the currently existing processes that conflict with the messages needed to build leadership capacity. For example, in one company the performance management system focused leaders on the financial results at the expense of qualitative measures that were important to leadership capacity. In addition, the compensation system reinforced individualistic leadership behaviors that were antagonistic to team-based leadership approaches. The company needed to revamp the "antagonistic" processes so that they were, at least, neutral to the key messages of leadership capacity.

WHAT IS LOST WHEN ONE OR MORE OF THE STRATEGIES TO EMBED HAVE NOT BEEN APPLIED?

The three strategies for embedding leadership—supply of talent, leadership stories and systemic anchoring—are each very important to embedding leadership in an organization. However, in combination, the three have a much greater likelihood of success. Here are the implications of not including one of the three:

• In the absence of a secure supply of leadership talent, the leadership story may be known through the anchoring, but the supply of leadership talent may remain underdeveloped.

- In the absence of a leadership story, the secure supply of leadership talent may be unfocused and the anchoring will lack clarity of purpose.

- Finally, if there is no anchoring, then the method of embedding leadership capacity will be inefficient and possibly not entrenched throughout the organization.

The challenge is significant, but the long-range benefit of using these strategies to embed leadership in the organization could mean the difference between an organization that achieves sustainable competitive advantage and one that cannot compete in new business environments.

CLOSING COMMENTS

The three strategies for embedding leadership are the foundation for the rest of Part Three of this book. They articulate what organizations must continuously do to implement leadership capacity and to build a sustainable process for supporting the development of leaders. The next three chapters explore additional organizational ways to bridge the leadership capacity gap and further embed leadership in the organization.

Embedding leadership will not be quick. It takes a relatively long time for an organization to be in a leadership gap predicament, and it will take some time and a constant commitment to get out of it. The challenge of embedding leadership is not insurmountable. With focused attention and planning, it can occur.

Focus on Critical Positions and Key Talent

This chapter explores the next critical success factor for effective implementation of leadership capacity—focus on critical positions and key talent (See Figure 12.1). More specifically, it explains what we mean by succession management, why the succession management focus should be on critical positions specifically and how the process is implemented. It also explores our recommendations to engage and retain key talent in the organization.

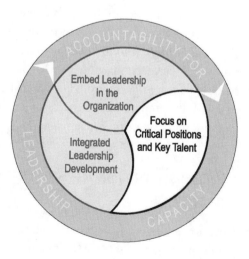

Figure 12.1   *Leadership Capacity Implementation*

Business strategy requires leaders to make choices. Most executive groups have limited access to capital and people to allocate to strategies. They need to choose the strategies that 1) are the best bet to deliver sustainable competitive advantage for the business and 2) remove the risk to the business by achieving competitive parity in areas where the business may be lagging behind the competition.

The same concept applies for the process of bridging the leadership capacity gap—choices must be made. In an ideal world, all leaders should be developed to maximize their potential. However, the costs associated with maximizing the potential of every leader in the organization are prohibitive. Executives need to make choices about which areas of the business are at the greatest risk because of the potential of either a current or future leadership capacity gap. The organization needs to give extra attention to those critical areas. That is our focused approach to *succession management*, which is the overall planning and development of "ready now" successors for targeted critical positions

We define a critical position as one in the organization that 1) is critical or vital to the organization in achieving sustainable competitive advantage (or competitive parity) 2) delivers significant value to customers (and/or key stakeholders), and 3) has characteristics unique to the organization and difficult to fill from the open marketplace. Organizations must ensure that they have a pool of potential "ready now" successors—those leaders who are able to move into a critical position and perform at the level comparable to what you would anticipate would be the level of performance from an external candidate. An organization that has fully prepared candidates for critical positions reduces its strategic risk of a leadership capacity gap.

THE FAILURE OF TRADITIONAL SUCCESSION PLANNING PROCESSES

Many view succession planning as a process to identify successors for every senior position in the organization. Unfortunately, this generic succession planning process results in valueless lists of people identified as future successors for executive positions. This kind of succession planning process gives a "vanilla" solution that overprotects some leadership positions that are not at great risk, and it underprotects some critical positions.

For example, Conger and Fulmer describe examples in which two companies implemented succession planning for the CEO position, and both of the heir apparent executives failed in their new roles.[1] One failed because the CEO development process did not prepare the prospective CEO for the challenge of handling Wall Street; the other failed because "not enough attention was paid to how his particular skills might apply to the broader role."[2] The succession planning process needs to be much more focused and intense for critical positions such as that of the CEO.

Succession planning also can fail for other reasons, including:

- It functions as a crisis management process to respond to key talent who may not be retained versus a thoughtful process focused on critical positions in the organization.

- Little distinction exists between positions that are critical to the future success of the business and those that are less crucial.

- There is little differentiation between leadership talent, and the talent assessment is unstructured and not defensible.

- The specific leadership development for the critical positions is not focused on the unique competencies required in those positions.

- It can be viewed as a Human Resources requirement rather than a business need.

- It is often a bureaucratic process characterized by lengthy forms and paperwork.

---

1. Jay Conger and Robert M. Fulmer, "Developing The Leadership Pipeline." *Harvard Business Review*, December 2003, p.76–94.

2. Ibid. p. 78.

FIVE METHODS OF IDENTIFYING SUCCESSORS TO FILL THE LEADERSHIP CAPACITY GAP

Organizations use a wide variety of methods to respond to the need to find successors to fill the anticipated leadership capacity gap. Figure 12.2 presents a continuum from the least to the most intensive methods.

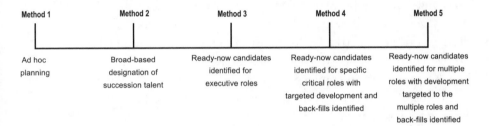

Method 1	Method 2	Method 3	Method 4	Method 5
Ad hoc planning	Broad-based designation of succession talent	Ready-now candidates identified for executive roles	Ready-now candidates identified for specific critical roles with targeted development and back-fills identified	Ready-now candidates identified for multiple roles with development targeted to the multiple roles and back-fills identified

Figure 12.2 *The Five Methods Of Identifying Successors*

Here is an analysis of each of the five methods:

- *Method 1: Ad hoc planning.* Many organizations do not do any planning for successors until it is too late. Many leaders do not like to talk about their potential departure, and very few people have the courage to ask them about their retirement plans. The "ad hoc planning" method is common in small- to medium-sized businesses and is characterized by "in the moment" crisis management. Although ad hoc planning is done by organizations, it really is not an advisable method even though many organizations have survived with this approach by informally tracking and attending to the internal development of high-potential talent.

- *Method 2: Broad-based designation of succession talent.* This is the pool approach to identifying successors. Essentially, organizations establish a talent pool as the group from which they identify internal successors. The organizations do very little differentiating between the candidates in the pool and almost no focused development for specific critical positions. Some organizations use this approach in the spirit of equality and fairness to all. However, the pool concept is often a detriment to identifying and developing specific successors for critical positions.

- *Method 3: Ready-now candidates identified for executive roles.* This method is the standard strategic planning approach used by larger organizations. Most of the time, this process is used because it is part of the HR checklist of processes that must be performed, including recruitment, training, employee relations and compensation. This method can be useful to: 1) identify successors for the broad set of senior positions, 2) quickly identify who should be the acting leader if an executive suddenly departs and 3) develop a short list of candidates for positions. However, this method does not focus on development of the candidates, and it does not allocate the resources to ensure that candidates will be "ready now" for critical positions if and when they are vacated.

- *Method 4: Ready-now candidates identified for specific critical roles with targeted development and with back-fills identified.* Method 4 is much closer to the succession management approach that is necessary for high-risk critical positions. This method involves the succession planning and targeted development for these critical positions. It also requires a significant investment of time and money because the organizations need to have significant depth of understanding of the critical positions and precision in assessing the candidates for focused development. Organizations identify very few critical positions when they use this method because of the cost and time of the ongoing implementation. Organizations often use this method exclusively for the critical positions for which they anticipate a leadership capacity gap in the near future. Method 4 also identifies back-fills for the candidates for the critical positions.

- *Method 5: Ready-now candidates identified for multiple roles with development targeted to the multiple roles and with back-fills identified.* This is a new and improved "Method 4." We recommend Method 5 rather than Method 4 for succession management for critical positions. Method 4 prepares candidates for *specific* roles, while Method 5 prepares them for *multiple* positions. High-performing, high-potential candidates can be disenchanted when Method 4 is used if the incumbent in a targeted position does not leave. The candidates went through intensive development and no senior opportunities opened up for them. These candidates could become retention risks. Method 5, developing the high-potential candidates for multiple positions (perhaps some that are critical and some that are senior but not critical), would increase the chances of their getting a new career opportunity.

THE RISKS OF NOT INSURING SUCCESSORS FOR CRITICAL POSITIONS

If a critical position is vacant for an extended period of time or if the incumbent makes mistakes or if the wrong person is in the position, the entire organization can be at risk. The risks may include a detrimental impact on productivity, financial/economic loss, customer service and/or the credibility and reputation of the organization.

Organizations can fill some critical positions by looking to external sources for hiring talent. In many cases, the new ideas and experiences from an external talent can be very helpful for an organization. However, it is often too unpredictable to rely on the availability of external talent sources for critical positions. We advise organizations to use assessment processes that will help them find talent that *can* maximize the potential of the position.

The critical positions that require the greatest investment by an organization are those for which there are very few external candidates, and, therefore, the successors for the positions must be developed from within the organization. These positions have unique characteristics to the organization and often are technically and/or politically complicated. In addition, the knowledge, skill and experience for the positions are passed down to the leaders in those positions through their internal mentors.

Five types of critical positions are difficult to fill with external candidates. These are:

1. *A position that is important to the business' short- and long-term strategic direction:* A position is critical if (1) it is designed to be a major contributor to achieving competitive advantage or competitive parity, (2) it delivers significant value to customers (and/or key stakeholders), and (3) it represents a position that has unique characteristics to the organization and is difficult to obtain in the open marketplace. Often, these positions are expected to change rapidly over time in order to meet the evolving nature of the strategic initiatives. For example, a company's core long-term strategy was to acquire three new companies in R&D to replenish its line of innovative products. They developed a general manager acquisitions position. This position was critical to the implementation of the strategic direction in a complex and unpredictable environment.

2. *A position that consists of multiple critical roles:* This kind of position is unique; the skill sets and experience required are not available outside the organization. It may require technical proficiency, managerial excellence and internal knowledge. For example, in a regulated company, the legal counsel position was deemed to be critical. The position required specialty knowledge about the regulated environment and tax law. The company expected the individual in this position to manage the other lawyers both within the organization and in the external law firms that supported this organization. The company needed to develop the succession talent from within the organization for this position.

3. *A position with extensive and deep networks to influence key stakeholders:* For example, in one environmental organization, the position of regional director of business development required an extensive network with the local elected officials, the environmental advocacy groups and major customer accounts. This position also required the trust within the region that the director was operating with integrity and in the community's interest. The organization

needed to develop the backup resources to insure they chose a successor for this critical position.

4. *A position that has a major impact on the organization if it is not adequately filled:* This type of critical position is of extreme importance to the credibility of an organization and its reputation with external and internal stakeholders. Significant damage could result from an individual's inadequate performance in this position. The organization would have to have a quick recovery from a loss of credibility resulting from inadequate performance. For example, a high technology company's financial reporting was under intense scrutiny by investors and governments. The CFO had complex reporting requirements. He needed to respond to the investor community and understand compliance requirements and the regulatory environment. This made the position very complex, high profile and critical to the organization. It was vital that the right leader be chosen for that role and that the best incumbents be prepared for assuming the role in the future.

5. *A position that will be required in the future because of the evolving business.* Here are three examples of this type of critical position:

- A fashion design company planned to expand its services to Europe. It needed an executive who would understand the European markets and variability of tastes and be able to work in multiple languages. The executive also needed to fully align with the business direction of the home office. The company set some criteria for the internal candidates for the critical position, which included working experience in more than two countries, experience working in the home office and comfort with multiple languages and diversity.

- A company had several business development positions. They decided to implement a client-focused strategy that would change the positions considerably. In preparation for the significant changes expected in those positions, the company treated them as critical.

- A company had several "mature" positions in old technology services that were not critical in the North American market. The company decided to pursue a strategy to grow in several underdeveloped countries that needed the old technology and skills. Their current mature positions would be leading edge in those underdeveloped countries and became critical positions in those new markets.

In each of these critical position "types," the organization had two choices: (1) they could put the effort into identifying candidates for the critical positions and developing the candidates to perform well in those positions or (2) they could take action to reduce the critical characteristics of the position.

Here are some examples of how to reduce the critical nature of a critical position:

- In the example given in the second type of critical positions, the legal counsel position could be divided into two positions: a legal counsel and a director of legal services who could manage the lawyers and the external service providers.

- In another organization, a vacancy suddenly occurred due to illness in a critical customer relations position that was company-wide. The executive decided to divide the position into five regional positions. By subdividing it, the executive reduced the critical nature of the position and also was able to fill the regional positions more easily because the regional roles were not as complex and, therefore, were less demanding.

- A financial investment firm had a managing director position that was accountable for the top three customer sectors, which represented over 60 percent of the firm's profits. The executives were concerned that the incumbent in that position was the only person who understood the customer sectors well. They also knew that their competition was actively pursuing the incumbent. The executives decided to remove the risk of this critical position. They reorganized the managing director position, dividing it into three positions. At the same time, they promoted the incumbent managing director to a VP position responsible for all commercial accounts.

WHY FOCUS SUCCESSION MANAGEMENT ON CRITICAL POSITIONS AND NOT ON KEY LEADERSHIP TALENT?

Succession management creates "ready-now" candidates for *critical positions* and not for *key leadership talent*. In contrast, retention strategies focus on key leadership talent and not on critical positions. Many executives and HR professionals miss this distinction. They often want to focus their efforts on replacement planning for key leadership talent.

For example, in one company a VP of Sales had trouble grasping why he was asked to focus succession management on critical positions. From his perspective he was concerned about his key talent and what he would do if his key talent were "hit by a bus tomorrow." He wondered whether he would have the backup talent to respond to that crisis. Most executives do think about their key talent. Their concerns about losing this talent should motivate them to develop very effective and tailored retention strategies for them. Succession management is needed for critical positions. Retention strategies are need for key leadership talent.

Finding successors for key talent is an elusive objective. Let's consider a sports analogy. In baseball the San Francisco Giants would not succeed in a succession management process to back-fill for the superstar, Barry Bonds. There is only one Barry Bonds, and no one could duplicate his achievements. Rather, the team needs to identify its critical positions and back-fill for the positions that if not filled could put them at risk.

In most cases, a key talent in an organization comes about by accident. *Key talent* refers to individuals who possess a unique combination of skills and abilities and who are able to consistently deliver remarkable results that others in the organization can't easily duplicate. Every manager dreams that each person hired or promoted will become a key talent, but predicting whether or not a leader will do this is very difficult. This means two things:

- It is unlikely that organizations can develop a candidate who would recreate a key talent's gifts.

- If an organization can afford to hire a known key talent, then they should do it regardless of whether or not a critical position currently exists to fill. Once the organization has hired the key talent, they can leverage the individual's capabilities and create a new critical position, or they can develop the key talent to fill the gap in a current critical position.

In contrast to key talent, a critical position is often purposely designed into the organizational structure. There is strategic intent in the development of the critical position because the multiple roles, complexities and stakeholders of a critical position need to be managed to ensure that the position delivers the required value.

Also, when executives debate the extent of the individual leaders' talents, the conversation often deteriorates into comments based upon personal loyalties, potential retention vulnerabilities and preconceived biases. An individual is an agent of the position, not the reverse. The focus on critical positions is a much less emotional experience for executives. They may even identify critical feeder positions that are important developmental positions candidates can fill for a time in order to develop their skills and knowledge.

In our experience, once executives get past their ingrained bias toward key talent, they can identify critical positions rather easily. The ultimate challenge is to identify the critical positions and put the key talent in those positions to maximize the potential of those positions to the organization. Also, if there are key talents who are not in critical positions, then the organization may want to consider developing those individuals for critical positions.

RETENTION STRATEGIES FOR KEY TALENT

In this section we discuss retention strategies for key talent, followed by a discussion of the five steps of succession management for critical positions.

In Chapter 6, Culture and Values, we explored the six factors that drive engagement. In our experience we have found that these six factors also drive retention of key talent.

Consider the six factors that drive engagement as they relate to the retention of key talent:

1. *Being part of a winning organization:* Key talent leaders have a strong desire to be part of winning organizations they deem to be the best in the field. These leaders want to be part of well-run organizations with an ambitious vision, core purpose and solid business strategy. Key talent leaders also want to be in an organization in which they can utilize and further develop their talents. A winning organization helps create for them a challenging environment that stretches their abilities in their fields of expertise. Winning organizations help key talent become even more talented.

2. *Working for admired leaders:* Key talent leaders are engaged when they have the opportunity to work for admired leaders, who will help them grow and develop. They want to work for leaders who are key talent themselves, who can add value to their own development and whom they can emulate. In fact, the Corporate Leadership Council found that the number one non-monetary motivator to attract and retain employees is working for admired leaders.[3]

3. *Having positive working relationships:* Key talent leaders are retained when they have positive working relationships with others but, more specifically, with other key talent. As one leader described, "I have the privilege of coming into work with such a dynamic and intelligent group of colleagues. It makes for a stimulating work environment that I know I will not be able to get anywhere else." Key talent leaders often are engaged and retained if their peers within their work units and across the organization (in "communities of interest"—see Chapter 8) stimulate them to continue to grow and produce exceptional outcomes from their work.

---

3. Corporate Leadership Council, *Crafting a "Compelling Offer": Overview of Results from Primary Research Into The Career Decisions of High Value Employees,* (Washington DC, Corporate Executive Board, 1998).

4. ***Doing meaningful work:*** Key talent leaders need to engage in meaningful work that impacts the organization. In some cases, a position may become very meaningful because of the key talent's unique set of skills. The person made the position meaningful. Critical positions are often the positions with the most meaningful work. Placing key talent in those critical positions will contribute to their engagement and retention.

5. ***Recognition and appreciation:*** Key talent also desire recognition and appreciation. Typically, they know they are key talent and that they make a distinctive contribution to their organizations. They also want to be developed. One common error is that organizations believe that key talent does not need development. The assumption is that they are terrific already, and the organization should invest its development funds in the weaker performers. However, our research has shown contrary findings. Key talent often want ongoing development, and the return on investment of the development expenditure is the highest when the investment is made in key talent.[4] Essentially, the development strategy should be to invest in the best rather than invest in the problem areas. We have repeatedly observed that organizations are often surprised when a key talent leader leaves them unexpectedly. In our experience one of the primary reasons they leave is because the organization that hires them away provides the appreciation, recognition and development they did not receive in their previous organization.

6. ***Living a balanced life:*** As we discussed in Chapter Six, work/life balance is an important factor that drives engagement in today's organizations. A common error is that all challenging work falls upon the key talent; however, they often complain that it is unfair that they are expected to work weekends (albeit on interesting projects), while less capable peers are not given the extra projects. Organizations need to be extremely sensitive to the fairness of the

---

4. See *High Performance HR* by Dr David Weiss (John Wiley & Sons Canada, Ltd., 2000). Chapter 9 focuses on the "Return On Investment In Human Capital" and includes the findings that the best ROI in development is when organizations "invest in the best."

distribution of workload among key talent and others. All employees deserve to lead balanced lives.

THE FIVE STEPS OF SUCCESSION MANAGEMENT FOR CRITICAL POSITIONS

Let's now turn our attention to the implementation process for succession management for critical positions. As mentioned earlier, *retention strategies should focus on key talent, and succession management should focus on critical positions.*

We recommend five steps for developing leadership capacity for critical positions through succession management:

Five Steps of Succession Management for Critical Positions

1. Identify critical positions.
2. Assess current incumbents occupying the critical positions to determine the vulnerability in those positions.
3. Identify the development pathways to build competence in critical positions.
4. Identify potential candidates for critical positions.
5. Implement development plans and evaluate outcomes.

Step 1: Identify critical positions.

Identifying critical positions begins with the organization analyzing what creates its business, customer value and stakeholder value. At this early stage in the process, it may be difficult to distinguish precisely between one position and another to determine which has the most significant value contribution. As a result, the preliminary list probably will include two to three times the number of positions that eventually will be the organization's critical positions.

Then, a list of criteria and category ratings is used to assess the potential critical positions.

Criteria to Assess the Critical Nature of Positions

1. Business Contribution of the Position (High, Moderate, Low):

- To what extent does this position impact the organization's ability to achieve its priority strategic objectives?
- To what extent does this position impact revenues?
- To what extent does this position impact the achievement of business results?
- To what extent would mistakes made in this position impact the success of the overall organization?

2. Stakeholder Relations (High, Moderate, Low):

- To what extent does this position impact relationships with stakeholders?
- To what extent does this position impact relationships with external customers?
- To what extent does this position affect the organization's credibility and reputation?
- To what extent does this position impact relationships globally?

3. Future Impact on the Organization (High, Moderate, Low):

- To what extent does this position impact the delivery of future products?
- To what extent does this position impact the making of strategic decisions, which affect the organization's success in the future?
- To what extent does this position influence strategic choices about the organization's direction in the future?
- To what extent is this position likely to become critical to the organization's success in the future?

4. Uniqueness of the Position (High, Moderate, Low):

- To what extent is this position so unique to the organization that it will be very difficult to recruit an external candidate successfully?

Based on the responses to the above criteria, the organization then needs to determine if some positions are more critical than others. This analysis will also expose areas of missing information about specific positions.

Step 2: Assess the current incumbents occupying the critical positions to determine the vulnerability in those positions.

The next step is to identify the current incumbents in those positions and determine if they are "vulnerable incumbents." This term refers to those people who have a high likelihood of vacating their positions in the near future. In many situations further research will be required (including one-on-one conversations and career planning with the incumbent) to determine the actual extent of the incumbent's vulnerability.

Here are the most common reasons why an incumbent may be vulnerable:

- The incumbent is near retirement, and she/he is likely to leave within the next few years.

- The incumbent is dissatisfied in his/her current role and he or she may be a retention risk.

- There are plans to promote the incumbent to a more senior position and this critical position will be vacated.

- The incumbent is not key talent and is suboptimizing the critical position. Even if the incumbent is performing at an acceptable level, that level of performance may make a critical position vulnerable for the organization.

After the organization determines which incumbents are vulnerable or not vulnerable, the leadership positions in the organization are then plotted on the following matrix.

Organizations should determine the priority positions on which to focus and to invest resources. In general, the focus should be on the critical positions with vulnerable incumbents.

	Critical Position	Other Positions
Vulnerable Incumbents	**Damaging Risk:** Highest Risk: Primary focus of succession	**Moderate Risk:** Regular back-up resource planning
Non-vulnerable Incumbents	**High Risk:** Develop longer-range succession management	**Contained Risk:** Monitor for changes over time

Figure 12.3 *Position by incumbent matrix*

Once the critical positions have been identified, they can then be summarized in the following summary chart:

Position	Name of Incumbent	Critical Position?	Vulnerable Incumbent?	Key Talent?	Overall Risk Assessment

The extent of the risk of having vulnerable and non-vulnerable incumbents in critical positions is then prioritized in the following categories:

- **Damaging risk:** Damaging risk applies to the critical positions with vulnerable incumbents. These are those positions that would put the organization at greatest risk.

- *High risk:* High risk applies to the critical positions with incumbents who are not vulnerable. The risk is designated as "high" for a number of reasons:

  - The assessment that the position is not vulnerable may be mistaken. If an incumbent does leave and the assessment of his or her vulnerability was incorrect, it could cost the organization greatly and could put it at great risk.

  - It is used for critical positions with vulnerable incumbents who have ready-now successors who can do the work at an acceptable level of effectiveness.

  - A candidate for a critical position may be vulnerable to leaving the organization if he or she does not receive an offer for advancement.

- *Moderate risk:* This level of risk applies to the "other positions" that are not deemed to be critical positions but have vulnerable incumbents. Plans need to be put in place to make sure the organization has back-fill candidates for these positions.

- *Contained risk:* This level of risk applies to the "other positions" with incumbents who are not vulnerable.

Organizations' top priority should be to conduct a detailed analysis of the potential "damaging risk" situations. However, if possible, they should also undertake an analysis of "high risk" situations as well. The preferred approach is for organizations to manage the risk associated with critical positions by having succession management plans for all of those positions (regardless of the incumbents' vulnerability). An added benefit of this approach is that it helps the organization identify the "moderate" or "contained" positions—those that don't require detailed succession management plans.

Step 3: Identify the development pathways to build competence in critical positions.

One of the major characteristics of people in critical positions is that they often require specialized knowledge, technical capabilities and influence skills in order to succeed. It is the specialized and unique capabilities that make the critical position so difficult to replace. Sometimes, a new employee in a critical position encounters a steep learning curve that requires years of skill and knowledge development before the employee can succeed in that role. In the meantime the loss for the organization could be extensive.

It may be useful to encourage a candidate for a critical position to take an academic course to gain preliminary information of what makes someone successful in that kind of position. However, critical positions require a more focused plan to develop a candidate's skills in order to replicate the critical position's unique characteristics.

Typically, a position is critical and difficult to replicate if one of the primary ways of learning how to fulfill the position is through mentorship. Mentorship is a very old method of learning. For situations in which the knowledge an individual needs for a job can only be transferred person-to-person, mentorship is very important.

One good test of the uniqueness of a critical position is to ask how the current incumbent learned to do the work. You will find that incumbents give answers such as the following:

- All the academic training for this job didn't really help me enough.

- What really taught me how to do this job was working with so-and-so who passed down the information.

- I learned most of what I know from my experiences and my mistakes.

- It took years to master all the various components of this position.

It is important though to emphasize that the intent is not to create candidates who are duplicates of the current incumbents. The focus is on the critical positions and not on the incumbents in those positions. Even if they are high performers the incumbents will have their own areas of strengths and weaknesses. The candidates for these positions will bring their own mix of skill and competencies that may add value to the positions and evolve them to another level of contribution to the company. In addition, the development pathway for incumbents may have been particular to their learning styles. The future candidates will probably find their own pathways that will fit their style of learning. As a result we suggest using multiple sources of data in order to understand the critical position and the developmental pathways to achieve competence in that position.

For example, one company found that the unique characteristics of the critical positions were not identified in competency analyses and job evaluation reports. Some of the critical positions required political astuteness, an influence capability and a network that made the positions and the incumbents quite unique. The company also identified what are called "critical feeder positions" that candidates for critical positions could be assigned to for a period of time and that would help them develop the skill and knowledge to eventually succeed at their critical positions.

Current incumbents and their immediate supervisors are major sources of information about critical positions. Their support is essential for determining the unique technical and leadership requirements for their critical positions. It also is very useful for organizations to interview previous incumbents who worked in critical positions prior to the current incumbents. The previous incumbents may have ideas about how to develop future incumbents, since they may have helped develop their successors. They also can provide additional insights into the unique characteristics of those critical positions. The organization also can interview direct reports, some peers and some customers/stakeholders to gather their insights into critical positions that are difficult to duplicate.

The interviewing process has three purposes:

• To identify how the critical position creates business, customer and/or stakeholder value.

• To determine the characteristics of this position that make it unique to the organization.

• To explore the pathway for developing a successor who will be able to perform the critical position effectively.

At the conclusion of the interviewing process, it is important to re-engage in a discussion with the current incumbents to validate the analysis of the critical position and the successors' development plans. Incumbents often find this information helpful to them in bridging their own skills gaps in their positions. Also, the incumbents can provide suggestions about who could be candidates for their critical positions.

These are several possible development pathways:

- *One-on-one internal mentoring:* The potential mentors are the following:

  - The current incumbents of the critical positions. The incumbent mentors should be able to transmit their knowledge, skills and insights to the candidate(s) directly. The current incumbents who are key talent should have, as a personal metric, the development of the successor candidates for their own positions.

  - The managers once removed from the candidates for the critical positions (especially when the incumbents of the critical positions are not key talents).[5]

- *External coaching for strategic, leadership and professional development:* A previous incumbent of a critical position can function as an external coach or mentor in the event the current incumbent is not suitable or unwilling to fulfill the mentoring role. Also, some external consultant coaches who understand the organizational dynamics well can function as effective external coaches.

- *Placement in critical feeder positions:* These are the positions that function as an important part of the learning experience for candidates to succeed in a critical position. They also can include temporary assignments to other departments or externally to provide the needed experience, exposure and training.

---

5. Elliott Jaques introduced the concept of Manager Once Removed (MoR) on page 52 of his landmark book *Requisite Organization* (Cason Hall and Co., 1989). He recommends that the MoR should "assess pro tem the current working-capacity of each subordinate-once-removed (SoR), and the likely working-capacity growth within the next three to five years." However, we have found that most MoRs do not have the time to fulfill this accountability effectively. As a result, we have focused the MoR assessment and career discussion specifically on the subordinates-once-removed who are key talent in their organization, which seems to be a more manageable request.

- *Lead cross-functional assignments:* These assignments help individuals understand the holistic leadership requirements for a critical position.

- *Lead customer value and/or stakeholder value research:* The candidate for a critical position can lead the research to better understand the value the critical position provides currently and its potential value for the future.

- *Exposure to internal and external executive programs:* These programs build the network of leaders in the organization and ensure that potential candidates meet leaders currently in critical positions.

Step 4: Identify potential candidates for critical positions.

The next challenge is for organizations to identify high-potential and high-performing candidates interested in the critical positions. Often, the current incumbents can help identify potential candidates for their positions. In this case, current incumbents must act out of the interest for the greater good of the organization. (This process can be impeded if the current incumbents feel threatened by discussions about identifying potential candidates who will ultimately replace them.)

The organizations then invite individual candidates to consider their personal involvement in this development process. The companies assess the candidates based on the core competencies and knowledge required in the critical positions.

Once the organizations identify the candidates for each critical position, the candidates are informed of their selection for this career track. If the organizations are using a Method 5 succession management approach, then the candidates may be considered for more than one critical position or other positions as well.

The assessment process for candidates proceeds as follows:

- Assess the candidates on the leadership elements that are a prerequisite for success in any leadership role (including critical positions).

- Assess the candidates on their capabilities in the unique characteristics of the critical positions.

- Identify the gaps between the current assessed performance and the required performance for the critical positions.

- Identify the parts of the developmental pathways the candidates need to emphasize to be effective performers in the critical positions.

Step 5: Implement development plans and evaluate outcomes.

Organizations need to implement development plans for succession management as part of their strategy. They need an allocated budget, resources and time to invest in the development of the potential successors. Also, if organizations use the Method 5 succession management approach, the development will need to be for multiple positions.

The evaluation of the succession management for critical positions should be based on agreed-upon metrics that are tracked regularly. The metrics should focus on reducing the risk of the overall leadership capacity gap for critical positions. Here are some metrics used by one organization that had already identified their critical positions and critical feeder positions.

- Ninety percent of critical positions have high-performing incumbents.

- Ninety percent of the identified candidates for critical positions are high-potential talent.

- Ninety percent of the identified candidates for critical positions are "ready-now" candidates for critical positions that are *damaging* risk.

- Fifty percent of the identified candidates for critical positions are "ready-now" candidates for critical positions that are *high* risk.

- The identified candidates for critical positions become "ready-now" for critical positions within three years.

- Ninety-seven percent of the identified candidates for critical positions are retained in the organization.

- Ninety percent of candidates for critical positions are in critical feeder positions. These positions will provide the experiences to develop the skill and knowledge required to perform well in the targeted critical positions.

- Career development plans are in place for 100 percent of the remainder of the leadership team (i.e., for those who are not candidates for critical positions).

FIVE KEY SUCCESS FACTORS IN SUCCESSION MANAGEMENT FOR CRITICAL POSITIONS

A number of key success factors will increase the probability of positive outcomes on succession management for critical positions. The five key success factors we have identified are:

1. *Ensure that the critical positions that are identified are the critical few.*

   Organizations have a tendency to want to include all positions as critical positions. It is important for them to reduce the quantity of critical positions to a manageable number. This includes creating a triage system to address the critical and vulnerable positions (damaging risk) first and then the critical and non-vulnerable positions (high risk) second. They need to invest the resources in the areas that have the greatest risk. Of particular note, it often requires significant maturity by an executive team to know that perhaps only a few of the positions on the executive level are actually critical.

2. *The method of identifying critical positions and candidates needs to be data-based.*

   In the worst-case scenario, the executives hold a meeting and advocate for their favorite employees to be the candidates for critical positions. This approach, although common, is highly unprofessional. It generates sub-par decisions, and it calls into question the integrity and justice of the entire process. The method of identifying critical positions, incumbent vulnerability and the future candidates for critical positions needs to be data-based, repeatable and beyond reproach. Often, psychometric leadership assessments reduce personal bias.

3. *Ensure the succession management process is "transparent."*
One way to ensure that succession management for critical positions is beyond reproach is to make the process transparent and objective. The method of identifying the critical positions, the incumbent vulnerability and the potential candidates should be communicated to everyone.

But are you required to be transparent and share the list of candidates who are identified for critical positions with everyone? Consider the ways organizations treat employee compensation, or the way they treat employee promotion issues.

- *A process similar to employee compensation:* If it is similar to the way that organizations treat compensation, then only the high-potential candidate and the executives would be told that the candidate has been identified for specialized development. In that case transparency is explicit, and it is understood that only the candidate will know. By virtue of making the level of exposure explicit, then the organization is being fully transparent.

- *A process similar to employee promotion:* If the transparency is compared to the process of promotion, then a promotion is communicated throughout the organization and everyone knows about it. The risk in this model is that it can create "haves" and "have-nots" and a perception by some people of inequality and favoritism.

Many effective organizations treat the transparency of this process much the way they treat compensation. Candidates know their own status (not making it known to them is an error); however, they do not broadcast the information throughout the entire organization. This level of transparency avoids the potential internal questioning of the choice of the high-potential candidates. It also saves face for the internal candidates for the critical position if, at a later point, they are no longer eligible to be candidates. (It might be difficult for candidates to step backwards if their candidacy is publicly known and then they do not meet the required standards.)

4. *Ensure that the executive group takes accountability to lead this process; do not vest this process strictly within the domain of Human Resources.*

The CEO and the executive team need to have active accountability in this process (as described in detail in Chapter 14).

- Use leadership talent reviews and progress reports on succession management for critical positions to regularly review the candidates' developmental progress for the critical positions. (Essentially, candidates for critical positions are viewed as "corporate resources.")

- The executives need to remove any systemic barriers to identifying and developing candidates for critical positions. For example, some executives might resist letting candidates apply for critical positions because they would lose one of their major talents from their functional areas. To offset this systemic barrier, consider allocating a special resource as a back-fill for these candidates so that the candidates can be developed properly.

- The incumbent leaders in the critical positions (including executive incumbents) need to be active participants in this process. The incumbent's expectation is to transfer the knowledge to the candidate so that the candidate will be developed effectively.

5. *Do not ignore the rest of the leadership—they need development, too.*

Notwithstanding everything said about developing candidates for critical positions and retention of key talent, organizations also need an integrated approach to leadership development that addresses their broader leadership. This will be explored in greater depth in the next chapter.

CLOSING COMMENTS

The goal is to protect the organization from the damaging risk of a vacancy in a critical position, with no one to fill that role. The investment in time and resources for succession management needs to be focused. When done properly, this investment ensures that the organization continues to have the leadership capacity in critical positions to deliver value to the business, key stakeholders and customers.

ACKNOWLEDGMENTS

Integrated Leadership Development

Many organizations are devoting considerable energy to building their leadership capacity to gain competitive advantage. However, as we explored in Chapter 2, this effort is a struggle for many. Current approaches to building leadership capacity are failing to hit the mark, and many senior leaders have little confidence in their organizations' leadership development programs.

Emerging research links an organization's ability to develop its leadership capacity to its competitive advantage.[1] A recent international study found that the more robust a company's approach to building internal leadership capacity, the greater the financial return in critical financial measures such as shareholder returns, growth in net increase, growth in market share and return in sales.[2] There are other financial implications of the development aspect of the leadership gap. For example, organizations now spend millions of dollars annually on leadership development.[3] Many also are dedicating a greater portion of

1. Watson Wyatt 2003. "Leadership: The Critical Key To Financial Success." *Drake Business Review*, 1,1. pp. 21–25; Richard S. Wellins & Peter S. Weaver Jr., "From C-Level to See-Level," *T&D Magazine*, September 2003.

2. Watson Wyatt, "Leadership: The Critical Key To Financial Success," p. 24. Found that the perceived quality of an organization's leadership development activities has a direct impact on financial outcomes (revenue growth, profitability, market share). 34 percent of organizations that had superior financial performance also had high-quality leadership development programs. In contrast, only 6 percent of those organizations that had below-average financial performance had high-quality leadership development programs.

3. Jennifer Merritt, "The Education Edge," *BusinessWeek*, October 2003.

their overall training budgets to leadership development programs.[4] Yet organizations are largely squandering this investment and are not generating the return on their investment.

This chapter continues the discussion on the implementation of leadership capacity (Figure 13.1) by examining how organizations can take an integrated approach to leadership development.

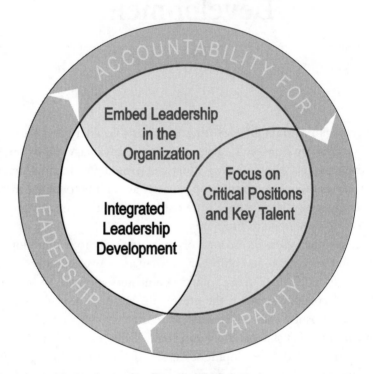

Figure 13.1 *Leadership Capacity Implementation*

First, we'll explore the traditional approaches to leadership development and consider their limitations. Next, we'll describe the steps to effectively implement an integrated approach to leadership development that builds strong leadership capacity.

4. Martin Delahoussaye, "Leadership in the 21st Century," *Training*, September 2001, pp. 60-72.

THE TRADITIONAL APPROACHES TO LEADERSHIP DEVELOPMENT

Traditionally, organizations have relied primarily on two approaches to building their leadership capacity. We refer to these as the single-solution approach and the multiple-solution approach.

The Single-Solution Approach

The most common approach has been the single-solution approach, where organizations rely primarily on one method to build leaders. Many organizations assume there is one answer, a so-called "silver bullet" that will solve their leadership gap problems. Consider the following case example of a manufacturing company that tried a single-solution approach to its leadership capacity challenges:

The CEO of a global manufacturing company returned to his job after attending a three-day industry conference. He was extremely excited because on the third day of the conference, he listened to a keynote speaker discuss the topic of leadership. The speaker was a "leadership guru" who had recently published a bestselling book. Based on the keynote, the CEO signed up for a post-conference workshop led by the leadership guru. He found the experience to be personally valuable, even "transformational." On the flight back, he read the leadership book from cover to cover. On his return the first thing he did was to drop by the office of the VP HR. The CEO could not contain his excitement. He told her about the book and the program he attended. He then told her that he wanted to bring this same program into the company and have it delivered to all 500 managers and supervisors worldwide. He said that this was the solution the company was looking for to revitalize its leadership and get the company back on track. The VP HR challenged the rationale for implementing such a program, but the CEO was too passionate about the idea and essentially told her to do it and make it her number one priority.

The VP HR contacted the consulting company, and together they developed a five-day residential training program that would be delivered to all five hundred leaders. Over a three-year period, the company was able to train all of its leaders. On the surface, it appeared that the leadership training program was a tremendous success. However, in reality, the program was not effective in building the leadership capacity needed by this organization. The leaders were confused about the "mandatory" program. Few knew why it was being implemented. Another problem was that the leaders saw the leadership model and many of the concepts of the program as too "touchy-feely" and not at all applicable to the production floor environment in which they worked. The program also included too many "silly training games" that simply wasted time. In addition, after leaders attended the program, there was little follow-up. In the end, the company spent over four million dollars on the initiative. The company had no way of determining whether the investment provided a return; the prevailing attitude was that it was a waste of time.

This case example illustrates some of the strengths, weaknesses and limitations of the single-solution approach. This approach does have some advantages in that it can be easy to implement. It also ensures a certain level of consistency, since all leaders receive the same content. It provides leaders the opportunity to come and learn together. Certainly these were some of the benefits derived in the case example above.

However, the single-solution approach also has several weaknesses and limitations that essentially make it ineffective as a sole strategy for building leadership capacity.

- *The over-reliance on the classroom as the primary method of developing leaders.* The classroom still predominates as a strategy for building leadership capacity.[5] This often creates a "one-size-fits-all" approach to leadership development. In his book *Managers Not MBAs*, Mintzberg correctly argues that leaders are not developed

---

5. Hewitt, *Leadership Development Ineffective.*

solely in the classroom.[6] The other limitation with classroom-based leadership training programs is that they are seen as being too time-consuming. Today, leaders are too busy and will not attend leadership programs that ask them to sit in a classroom for long periods of time. Leaders also will not sit through classroom experiences that are full of "training games." Increasingly we are finding that leaders are tired of this approach and see lengthy training games as silly and irrelevant.

- *An overemphasis on generic leadership models.* In many cases a single-solution approach to leadership development also has had a tendency to adopt generic leadership models that overemphasized personal traits and characteristics of individual leaders.[7] Many of these models provide valuable insights, but leaders typically find them to be too theoretical and often disconnected from day-to-day realities. These models also focus too heavily on the individual leader or personal leadership and do not adequately address other important elements of leadership. This has led many organizations to think of leadership as a product or event.[8]

The Multiple-Solution Approach

Many astute organizations have recognized that the single-solution approach to leadership development is insufficient to build leadership capacity. These organizations implement a more evolved approach by utilizing an array of leadership development options. We refer to this as the multiple-solution approach to leadership development. Today, organizations have a wide array of development options available.[9] In the section below we briefly review some of the more prominent development options emerging in the leadership development landscape.

6. Henry Mintzberg, *Managers Not MBAs* (San Francisco: Berrett-Koehler, 2004).

7. Ulrich, et al., *Results-Based Leadership*.

8. Ready & Conger, "Why Leadership Development Efforts Fail".

9. Saratoga Institute, "Leadership Development: Programs and Practices, Future Directions, Examples and Models." (Santa Clara, CA., 1998) Also see Cynthia McCauley, Russ S. Moxley, Ellen Van Velsor, *The Center for Creative Leadership Handbook of Leadership Development*, (San Francisco, CA: Jossey-Bass Publishers, 1998).

THE FOUR TYPES OF LEADERSHIP DEVELOPMENT OPTIONS

Organizations can use four broad types of leadership development options when developing their leaders: 1) assessment options, 2) coaching options, 3) learning options and 4) experience options. These will be described in more detail below and are summarized in the following table.

ASSESSMENT	COACHING	LEARNING	EXPERIENCE
• Psychometric Assessment • Multi-Rater Feedback • Competency Assessment • Assessment Centers	• Internal Coaching • External Coaching • Mentoring	• Individualized Development Planning • High Profile Learning Events • Technology-based Learning Options • Leaders Developing Leaders • Partnering with Thought Leaders • Business School Affiliations • Development for Intact Teams	• Stretch Assignments • Outside Positions/Projects • Action Learning

1. Assessment Options

Assessment options provide leaders the opportunity to get objective feedback on their current and potential leadership capability. Here are some of the assessment options:

- *Psychometric assessment:* This includes the use of valid, reliable and normative psychometric instruments to assess a variety of underlying traits and aptitudes associated with leadership capacity.

- *Multi-rater feedback:* This approach to assessment provides leaders with behavioral feedback received from managers, peers and direct reports.

- *Competency assessment:* This development option assesses leaders on a variety of core leadership competencies identified by an organization. It provides organizations the ability to create a baseline measure on the leadership competencies, identify gaps among leaders and measure improvement over time.

- *Assessment centers:* Assessment centers combine psychometric assessments, multi-rater feedback and competency assessment with expert observation in a simulated case example environment.

Collectively, these assessment development options are valuable because they enable organizations to effectively evaluate a leader's strengths and weaknesses. This evaluation data helps organizations understand the status of its leadership capacity. Furthermore, the organization can make better-informed decisions regarding a leader's future growth potential and the gaps that need to be overcome. The aggregate data also acts as a baseline to guide the measurement of changes in the organization's leadership capacity.

2. Coaching Options

Coaching is another important development option available to organizations.[10] Organizations are utilizing several types of coaching to develop leaders:

- *Internal coaching:* Through the use of internal coaching, organizations ensure that leaders have the skills to effectively coach others in the organization. Organizational support for coaching is an important success factor that determines how successful an organization will be in building its leadership capacity. All development options are fully optimized in an organization where leaders are able to coach, do it on a regular basis and are held accountable for having development conversations with their direct reports.

- *External coaching:* Many organizations also are using external coaching as a development option for leaders. Professionals outside the organization are retained to work with leaders through one-on-one sessions to address key development needs. This is an

10. Marshall Goldsmith, Laurence Lyons & Alyssa Freas, *Coaching for Leadership: How the World's Greatest Coaches Help Leaders Learn,* (Jossey-Bass/Pfeiffer Publishers, 2000).

especially useful solution because it can easily accommodate leaders' busy schedules and can complement other leadership development options. One area where external coaching (often referred to as "executive integration" coaching) is proving to be extremely valuable is in helping leaders effectively integrate into new leadership roles. Coaching also is becoming an important development approach to increase leaders' ability to deliver results in their new roles. In one financial services company, external coaching was offered as a development option for high-potential leaders. Through our experience we have found that the use of external coaching works best when it is focused on the development of leaders, rather than when it is used as a "punitive" approach to turn around a leader's performance.

- *Mentoring:* Mentoring is a relationship that exists between a seasoned and respected leader and an aspiring high-potential leader. One of the challenges that the leadership gap presents to organizations is the needed transfer of knowledge and experience from senior leaders to the leaders of the future. Mentoring provides a process where mentors can transmit their knowledge, skills and insights to future leaders directly. Organizations can implement mentoring in formal and informal ways. Typically, mentoring is as much a practice as it is a value. We have found that mentoring works best in organizations that value it and understand the importance of knowledge transfer to building strong leadership capacity. In the absence of this understanding, senior leaders will not make the time for mentoring.

3. Learning Options

Learning options dominate the leadership development landscape. They represent education-related events or programs designed to impart the skills, knowledge and ideas to build strong leadership capacity. Below we review some of the learning options that we see gaining prominence in years to come.

- *Individualized development planning:* This development option is used to ensure that leaders have individual learning plans to guide their development. This option also helps organizations better identify and respond to leaders' individual learning needs.[11]

- *High-profile learning events:* Increasingly, organizations are reinventing the classroom experience by holding high-profile learning events. During these events, senior leaders meet with current and aspiring leaders to explore strategic business issues and connect leaders across organizational boundaries. Often, the focus of these learning events is less on individual development of skills and talents and more on imparting a collective ethos and leadership story. Another key benefit of these high-profile learning events is the "socialization" among the leaders to develop a shared understanding of what the organization is about and where it is going. The socialization requires an investment of time to engage leaders through networking and interpersonal relationships.[12] One large pharmaceutical company effectively utilized high-profile learning events by holding "leadership summits" on a quarterly basis. The company brought together all the company's senior managers and directors to work with the executive team. The meetings focused on aligning and engaging the senior leader group to the strategy and developing a common understanding of business and organizational priorities.

- *Technology-based learning options:* Organizations have increasingly been using technology-based learning options such as e-learning, performance support systems and simulation-based learning. These options appear most suited when large organizations need to provide development to leaders distributed in locations around the world.

- *Leaders developing leaders:* In many organizations senior leaders are beginning to take an active role in developing future leaders.[13] As senior leaders understand the strategic importance of their leadership

11. Jay A. Conger & Beth Benjamin, *Building Leaders*, (San Francisco, CA: Jossey-Bass, 1999).

12. Tichy, *The Leadership Engine, How Winning Companies Build Leaders at Every Level.* (Harper Collins Publishers, 1997).

13. Ibid.

capacity, they are beginning to invest more personal time to guide program development, assess leadership capability, deliver content and facilitate discussions with future leaders. We anticipate that in coming years, senior leaders will be expected to have the ability to develop future leaders. We also believe that boards of directors and executive teams will be recruiting senior leaders who demonstrate track records for developing leaders.

- *Partnering with thought leaders:* One CEO of a technology company believed that in order for her company to remain leading edge, it needed leaders who were continuously exposed to new ideas. She established a partnership with several thought leaders in various areas of expertise that would bring their ideas to this technology company. Such thought leaders can come from academia, consulting, and other companies and are able to provide innovative and stimulating ideas to organizations. Establishing such a partnership creates a special relationship where the external thought leader comes to know the organization intimately and is then able to present ideas in the context of the company story and how leadership can deliver competitive advantage. The thought leaders provide the best of two worlds—external freedom of thought with internal understanding of the company's reality, so that the new ideas will be useful and applicable.

- *Business school affiliations:* Many organizations also establish close affiliations with business schools. We anticipate that this development option will continue in the future. Organizations increasingly will look for opportunities to affiliate with educational institutions that can demonstrate an impact on the organization's bottom line. Another important requirement will be the need for external partners not to merely customize off the shelf products but rather fully develop customized leadership development learning programs.

- *Development for intact teams:* Many organizations also are redefining the classroom experience by conducting leadership development for intact teams, departments and business units.[14] By working with

---

14. J. Schettler, "Exclusive Leadership Research." *Training Magazine.* Vol. 40. #6, 2003, pp. 70–75.

intact teams, learning outcomes can be focused to drive specific business results for the teams. The added benefit is that intact teams work more effectively with other teams across the organization. Furthermore, specific behavioral change can be increased because the entire team holds itself accountable and works with other teams in the organization to effect change.

4. Experience Options

Experience options provide leaders with a variety of opportunities that enhance their current performance or prepare them to assume future leadership roles. As we discussed earlier in this book, experience may be the best teacher when it comes to developing leaders. However, experience is only an effective teacher when leaders have the time to reflect on their experiences, when they can learn from other leaders in their organizations and when they can work with mentors who help transfer their own knowledge to future leaders. Therefore, for organizations to derive the value that experience options have the potential to generate for a leader's development, those options must be carefully planned.

Organizations can implement many types of experience options:

- *Stretch assignments:* Many organizations use "stretch" assignments and job rotations to develop leadership capacity. They use lateral moves to expand the breadth of knowledge of a leader within an organization. They also use vertical moves designed to expand a leader's ability to handle increased senior leadership responsibility. Organizations also utilize cross-functional or corporate-wide project teams to help develop an enterprise-wide perspective.

- *Outside positions/projects:* Organizations also have started to look outside their organizations for experiences that develop their leaders by creating short-term assignments with clients or companies within the supply chain. Leaders assume new roles and experiences that enable them to deepen their understanding of the industry and overall business.

- *Action learning:* Action learning involves linking leadership development with the company's need to solve an important business
problem. The process generally begins by having the company identify a problem that affects the entire organization. Teams are created,
and then they receive the tools and skills needed to solve the problem.
Over time, the teams come together to develop solutions to the problem. The teams then report back to senior management with
proposed solutions. In our experience we have found that action-
learning projects succeed because they enable leaders to transfer
learning immediately through ongoing real-time work projects. The
organization typically realizes cost savings from the recommended
solutions emanating from action-learning teams.

THE STRENGTHS AND LIMITATIONS OF THE MULTIPLE-SOLUTION APPROACH

The development options we've described represent a more evolved
approach to leadership development. Since leaders are exposed to a
greater number of development options, organizations are more effective at building their leadership capacity. Unfortunately, we have
observed through our experience that these options are implemented in
a fragmented manner, thereby limiting their potential value. Consider
the experience of the following organization:

> *A large insurance company prided itself on investing consider-
> able resources in developing its leaders. Over the years it had
> used an impressive number of options to build its leadership
> capacity. These included internal leadership development pro-
> grams, the use of external coaches for high-potential leaders,
> robust 360-degree assessment practices and a succession plan-
> ning process. The highest-profile development option was a joint
> program the company developed with a prestigious business
> school that offered selected leaders the opportunity to complete
> an MBA.*

Collectively, the financial commitment to implement these options was considerable, and the company's CEO was starting to scrutinize them. During an executive team meeting, the CEO ask the SVP of HR to explain why the company was spending almost three million dollars annually on tuition for MBA programs. The SVP of HR struggled to provide an answer. It soon became apparent that the investment in MBA programs was not guided by an overall strategy. Furthermore, the company had no internal process to assess the caliber and quality of the academic courses. Upon closer examination, the organization realized that many of the leadership development practices were largely disconnected from one another.

The insurance company needs to be congratulated for taking leadership capacity seriously and for making it a priority. However, the significant financial investment it made was not fully realized because many development options were implemented in an unplanned and fragmented manner. This case example illustrates some of the potential limitations of the multiple-solution approach to leadership development:

- *Lack of an overall strategy.* Many times the multiple-solution approach is not guided by an overall strategy. This leads to a lack of coordination and a disjointed approach to leadership development. It also becomes difficult to see how the development options add value to each other or connect to the overall business strategy.

- *Confusion among leaders.* When organizations implement a multiple-solution approach in a fragmented manner, it routinely leads to confusion among leaders. Leaders experience the development options as a hodgepodge of discrete courses, seminars or programs.

- *Failure to generate value for the organization.* The multiple-solution approach to leadership development can fail to generate value for the organization. The investment is not leveraged to its fullest extent.

THE NEED FOR AN INTEGRATED SOLUTION

The leadership gap often persists in organizations that implement either single-solution or multiple-solution approaches to leadership development. However, several factors are creating a new sense of urgency for organizations to evolve to an integrated solution to leadership development:

- *The complex business environment:* Organizations need to understand that the emerging environment (E2) in which leaders operate today is more complex and intense. It is placing greater pressure and demands on leaders. As a result single-solution and multiple-solution approaches to leadership development are not robust enough to build the leadership capacity required today. Leadership development in today's world needs to be more integrated and sophisticated.

- *The need to deliver results on many levels:* Today, the stakes are higher, and leadership development must deliver on many levels. It must not be done just for the sake of doing it but must achieve the following:

  - Transfer vital skills and ideas to leaders.

  - Enhance performance.

  - Reinforce corporate culture and values.

  - Drive business results.

  - Adapt to changing business realities.

  In essence leadership development must be relevant, align to business strategy and add value to leaders.

- *The high expectations of leaders.* Higher expectations are being placed on organizations. First, senior executives want to ensure that their investment in leadership development is maximized and delivers on the promise to build the leadership capacity needed. Second, the leaders who are the participants in leadership development also have extremely high expectations and want their organizations to implement integrated and high-value leadership development options. Consequently, HR and leadership development practitioners are under tremendous pressure to deliver results. A common "failure" path is to embrace the single- and multiple-solution approaches to leadership development.

- *The need to sort through a maze of leadership development options.* Leadership development is big business, and there is no shortage of development options for organizations to consider. At times, the number of development options can be overwhelming, and business leaders may be ill equipped to identify the best ones effectively. The maze of leadership development options actually reinforces the conditions for fragmented multiple-solution approaches in organizations. Therefore, organizations need to develop the internal expertise or rely on external guidance to help them sort through the maze and identify the options that have the potential to be offered in their organization in an integrated manner.

THE INTEGRATED–SOLUTION APPROACH TO LEADERSHIP DEVELOPMENT

The field of leadership development is in the midst of an evolution. This evolution is depicted in the figure below.

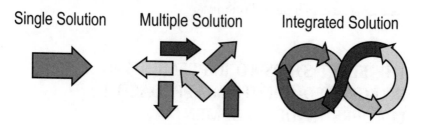

Figure 13.2 *The Evolution in Leadership Development*

We believe that organizations must implement what we refer to as an "integrated-solution" approach to leadership development. We define this approach as one that brings together and unites an array of development options so that they add value to one another. But there is more. The integrated-solution approach is more comprehensive, rigorous and long-term in focus. It also is more complex and requires greater commitment on the part of organizations. In the end, it is the most effective approach to building leadership capacity and overcoming the leadership gap. There are three reasons, summarized in three S's:

- *Strategic:* The integrated-solution ensures that all development options are focused on helping the organization gain competitive advantage. This approach involves creating a comprehensive strategy for leadership development and implementing the strategy effectively.

- *Synergistic:* Instead of implementing a hodgepodge of discrete development options, the integrated-solution approach is more synergistic. It strives to select and implement development options in a seamless manner so that they add value to one another.

- *Sustainable:* The integrated-solution approach is sustainable in that it takes a long-term perspective to leadership development. It recognizes that leadership development today is an emergent and iterative process that needs constant attention, focus and resources. It needs to become an organizational priority.

THE EIGHT STEPS TO IMPLEMENTING AN INTEGRATED-SOLUTION APPROACH TO LEADERSHIP DEVELOPMENT

Below we explore the eight steps to successfully implementing an integrated-solution approach to leadership development.

Eight Steps to Implementing An Integrated-Solution Approach to Leadership Development
1. Develop a comprehensive strategy for integrated leadership development.
2. Connect leadership development to the organization's environmental challenges.
3. Use the leadership story to set the context for development.
4. Balance global enterprise-wide needs with local individual needs.
5. Employ emergent design and implementation.
6. Ensure that development options fit the culture.
7. Focus on critical moments of the leadership lifecycle.
8. Apply a blended methodology.

Step 1: Develop a comprehensive strategy for integrated leadership development.

The integrated solution approach begins by developing a comprehensive strategy. As we discussed in Chapter Five on business strategy, most organizations have limited access to capital and people to allocate to their business strategies. The same is true when it comes to leadership development. Organizations do not have unlimited resources; they need to develop a strategy for integrated leadership development that delivers sustainable competitive advantage for the business. It must also ensure that the integrated leadership development strategy mitigates risk to the business that might emerge from the existing leadership gap. One way this is accomplished is by ensuring that leadership development is not just done for the sake of doing it; instead, it supports the organization's overall business strategy. The comprehensive strategy also ensures that development options are relevant, align to business needs and add value to leaders. Another critical element of the leadership development strategy is a comprehensive communications plan that regularly sends messages to leaders about the organization's efforts in building leadership capacity and also inculcates the organization's leadership story.

Step 2: Connect leadership development to the organization's environmental challenges.

The integrated-solution approach is effective because it connects leadership development to the organization's new environmental challenges (E1 vs. E2—see Chapter 1). It focuses its effort on helping leaders develop the capacity needed to lead effectively in future environments. Consider the following example:

> *A global technology company was a leader in its marketplace. The company had several years of consistent growth, but in recent years growth began to decline and become stagnant. Past success was a function of the company successfully being a niche player in its market (E1). The senior leadership team recognized it was time to change the business strategy and implemented a volume market strategy (E2). This change created a leadership gap in the organization because the new business model established a new set of expectations for leaders (L2). Now they needed to be more externally focused. Leaders needed to identify new customers and create a new stream of products for these new customers.*
>
> *The VP HR was charged with the responsibility to build the leadership capacity needed to help the organization succeed and implement the new business model. However, with the downturn in the technology sector, the parent company of this technology organization slashed training and leadership development budgets considerably. Many long-held leadership activities were cut. This created a significant problem for the VP HR; however, they responded in a focused manner. Given the financial constraints, they identified three core leadership skills that had the greatest potential to contribute to the business from a strategic perspective. The first was the ability to understand*

the new business environment and expectations of new customers. The second was the ability to lead change internally within the organization. The third was the ability to coach and engage staff in the new business model. They decided to launch a company-wide coaching initiative. This approach was directed to all leaders, but delivered to intact departments and business units to ensure the learning immediately transferred to key business priorities. They also implemented a blended approach which included self-assessment, learning sessions, webcasts, and follow-up "booster sessions" to sustain the learning.

Connecting leadership development to an organization's E1-E2 environmental challenges creates focus and ensures that leadership development is being used to prepare leaders to succeed in the future.

Step 3: Use the leadership story to set the context for development.

As we discussed in Chapter 11, organizations need to have a compelling story that communicates to employees the organization's philosophy and its approach to leadership. The story becomes part of the folklore of the organization and creates an expectation of leadership to behave consistently with the story and its message. An integrated-solution approach to leadership development uses the leadership story to set the context for development. The story tells the organization why leadership is important and how leaders will be developed. The story also creates a well-delineated leadership model that clearly articulates what leadership means to the organization. The model then serves as a focal point for defining development options. The leadership story is also important because when it comes to developing leaders, there are ideas, concepts and skills that can be taught directly to leaders. In many other cases, leaders learn best when they are in a positive environment that facilitates their ability to learn important leadership values on their own. A strong leadership story plays a pivotal role in creating such an open environment for self-learning.

Step 4: Balance global enterprise-wide needs with local individual needs.

In *Managing Across Borders*, Bartlett and Ghoshal explain the need for global businesses to balance the forces for global efficiency with the forces that require local responsiveness within a marketplace.[15] This is an important concept that also is relevant to integrated leadership development. Organizations must strive to balance the global or enterprise-wide development needs of an organization with local responsiveness to a leader's individual development needs. Organizations must identify development options that are needed by all their leaders—for instance, creating a common leadership culture, enhancing core leadership competencies and responding to changes in the business environment. The organization must also identify development options which target individual needs of key talent and future candidates for critical positions, and of leadership in specific departments and business units.

Step 5: Employ an emergent way to design and implement leadership development.

A VP HR for a large professional services firm recently commented, "Effective leadership development is a marathon!" In fact, one of the reasons the single-solution approach still exists is that it is fairly easy to implement. The integrated-solution approach is far more complex and challenging to implement.

> **The integrated-solution approach suggests that effective leadership development is emergent in that organizations must continually be in touch with what is happening in the business and be ready to respond to it.**

---

15. Christopher A. Bartlett & Sumantra Ghoshal, *Managing Across Boarders*. (Harvard Business School Press. 1989).

The organization must constantly be looking for opportunities to improve the development options because leaders learn through a constant process of learning, relearning and unlearning. The plan needs to be emergent rather than static; it needs to be flexible and fast, because the business world moves fast and leadership solutions must keep up.

This emergent way of designing and implementing leadership development is reflected in the following case example of a management consulting firm. This firm effectively used a change in organizational structure as an opportunity to build the leadership capacity of its future leadership talent.

The senior leadership was concerned that their partners' average age was close to 50 years old. The firm was very successful and so was its partners' performance. However, they worried about the viability of the firm in five to ten years as the partnership aged. They also realized that they had become partners in their early 40s, but they in turn were not providing leadership opportunities to the current 40-year-old leaders. They needed to expose their younger talent to the full scope of the leadership challenges in a management consulting firm without dismantling the successful leadership model that was in place.

They decided to create another kind of management role for the future leaders. They structured them regionally with managing partners and partners leading each of the regions across the country. They decided to create a parallel structure of "national practice leaders" who would have cross-country practice area leadership responsibilities. The younger leaders were given these roles, reporting directly to the president of the entire firm. The national practice leaders were responsible for the development of the next evolution of products and services in that practice area and the country-wide sales performance for the practice area, and they participated in the annual strategic planning process.

Step 6: Ensure that development options fit the culture.

At times organizations fail at building leadership capacity because they implement development options that do not fit their culture. The integrated-solution approach strives to ensure that the development options fit both the culture and the organization's "readiness." Consider the following example:

> In a large engineering firm, the VP of HR wanted to implement an Assessment Center process to launch a significant leadership development initiative. In initial discussions with members of the executive team, the VP of HR found significant resistance to the idea. The executives were concerned about the level of financial commitment required and the ability of the firm to do this well, given the other organizational priorities. Upon further reflection, the VP of HR recognized that the organization was not ready for this type of solution. The organization did not yet have a culture in which leaders were open to receiving the feedback that an Assessment Center would generate.
>
> Rather than force this upon the leaders and risk failure, the VP of HR introduced a staged approach. In the first year of the initiative, an online self-assessment tool was implemented that gave leaders the opportunity to assess themselves based on the organization's leadership competencies. This was an important first step because it was the first time the leaders had ever done this kind of self-assessment. The value that was provided was in the individual reports given to each leader. Not only did leaders receive a summary of their own ratings, they received a summary of the overall averages for all the leaders in the company, as well as the leaders within departments. This provided individuals an opportunity to compare themselves to their colleagues. This approach proved effective and laid the foundation for more robust assessment. In the second year of the initiative, the VP of

HR implemented a multi-rater assessment. Now leaders were assessed on the leadership competencies by direct reports, managers and peers. This also proved effective. In year three, the VP of HR introduced an assessment center process and focused it first on the high-potential candidates. Though this approach was more complex and took considerably longer to implement, it was in the end more effective because it respected the culture and readiness of the engineering firm.

Step 7: Focus on critical moments of the leadership lifecycle.

The integrated-solution approach also focuses its attention on critical moments along a leader's lifecycle. As we discussed in Chapter 9, these are times when leaders transition to new roles, such as the first time an employee becomes a manager of people or the first time a leader becomes an executive. Each transition in role presents new challenges and pressures. To succeed, new leaders need to develop new ways of thinking about their roles. These also are moments when leaders are at the greatest risk of failing or derailing. The integrated-solution approach concentrates activities to support leaders through the transition points in their leadership lifecycle.

Step 8: Apply a blended methodology.

The blended methodology suggests that development options from assessment, coaching, learning and experience are selected and organized to seamlessly add value to one another. They are parts of an overall integrated approach to leadership development. This does not mean that all development options need to be blended. However, increasingly we are seeing organizations take a blended approach to leadership development and create robust offerings that combine some form of assessment, coaching, learning and experience. Consider the following example:

Traditionally, a public-sector organization conducted much of its leadership development via the classroom. Leaders attended the classroom training; however, the program required little pre-work or follow-up. The organization revamped the program to be more integrated. For example, they developed an online performance support system for leaders that provided them with just-in-time content on a variety of leadership topics. They delivered a series of online learning modules through webcasts facilitated by senior leaders. They also developed a chat room to foster collaboration with peers on leadership issues. They redesigned the classroom experience as a "laboratory" for leaders to practice their leadership skills. The feedback from participants was extremely positive. The use of technology cut down on travel time, and the learning was more effective because it was not a one-time event.

CLOSING COMMENTS

The integrated-solution approach to leadership development represents a more strategic, synergistic and sustainable way for organizations to build the leadership capacity they require to gain competitive advantage. The integrated solution is intense. It requires serious commitment on the part of organizations, their senior leaders and from HR. The process also is more complex. In the long term, though, the integrated-solution approach delivers greater value to organizations and ensures that their investment in leadership development is optimized.

CHAPTER FOURTEEN

Accountability for Leadership Capacity

One of the key reasons the leadership gap continues to exist is the confusion over who in an organization should own accountability for

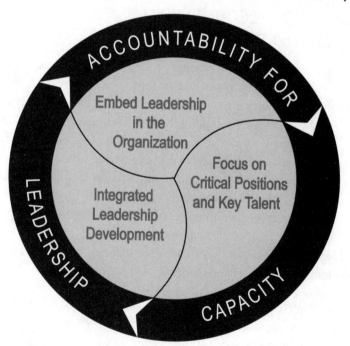

Figure 14.1 *Leadership Capacity Implementation*

leadership capacity. This accountability needs to be owned primarily by the executives, with senior leaders and Human Resources (HR) professionals accepting specific areas of accountability. Each group needs to do its part to bridge the leadership capacity gap.

This chapter focuses on three issues:

- Executive and senior leader accountability for bridging the leadership capacity gap.

- HR professionals' accountabilities, including their responsibility to conduct an annual leadership capacity audit.

- A set of questions to 1) guide the audit process, and 2) function as an overall summary of the essential issues in developing holistic leaders and for ensuring systemic implementation of leadership capacity.

EXECUTIVE ACCOUNTABILITY FOR LEADERSHIP CAPACITY

Executive accountability for bridging the leadership capacity gap is a key success factor for organizations. However, examples of executive leadership in this area are not common. There are some "early adopt" executives who assume accountability for leadership capacity and understand the strategic importance of strong leadership. As a result, they take personal accountability and invest the needed time to assess leadership capability and to be involved directly in building leadership capacity. Books have been written about these individuals, but they are not sufficient to motivate other executives to take accountability for the leadership capacity in their organizations.

Here is an example of an executive team that struggled with its accountability for leadership capacity.

A high-tech company quickly rose to great profitability and success only to suffer an overwhelming downturn during the technology meltdown in 2001. They laid off over half their employees. Stock prices dropped by 80 percent, and the board appointed a new executive group to lead the turnaround. After two years the company started to solidify its financial position and showed some modest profit again. The turnaround strategy focused on bundling products for customers and on customer loyalty initiatives.

The new executives realized they needed to develop the leaders in their organization. Their leaders had been exposed to only two kinds of business experiences: phenomenal growth and dramatic downturn. They did not know how to lead in a more stable, managed growth environment. The executives decided to conduct an in-depth training program for all of the top 120 leaders. The one-year program included three sessions for each group of thirty leaders, action-learning projects for small groups and benchmark visits to other companies to learn from them how to lead businesses globally. The executive group asked their VP HR to take accountability for this process. The executives themselves were prepared to participate in a half-day overview session so they would know what would be taught to their leaders. They did not think they needed the development themselves.

The initial step of the process was an in-depth needs analysis. The data were collected globally by a highly respected group of academics and consultants in Europe, Asia Pacific and North America. They met to prepare an aggregate report of what they found.

The data from the needs analysis was alarming. The 120 leaders (not including the executives) were overworked, disaffected and very upset with the leadership approach of the executive group. They claimed that the executive group needed to change if the company was going to succeed in the future. Apparently, the president's style during the turnaround was to give orders, and the rest of the executives and the company followed. All issues escalated to the president for his decision. He managed each of the executives individually and then made all of the key decisions for the company independently. This style worked well to turn the company around, but it was not perceived to be an effective leadership style for the continued growth of the business. Most leaders did not believe the company was going to survive another three years.

The executive team attended the planning session to debrief the needs analysis and to determine the next steps for developing leadership capacity. The president was briefed on the contents of the needs analysis before the session.

A number of the professionals who conducted the needs analysis attended the session to add depth to the report and to provide further insight into the next steps that were required. The executives responded defensively to the needs analysis report. One said that the executive group needed to operate as it did to turn the company around. Another executive questioned the validity of the report because it was so negative. After some discussion, the president articulated the real issue and asked: "Is this a training program or is this a change process?" He thought initially that it was a training program to keep leaders happy in a chaotic business environment. However, now he was beginning to realize that this was a strategic change process.

The executive group agreed to change the objectives of this process to focus on the following: (1) build the leadership capacity for sustained growth, (2) launch a disciplined process of implementing change, (3) create cross-functional and cross-business unit team effectiveness to bundle solutions for customers, and (4) identify critical positions and ready-now successors.

Through the process the executive group came to the realization that they too would need to evolve as well. The executives agreed to participate in a more extensive executive development process to determine how they wanted to operate as a team, how they could collectively add value to the organization, and how they could model the leadership approach they wanted others to emulate. They also decided to participate in parts of the leadership development program themselves in order to build their own leadership capabilities, to share future business directions and to understand the leadership capabilities of the 120 senior leaders in their organization. But perhaps the most important *development was that they realized leadership capacity was a strategic imperative and that they needed to own the process as an executive accountability. Rather than delegating leadership capacity to HR, they decided that leadership capacity was the president's priority. Of course, the president expected all of the executives, including the business unit leaders and HR, to do their part to make this process succeed.*

This case example illustrates the challenge for many organizations. The executives need to determine if the leadership challenge is a strategic imperative—and if it is, they need to take the accountability to address the issue as they would address any other major threat to the ongoing success of their business.

Indeed, in the absence of acceptance by executives to take accountability for leadership capacity development, some boards of directors are compelling the executives to put it on their agendas. More CEOs are facing questions from their boards on their key talent, successors for critical positions and overall leadership capacity. Some boards are requesting leadership capacity audits of their existing organizations and for companies they plan to acquire.

Once executives accept the accountability for leadership capacity, they need to spread the accountability to the other levels of leaders. Line managers need to focus on delivering both leadership capacity and specific performance outcomes. One without the other is inadequate performance. Line managers need to be selected, developed, evaluated and given new career opportunities based on their capability to achieve performance outcomes and to build leadership capacity throughout their organization.

Here are seven ways for executives and senior line managers to demonstrate their accountability for leadership capacity:

1. *Position leadership capacity as a strategic priority for executives:* The executives should declare publicly their commitment to leadership capacity as a strategic challenge for the organization and demonstrate that commitment.

2. *Executives conduct annual talent reviews:* The executives need to take accountability for conducting annual talent reviews that explore retention strategies for key talent and succession management for critical positions.

3. *The executives personally continue to develop their leadership capabilities:* The executives need to be part of the learning process and not see themselves as above it. Excluding executives from leadership development implies that leadership development is only for promotion purposes, and that since the executives are at the highest positions, they do not need to be developed anymore. However, delivering the required leadership capacity is a challenge for all leaders, including executives. In fact, if the executives believe that it would be a waste of their time to participate in the entire program (and that they only need an overview), then it is quite possible that the leadership development program would be a waste of time for their direct reports as well.

4. *The executives need to model the required leadership capacity and holistic leadership:* Collectively and individually, the executives should be the example of what is expected of leaders in their organization. Others watch them closely. If they do not take leadership capacity seriously, then their direct reports often conclude that they do not need to take it seriously either. Executives' behaviors function as a model for others to emulate regardless of whether or not the executives model exceptional or inadequate leadership capability.

5. *Executives need to provide the time and resources to build leadership capacity:* Some of the ways to do this are:

   - Allocate internal people resources to support the development of leadership capacity.

   - Use the right mix of internal and external talent to develop their leaders.

   - Allocate the financial resources to build leadership capacity and protect it so that it is not sacrificed during a climate of constraint.

6. ***Executives make leadership capacity development a priority for their direct reports:*** Executives need to provide the time for leaders to participate in the leadership development process—and whenever there is a business need that conflicts with that process, avoid the urge to pull those leaders from leadership development.

7. ***Executives need to be leaders who develop other leaders:*** Executives should become excellent coaches of direct reports and mentors for high-potential talent that are two levels below them. Also, at least once a month, executives need to signal their commitment to be leaders who develop other leaders. Some examples of what they can consider doing are:

- Present ideas and dialogue at leadership development sessions and other development programs.

- Conduct town hall meetings with their entire organization or conduct skip-level meetings with groups below their direct reports.

- Encourage other leaders to job shadow them to learn about their role.

- Encourage leaders to present at staff meetings of other leaders in the organization to share ideas and to provide a broader perspective to the other units.

- Present externally at conferences to share their personal leadership story and the company's innovations in building leadership capacity.

HUMAN RESOURCES PROFESSIONALS PART OF BUILDING LEADERSHIP CAPACITY

Human Resources professionals often resist accountability and suffer from the "enabler" crisis. Many HR professionals have come to believe that it is not appropriate for HR to own anything; their role is to enable others to act. Unfortunately, the unwillingness to take accountability only serves to marginalize HR and reduce its value to the organization. Traditionally, accountability for leadership development has rested with the Human Resources function. This is no longer sufficient. HR needs to partner with the senior leaders of their organizations. However, HR needs to also carefully reflect on their part of the accountability when leadership development becomes strategic and focuses on the leadership capacity gap.

What Are the Areas of Accountability for HR?

HR needs to take accountability for the following three overall outcomes:

1. All people and organizational initiatives are aligned and eventually deliver external customer value.

2. The organizational conditions are created for every manager to function as a people manager and every employee to be self-reliant.

3. HR has value as a center of excellence that enhances the capability of people and the organization in alignment with the overall business strategic direction and core values.

It would follow then that HR's accountability in building leadership capacity would be as follows:

- To ensure that all HR initiatives in developing leadership capacity are aligned and eventually deliver value to the external customer.

- To create the conditions for line managers and executives to take accountability for building leadership capacity.

- To be the center of excellence for technical accountabilities that help build leadership capacity, such as best practice in succession management, integrated leadership development, finding and retaining talent, and developing alliances with key external service providers.

Other examples of HR roles are:

- Ensures that the executives own the leadership capacity gap in "words" as well as in "deeds."

- Enlists the commitment and accountability of the executives, line managers and eventually all employees to bridge the leadership capacity gaps.

- Audits the extent to which the required leadership capacity is developed.

Overall and Technical Accountabilities

In today's business environment, line executive ownership of leadership capacity is more important than HR-owned.[1] The paramount responsibility for bridging the leadership gap must rest with the top executive in an organization. However, most CEOs and other executives do not have the expertise or the time to develop comprehensive programs.[2]

Developing overall leadership capacity is not a luxury that can be delegated to a specialty HR group. It is a strategic necessity and an investment in the future. To be successful this investment must be a long-term commitment of time, money and resources during both economic prosperity and economic downturns.

HR's role is an important one—as a strategic co-creative partner with the CEO and the executive team to build leadership development strategies that drive business results.[3] The executives must be accountable for overall leadership capacity and HR for technical leadership capacity.

- *Executives are accountable for <u>overall</u> leadership capacity:* An important aspect of developing leadership capacity is to create a leadership story that reflects the future state of the capacity you wish to achieve. Executives must own the accountability to do this. They should also find ways to 1) visibly champion the importance of leadership capacity throughout the organization, 2) participate actively in leadership talent review processes, and 3) informally develop leaders through modeling, coaching, mentoring of high potential talent, developmental experiences, etc.

1. Ulrich, et al., *Results-Based Leadership*.

2. Conger & Benjamin, *Building Leaders*.

3. Weiss, *High Performance HR: Leveraging Human Resources For Competitive Advantage.* (John Wiley & Sons Canada, Ltd., 2000).

- ***HR is accountable for <u>technical</u> leadership capacity:*** HR needs to develop the tools and processes that can be leveraged across the organization to enhance overall leadership capacity. Technical processes include succession management, leadership development, finding the best talent, lateral transfers and promotion programs, formalized coaching, performance management, etc.

The organizations that have the right balance of executive and HR accountability will be in a position to succeed.

Executives should also signal the importance of leadership capacity by including a leadership or talent-related issue as a strategic initiative for the entire organization. Also, HR can reflect the leadership capacity strategic initiative by specifying it as an "HR strategic banner." For example, a professional services firm made building leadership capacity a strategic priority. This was driven largely by the need to build a strong pool of candidates to assume senior executive roles because of impending retirements. Building leadership capacity became mission critical to this organization. The CEO personally made it his number one priority and it became the "strategic banner" for HR, who in turn diverted resources to building leadership capacity for the firm.

The HR strategic banner is often the people and/or organizational challenge that can cause the greatest risk to continued organizational success. In other words, HR must focus its effort on this strategic issue because if it is not effectively addressed it can put the organization at risk. It is that strategic banner that becomes the strategic value proposition of Human Resources.

The figure on the next page illustrates this important point. This HR strategic banner is positioned at the top of the triangle that appeared in the book *High Performance HR*.[4] It is the strategic people and/or organizational issue that is essential to the competitive advantage of the business.

In our current business environment, we have found that bridging the leadership gaps (i.e., talent, capability, development, and values

---

4. David S. Weiss. *High Performance HR* (John Wiley & Sons Canada, Ltd., 2000), explored the wide range of dynamics and economic challenges related to organizational and people processes. The book identified four strategic challenges: culture, alignment, change and ROI of human capital. Most organizations are able to focus on only one HR strategic banner at a time. The proposition is that the new HR strategic banner in our current environment should be to build leadership capacity.

Figure 14.2 *The HR Strategic Banner: Building Leadership Capacity*

aspects) is the high-risk HR strategic banner that needs special attention from executives and HR. As a result, for many organizations, the top of the HR triangle would specify "leadership capacity" as it does in the figure above.

In many organizations, HR has been charged with the new challenge to elevate what they have done in the area of leadership development from simply implementing leadership training programs to creating a leadership capacity strategy and building a culture of leadership. They are challenged to champion the technical processes of building leadership capacity and its implementation to achieve organizational success.

Another important role for HR is to specify metrics that define the leadership capacity the company needs to achieve. Outcome metrics do not measure the input side or the work that is done; instead, they measure those specific results that the organization expects will fulfill the strategic initiative.

To develop the outcome metrics, HR must seek the answers to five outcome metric questions:

- What is the leadership capacity outcome needed to meet current and future business needs?

- What is the current state of leadership capacity in the organization? (Note: In the next section we provide the questions HR can ask when conducting a leadership capacity audit.)

- What is the extent of the leadership capacity gap between the capacity needs and the current leadership capacity?

- What are the change metrics to track the reduction in the leadership gap?

- What are the organizational systems, structures and HR processes that need to be in place to enable the required leadership capacity to occur?

HR ACCOUNTABILITY TO AUDIT THE CURRENT STATE OF LEADERSHIP CAPACITY

A key technical accountability for HR professionals is to conduct a leadership capacity audit on an annual basis. We've developed audit questions associated with the elements of the holistic leadership framework that will enable HR to assess the extent to which organizations and their leaders demonstrate holistic leadership. We've also developed audit questions based on the critical success factors needed for the implementation of leadership capacity. These questions enable organizations to audit the extent to which they are doing their part to implement the required leadership capacity to achieve organizational success.

Audit of the Extent to Which Leaders Lead Holistically

Here are the audit questions that use the six elements of the holistic leadership framework as a guide:

Figure 14.3   *The Holistic Leadership Framework*

	Area of Strength	Area of Development
Customer Leadership Overall (See Chapter 4) 1. To what extent are your leaders focusing on delivering external customer value? 2. To what extent are your leaders delivering the required level of value to your customers? 3. To what extent are you distinguishing your company by delivering a higher level of value to achieve customer loyalty?		
Business Strategy Overall (See Chapter 5) 1. *Architect:* To what extent have you crafted a strategy that delivers competitive advantage or competitive parity? 2. *Balance:* To what extent have you balanced the emphasis on growth in new initiatives with the optimization of current work to create space for new initiatives? 3. *Contingency Plans:* To what extent do you have an effective Plan B in the event that your Plan A strategy cannot occur? 4. *Deploy:* To what extent is your organization quickly and effectively implementing the strategy and the changes it has developed? 5. *Evaluate:* To what extent are you evaluating achievements and disappointments and focusing on continuous improvements to the strategy and its implementation?		

	Area of Strength	Area of Development
Culture & Values Overall (See Chapter 6) 1. To what extent is the leadership mindset focused on building the culture? 2. To what extent do your structures and organizational system support the creation of the desired culture? 3. To what extent are the rewards, incentives and consequences suppporting the desired culture? 4. To what extent are values integrated into the organizational practices? 5. To what extent are leaders selected, developed and promoted based upon whether they live their values? 6. To what extent do leaders create a compelling place to work? 7. To what extent do culture and values drive employee engagement?		
Organizational Leadership Overall (See Chapter 7) 1. To what extent is your organization aligned to drive the business strategy and customer loyalty? 2. To what extent are your employees engaged with the causes of the entire enterprise (i.e., deeply committed and personally invested?) 3. To what extent do your leaders operate with an enterprise-wide perspective and work in the interest of the whole organization? 4. To what extent are you able to balance authority with the abilty to influence key stakeholders? 5. To what extent are you able to collaborate and integrate cross-functionally?		
Team Leadership Overall (See Chapter 8) 1. To what extent are you operating the organization with the right mix of traditional teams, self directed teams, cross-functional teams or communities of interest? 2. To what extent are your teams functioning as high-performing teams? 3. To what extent do team leaders implement the tactics that build strong team leadership?		

	Area of Strength	Area of Development
Personal Leadership Overall (See Chapter 9) 1. Do leaders Cultivate personal credibility?		
2. Do leaders Achieve results?		
3. Do leaders Practice humility?		
4. Do leaders Acquire a broad perspective?		
5. Do leaders Build others into leaders?		
6. Do leaders Leverage employee conversations?		
7. Do leaders Exercise work-life balance?		

Audit of the extent to which the organization is effective at systemically implementing leadership capacity

This part of the audit explores the extent to which the organization is doing its part to implement and support the development of leadership capacity. We first present the implementing leadership capacity model followed by the specific audit questions.

Figure 14.4   *The Leadership Capacity Implementation Framework*

	Area of Strength	Area of Development
Embedding Leadership in the Organization Overall (See Chapter 11)		
1. To what extent to do you have a secure supply of leadership talent to meet your future leadership capacity needs?		
2. To what extent do you have a compelling organization-specific leadership story that galvinizes the workforce?		
3. To what extent does your organization have well-established processes on which you can embed leadership capacity?		
4. To what extent are executives focused on embedding leadership capacity?		
Focus on Critical Positions and Key Talent (See Chapter 12)		
1. To what extent have you identified the critical positions that have unique characteristics in your organization?		
2. To what extent are the incumbents of critical positions vulnerable to leaving the organization?		
3. To what extent do you have ready-now candidates to backfill incumbents in critical positions?		
4. To what extent have you defined clearly the developmental pathways for candidates to be able to be successful in those critical positions?		
5. To what extent do you have a well-developed key talent retention strategy and measurement process in place?		
6. To what extent do executives take accountabilty for reviews of critical positions, succession candidates and key talent management?		
Integrated Leadership Development Overall (See Chapter 13)		
1. To what extent do you have a comprehensive strategy for integrated leadership development?		
2. To what extent do you connect leadership development to the organizations environmental challenges?		
3. To what extent do you use the leadership story to set the context for development?		
4. To what extent do you balance global enterprise-wide needs with local individual needs?		
5. To what extent do you employ emergent design and implementation?		
6. To what extent do you ensure that development options fit the culture?		
7. To what extent do you focus on critical moments of the leadership lifecycle?		
8. To what extent do you apply a blended methodology in building leadership capacity?		

	Area of Strength	Area of Development
Accountability for Leadership Capacity Overall (See Chapter 14)		
1. To what extent do your executives see leadership capacity as a compelling strategic issue for your organization?		
2. To what extent do your executives allocate the required resources to build leadership capacity and don't reduce the allocation during a climate of constraint?		
3. To what extent are your leaders visibly involved in leadership development and building leadership capacity?		
4. To what extent are all leaders in the organization taking accountability for building leadership capacity to the same extent as they see their accountabilty to deliver performance outcomes?		
5. To what extent are your Human Resources professionals able to create the technical mechanisms (e.g., performance management, learning sessions, coaching, etc.) that create the necessary context for the organization to build leadership capacity?		
6. To what extent does HR audit its leadership capacity (i.e. annually)?		

WHAT IF THE EXECUTIVES ARE NOT INTERESTED IN LEADERSHIP CAPACITY

In one company, the HR group realized that the senior executives did not understand the idea of leadership development and succession management. The senior executives had all worked their way up through the company. Most did not have higher education, and all but one were within two years of retirement. Their executive meetings focused on responding to their board of directors' demands and on maximizing shareholder value. In contrast, the VPs who reported to the senior executives were much younger and passionate about leadership capacity. These future leaders all attended professional management schools, worked in other companies and had broader experiences that they introduced to this company.

The HR group needed to determine how they could generate senior level accountability for leadership capacity. They knew they could not do it alone. So they worked with several of the VPs to create a Leadership Task Force. The Leadership Task Force took the accountability for bridging the leadership capacity gap. They also discussed the extent to which they could advance this challenge without full senior executive support. They needed to identify how to involve the senior executives so that they would not sabotage the process.

The Leadership Task Force members also were astute enough to scale back the magnitude of the initiative to withstand the minimal support from the senior executives. As one VP said, "We need to balance the effort put into leadership capacity with the level of senior executive commitment. Otherwise we could be wasting our time."

The HR group made a choice. Instead of focusing all of its effort on the senior executives, they instead concentrated on building a base of support with the future leaders of the company (most of whom were on the task force). The future leaders on the Leadership Task Force were very open to the HR leadership capacity ideas and to how leadership capacity needed to be developed. HR then was able to start the process of investing in building leadership capacity through the Task Force. Slowly, members of the Task Force were able to influence the senior executives. HR ensured their approach would be one that the senior executives would value and so they tied their leadership development strategy to other business priorities, such as demonstrating an ROI on human capital, which was of great interest to the senior executive group.

CLOSING COMMENTS

Leadership capacity accountability needs to exist throughout the organization, but its primary locus of accountability is with the executive group. The executives are accountable for overall leadership capacity, and HR is accountable for the technical aspects for building leadership capacity.

The executives and HR need to know when to lead each other and when to follow. They need to be open with their intentions and plans to create an aligned response to the leadership capacity gap. The executives and HR also need to help each other succeed as they each do their part to protect the current and future value proposition of the organization.

The Leadership Economy

Strong leadership capacity is one of the scarcest resources in the world today.[1] Many organizations are struggling to build the leadership capacity they need to thrive in changing business environments. As we have explored, this is a critical business issue because leadership capacity has now become a primary source of competitive advantage for organizations.

Throughout this book we have presented a road map to help bridge the leadership gap. In essence, a dual response is required:

1. Individual leaders in organizations must strive to become holistic leaders by integrating the six elements of the Holistic Leadership Framework (discussed in Part Two). They also must work with other holistic leaders to bring about a new way of thinking about leadership—one that more effectively helps leaders deal with the pressures and complexity of the changing business environment.

2. Organizations must strive to build strong leadership capacity through the four critical success factors of the implementing leadership capacity framework (discussed in Part Three). This requires a comprehensive approach that demands a significant commitment on the part of organizations.

---

1. Noel Tichy, *The Leadership Engine*. (New York: Harper Collins Publishers Inc., 1997).

In this final chapter we look forward and consider the broader societal implications of the leadership gap. More specifically, we examine the role of business, government and academia in building strong leadership capacity to create vibrant communities throughout society.

WELCOME TO THE LEADERSHIP ECONOMY

Over the past decade, organizations have invested considerable resources in trying to become employers of choice in their industries. This strategy has been adopted primarily as a way to attract key talent. We believe that in coming years this strategy will become more targeted and focused around the issue of leadership capacity. We refer to this as the "leadership economy."

Consider the following example:

The senior leaders of a biotechnology company were holding a strategic planning session. One of the issues they were discussing was how to make their organization an employer of choice in their sector. They quickly realized that as an organization, they were very similar to their competitors. Like most companies in this sector they had very progressive HR practices and had built dynamic cultures that attracted and retained top talent. In the end, the group of leaders realized that their key strategic differentiator was the quality of their leadership. The CEO summed up the group's thinking best when he said, "What if we put a stake in the ground today and commit to do everything possible to make our company known for the quality of its leaders. Imagine telling our employees that we are going to develop the best leaders in the industry. Imagine telling prospective employees that if they join our company they can be assured that they will work for the best leaders anywhere in business, not just our sector. If we can successfully do this, it will clearly set us apart and differentiate us from our competitors."

The leaders of this biotechnology company have realized they are now competing in the leadership economy. This shift in thinking also is beginning to occur among a handful of companies. These companies recognize that strong leadership capacity is a critical strategy for success in the leadership economy. With a strong leadership capacity, they can differentiate themselves from their competitors and attract and develop top talent.

Once organizations make this shift, they quickly broaden their perspective and consider the societal implications of leadership capacity. The leadership economy is deeply rooted in the broader society in which the companies operate. Leadership capacity is not only a concern for companies but it also is a concern for other stakeholders in society.

Research conducted by Richard Florida and described in his book, *The Rise of the Creative Class*, provides some valuable insights that are helpful in understanding the connection between leadership capacity and the broader society.[2] Florida has observed the emergence of a "creative class." This class represents a large segment of society and of talent within organizations today. They are described as being highly creative, intelligent, and entrepreneurial. What is critical about this creative class is that they also seek to live in communities that are open to diverse ideas and provide a vibrant opportunity to live a fulfilling life. To that extent, Florida argues that cities need to create communities that will attract top talent. The implication is that organizations will need to go to communities where the top talent chooses to live. This is in sharp contrast to what occurred in the past when talent moved to where organizations established their operations.

A critical link then can be made between leadership capacity and the broader society. For example, in our experience we have found that top leadership talent share many of the characteristics of the creative class. These individuals are very selective of the organizations in which they choose to work. In fact, we predict that increasingly top talent will seek to work in organizations led by holistic leaders. Poor leaders will actually be a risk to organizations because today's talent will not put up

---

2. Richard Florida, *The Rise Of The Creative Class*, (Basic Books, 2002).

with organizations filled with poor leaders. They seek opportunities for creative growth and development, and holistic leaders who can provide this will attract and retain talent.

The desire of top leadership talent to work for organizations led by holistic leaders makes it a significant reason for companies to strive to build strong internal leadership capacity. In addition, many organizations will benefit from collaborating with other stakeholders—government and academia—to build both strong leadership capacity in the broader society and vibrant communities that will attract top talent.

THE IMPLICATIONS OF THE LEADERSHIP ECONOMY FOR BUSINESSES, GOVERNMENT, AND ACADEMIA

In the book *Excellence*, Gardner states that society needs a continuous flow of leaders.[3] Leadership capacity must be strong in every area of society for that society to be healthy and vibrant. If organizations are currently experiencing significant leadership gaps, then it stands to reason that society as a whole is challenged by the same problem. The broader society also is struggling with the leadership capacity essential for it to thrive in an ever-changing environment.

The leadership economy and bridging the leadership gap are issues that businesses are beginning to address, but it is time that legislators, regulators, political leaders and academic institutions also begin to understand this issue. Business, government, and academia need to partner to bridge the leadership gap in the broader society.

- *The role of business in the leadership economy:* Businesses collectively have a vital role to play in the leadership economy. Harman observed that business has become the dominant institution in our

---

3. John Gardner, *Excellence*, (New York: Harper & Row, 1961).

society today.[4] Organizations need to develop holistic leaders capable of thinking of their leadership role from a broader societal context. There is a reciprocal relationship between holistic leaders within organizations and the communities in which they live. Holistic leaders within organizations strengthen the leadership capacity of their communities and in the broader society, and a robust leadership economy feeds the leadership talent required for organizations to succeed.

- *The role of government in the leadership economy:* Traditionally, the role of governments is to build the necessary infrastructure (such as roads, healthcare and education systems) needed to sustain society. Leadership capacity is now a crucial element of the infrastructure needed for a leadership economy. Governments need to play their part to ensure that the necessary leadership capacity is in place for society to flourish. Along with creating jobs and sustaining communities, the leadership economy should be a priority agenda item. Local and national governments need to develop policies that support businesses and academic institutions in their investment in the leadership economy. Governments also have an important role in helping to create vibrant cities that attract talent. This in turn will attract the best organizations committed to building leadership capacity.

- *The role of academia in the leadership economy:* Academic institutions have an important role in building leadership capacity. At present, this role is being questioned because academic institutions, such as many business schools, are still too focused on developing leaders with the traditional functional leadership mindset.[5] Business schools must work with the stakeholders in universities and the business environment to develop more holistic leaders capable of leading organizations effectively.

---

4. Willis Harman, *Approaching the Millennium: Business as vehicle for global transformation*, in M. Ray & Al Rinzler (eds.), *The New Paradigm in Business* (New York: Jeremy P. Tarcher/Perigee Books, 1993).

5. Mintzberg, *Managers Not MBAs*.

Consider the following example of a city that survived the plant closure by a major employer because businesses, government and academia worked together to bridge the leadership gap:

The city's economy was built mainly on the taxation received from the one major employer of a local manufacturing facility owned by a global employer. For many years the manufacturing facility operated profitably, and the city and its other smaller businesses thrived. Most of the citizens were employed, and the city was vibrant and positive. The city's academic institutions trained students needed for the manufacturing facility and to meet other local needs. The company was good to the community, building sports complexes and giving generously to local agencies and charities. However, the global employer began to experience stiffer competition and started consolidating its manufacturing facilities to maximize capacity in its remaining plants. Many thought that a plant closure would mean the demise of the city. However, the many years that the stakeholders—the business, government and educational institutions—had invested in the leadership economy within the city paid off. While some of the leadership talent who worked in the plant did leave the city when the plant closed, many decided to stay. The city banded together to purchase the manufacturing facility and reopen the plant as an employee-owned business. The city and its leadership succeeded at leveraging the leadership capacity in the manufacturing facility, which protected it against the loss of the leadership due to the plant closure. The city and its business community continued to thrive because they built a strong leadership economy that could survive the loss of its major employer.

The political, academic and business leadership in this city prepared for this kind of change. The departure of the plant could have meant the demise of the city. They survived because they had a commitment to continually build the leadership within the city.

THE ROAD AHEAD

The two primary frameworks discussed in this book are applicable to both the leadership gap in organizations and within society. These frameworks provide a road map for business, government and academia to develop leadership capacity in society. Consider the applications of these frameworks to both organizations and to society as described in the following chart:

The Primary Frameworks	Leadership Capacity Gap Within Organizations	Leadership Economy Gap Within Society
 The Holistic Leadership Framework	The Holistic Leadership Framework within organizations is the comprehensive perspective that leaders need to meet the future leadership capacity needs of organizations. Leaders need to integrate the six elements of the holistic leadership framework: - Customer Leadership - Business Strategy - Culture & Values - Organizational Leadership - Team Leadership - Personal Leadership	On a societal level, this Framework applies as well. The leadership economy reflects the need to: 1. Have effective interrelationships among governing bodies, 2. Deliver value in the public interest, 3. Meet the need for economic development and 4. Create the internal organizational alignment to deliver the required leadership economy.
 The Leadership Capacity Implementation Framework	The Leadership Capacity Implementation in organizations is achieved through four critical success factors. These are: - Embedding leadership, - Focusing on critical positions and key talent, - Integrated leadership development, and - Executive accountabilities	The same critical success factors are appropriate to society in general as well. 1. Leadership needs to be embedded in society's culture along with its other infrastructure commitments. 2. Society also needs to plan for critical leadership capacity shortages, support integrated leadership development and take accountability to ensure it occurs.

Building strong leadership capacity is necessary for businesses and for the leadership economy within society. The benefits of applying the holistic leadership framework in organizations and in communities can mean the difference between sustaining high organizational performance and vibrant communities or the demise of both.

IF NOT NOW, THEN WHEN?

The leadership capacity gap and the need for a leadership economy are mission critical issues and require immediate attention. Business executives need to recognize that the leadership gap is a critical priority for the next decade and beyond. Leaders in government and academia must also recognize their part in working with organizations to build the leadership capacity needed to build vibrant businesses and communities. As a great scholar once said, "If not now, then when?"[6] The time to act is now. Building leadership capacity and a leadership economy will yield benefits that eventually can secure the future of the organization and the societies in which we live. It can be done! It must be done!

6. Hillel is quoted as saying this in the *Ethics of The Fathers*, Chapter 1:14, in 200 CE.

Index

About the Authors

Dr. David Weiss is Vice President and Chief Innovations Officer in the firm of Knightsbridge. David has been providing consulting services in the field of leadership and HR consulting for the past twenty years. He has developed an extensive practice in strategic and business planning, integrated leadership development, human resources strategy, organizational consulting and executive coaching to a wide range of clients throughout North America and Europe.

David received his Doctorate from the University of Toronto and has two Masters degrees from Columbia University in New York. He also has achieved the following:

- Faculty member of the Technion Institute of Management
- Senior Fellow of the Industrial Relations Centre of Queen's University
- Editorial Board Member of the *Canadian Learning Journal*
- Honoured as a life-time "Fellow CHRP" of the Human Resources Professional Association of Ontario
- Past President of the Section Of Industrial Organizational Psychology of the Ontario Psychological Association

- Honored member of the "International Who's Who of Professionals" 1998

David is a sought-after keynote speaker and organizational consultant for all of the concepts and practices presented in *The Leadership Gap* and *High Performance HR*. He has published on many topics, including: High-Potential Leadership Development, The Leadership Capacity Gap, Strategic Human Resources, High Impact Action Learning and Contextual Negotiations.

He is also the author of *Beyond the Walls of Conflict* (McGraw Hill, 1996), its revised version, *In Search of The 18th Camel* (IRC Press, 2003), and the HR bestseller *High Performance HR: Leveraging Human Resources For Competitive Advantage* (John Wiley & Sons Canada, Ltd., 2000). *The Leadership Gap* is his third book. David is a citizen of the USA and Canada and works extensively in both countries. See www.knightsbridge.ca for more information about Dr. David Weiss and his firm, Knightsbridge.

Dr. Vince Molinaro is a Principal and National Practice Leader, Leadership Capability, with Knightsbridge. Vince has been providing consulting services in the field of leadership and organizational development and executive team development for the past fifteen years. He has worked with an extensive list of clients within private sector companies (pharmaceutical, telecommunications, financial services) and public sector organizations (provincial and municipal government, health care, education).

Vince received his Doctorate from the University of Toronto and has degrees from Brock University and McMaster University. He lectures frequently at leading business schools on the topic of building leadership capacity and is an Adjunct Professor at Brock University. Vince has conducted pioneering research of holistic leadership.

The media frequently calls him for his opinions on how organizations can build leadership capacity for competitive advantage. Vince is a provocative speaker and conducts keynote presentations on the topics of Building Leadership Capacity, Holistic Leadership, Creating High-Performance Cultures, and Executive Team Development.

Vince has also published extensively in journals and business magazines. *The Leadership Gap* is his first book. See www.knightsbridge.ca for more information about Dr. Vince Molinaro and his firm, Knightsbridge.

About Knightsbridge

Knightsbridge provides integrated human capital management solutions to help organizations optimize performance through people.

Knightsbridge was created by bringing together best-in-class companies in the key disciplines of human capital management – all long established and with track records of success in their respective fields – to create a unique, integrated human capital solutions firm. With more than 80 years of collective experience, Knightsbridge has unparalleled depth and breadth of expertise to assist organizations at any point of the employment or business lifecycle:

Business Strategy & Organizational Development

Recruitment & Selection

Leadership Capability

Career Management

Career Transition

Today, Knightsbridge is the Canadian leader in providing integrated human capital management solutions, with 14 offices in major centres across Canada, and a network of proven associates in smaller centres. Internationally, Knightsbridge augments its geographic reach through strategic alliances with Penna Plc in the UK, and Lee Hecht Harrison globally.

Knightsbridge brings expertise together across the employment cycle in a way that allows for the development of unique and holistic solutions for specific business challenges. Whether you have need of a comprehensive human capital solution or a single service, Knightsbridge can help.

For more information, visit www.knightsbridge.ca